HOME OWNERSHIP IN A RISK SOCIETY

A social analysis of mortgage arrears and possessions

Janet Ford, Roger Burrows and Sarah Nettleton

The POLICY PRESS

First published in Great Britain in July 2001 by

The Policy Press
34 Tyndall's Park Road
Bristol BS8 1PY
UK

Tel +44 (0)117 954 6800
Fax +44 (0)117 973 7308
e-mail tpp@bristol.ac.uk
www.policypress.org.uk

British Library Cataloguing in Publication Data

A catalogue record for this book is available from the British Library

ISBN 1 86134 261 6 paperback

A hardcover version of this book is also available

Janet Ford currently holds the Joseph Rowntree Foundation Chair in Housing Policy at the University of York, where she is also the Co-Director of the Centre for Housing Policy and the Head of the Department of Social Policy and Social Work. **Roger Burrows** is a Reader in Social Policy and Co-Director of the Centre for Housing Policy, University of York. **Sarah Nettleton** is a Senior Lecturer in the Department of Social Policy and Social Work, at the University of York.

Cover design by Qube Design Associates, Bristol.
Front cover: Photograph of woman reading a repossession order by Tom Hunter.

Printed and bound in Great Britain by Hobbs the Printers Ltd, Southampton

Contents

List of figures and tables		iv
Preface		vi
one	The risks of home ownership	1
two	The 'epidemiology' and 'aetiology' of mortgage arrears and possessions	21
three	Owner-occupation and the impact of economic transformations	53
four	Unsafe safety nets	83
five	The costs of mortgage arrears and possessions	107
six	Experiencing mortgage possession	125
seven	Mortgage arrears and possession as public health issues	153
eight	Summary and conclusions	169
Bibliography		181
Index		195

List of figures and tables

Figures

2.1	Number of possessions as a percentage of all current mortgages in Britain (1980-99)	25
5.1	Some consequences of mortgage possession	111
5.2	Mortgage interest taken into account for Income Support and Job Seekers' Allowance (1980-99)	115
5.3	Number of local authority homelessness acceptances due to mortgage arrears in England (1990-99)	115

Tables

1.1	Attitudes to home ownership in Britain: % saying that they would advise a young couple both in secure employment to buy a property 'as soon as possible' (1986-99)	3
1.2	Mortgage transactions and lending in Britain (1980-99)	11
1.3	Mortgage borrowing in Britain (1980-99)	11
1.4	Socio-economic characteristics of mortgagors in Britain (1980-99) (%)	13
2.1	Mortgage possessions and mortgage arrears in Britain (1970-99)	23-4
2.2	Proportion of households in England in 1998/99 containing a member who has experienced possession (%)	28-9
2.3	Percentage of households in England with a mortgage in arrears of any sort (1993/94, 1994/95, 1995/96, 1996/97, 1997/98 and 1998/99)	33-4
2.4	Percentage of households in England with a mortgage in arrears of any sort or finding current mortgage payments 'difficult' or 'very difficult' (1993/94, 1994/95, 1995/96, 1996/97, 1997/98 and 1998/99)	35-6
2.5	Odds ratios and adjusted odds ratios of household being in arrears (1993/94 and 1998/99)	37-8

2.6	Reasons given for mortgage arrears in England (1995/96, 1996/97, 1997/98 and 1998/99) (%)	45
2.7	Tenure of the lowest equivalised income decile of household members in Britain before (BHC) and after (AHC) housing costs (1979, 1990/91 and 1997/98) (%)	47
2.8	Mortgage as a percentage of gross income	48
3.1	Composition of employment in Britain (1981, 1991, 1996, 2001 and 2006) (%)	54
3.2	Employment status of homebuyer household heads in Britain (1991/92, 1993/94, 1995/96 and 1997/98) (%)	58
3.3	Employment status of adult members of homebuying households in Britain (1997/98) (%)	60
3.4	Employment continuity and change for heads of mortgagor households (1991-94 and 1995-98) and tenure at end date (1994, 1998)	61
3.5	Employment continuity and change for all heads of mortgagor households and their partners (if any) (1991-94 and 1995-98) and tenure at end date (1994, 1998)	63
3.6	Job histories	72
4.1	Reasons for mortgagors claiming on public or private safety nets, compared with reasons for arrears (%)	89
4.2	Mortgagors' knowledge of ISMI provisions (%)	92
4.3	Relationship between MPPI take-up and the propensity to insure (%)	95
4.4	Reasons for arrears among successful MPPI claimants	101
4.5	Meeting mortgage payments in the ISMI wait period (%)	103
4.6	Reasons for ISMI meeting only part of mortgage interest (all with shortfall) (%)	104
4.7	Mortgage arrears among ISMI recipients (all receiving ISMI and in arrears) (%)	105
5.1	Typology of the potential range of costs associated with mortgage arrears and possessions	109
5.2	Accumulation of financial costs by a hypothetical mortgagor in default	118
5.3	Residual debt and costs of home ownership period using the same loan/sale details as in Table 5.2	119

Preface

This book brings together in one place a number of different pieces of research undertaken by the three authors over the last few years on the topic of mortgage arrears and possessions. It examines the causes, costs and consequences of a radical realignment that has occurred between the spheres of work, welfare and housing over the last two decades; a realignment that has made home ownership a far riskier undertaking than was hitherto the case. This research has been published in various formats, as reports, articles and chapters, and has been aimed at different audiences – policy makers, social scientists and housing market specialists. The book thus represents an opportunity to synthesise and update this otherwise scattered material and to place it all within a broader context.

Some of this research was initiated by us, or commissioned from us, in response to what appeared to be 'crisis' circumstances in the economy and home ownership market. However, both the earliest and most recent research took place in more benign economic circumstances and was informed by a recognition that the nature of owner-occupation was changing because social, economic and political structures were changing. Thus, increasingly, we have sought to embed the study of arrears and possessions within an analysis of the changing nature of contemporary society. This has led us to argue that arrears and possessions are, and are likely to remain, a more enduring feature of the home ownership market than has sometimes been suggested. A further characteristic of much of our research has been the focus on the lived experiences of those who have arrears and/or who lose their property as a result of possession. The long-established tradition of recognising the nature of 'personal troubles' but their connectedness to 'public issues' (Mills, 1959) has frequently been one of the important themes in our work.

By necessity then, the book draws on some material that is already in the public domain, the main details of which are provided, as appropriate, at the end of each chapter. The research from which we draw was funded by various organisations: the Department of Environment, Transport and the Regions (DETR), the Department of Social Security (DSS), the Council of Mortgage Lenders (CML), the National Centre for Social Research (NCSR), Shelter, and the Joseph Rowntree Foundation (JRF). Again, we make explicit sources of funding, as appropriate, at the end of each chapter. Some of the studies were carried out with other colleagues from the University of York and elsewhere, and include a number of people with whom we have worked over a considerable period of time: John Doling, Jude England, Elaine Kempson, Deborah Quilgars, Jenny Seavers, Christine Skinner, Steve Wilcox and Marilyn Wilson. We are very grateful to the organisations who have funded the research reported here, and we would also like to thank our colleagues who have allowed us to draw on their labours here. We are also very grateful to the support staff at the Centre for Housing Policy (CHP) – Jane Allen, Margaret Johnson and Lynne Lonsdale – for all of their work in both facilitating the research on which we report here, and for their help in producing this particular text.

Throughout the book we subject two statistical data sets to secondary analysis of various sorts. First, the Survey of English Housing (SEH), which was made available to us by the Office of National Statistics (ONS) and the DETR. Second, the British Household Panel Survey (BHPS), which was made available through the Data Archive at the University of Essex. These data were originally collected by the ESRC Research Centre on Micro-Social Change at the University of Essex. Neither the original collectors of the data nor the Archive bear any responsibility for the analyses or interpretations presented here.

Throughout the book we use a number of terms which it might be helpful to elaborate on at the outset. First, throughout, we use the term *possession* to refer to the compulsory or voluntary return of a mortgaged property by a borrower to a lender (see Ford, 1993, for a discussion). In common parlance this is often referred to as a process of *repossession* and this is the term which is used by many of the people from whom we quote throughout this book. Second, we use the term *unsustainable* home ownership as a shorthand term to refer to circumstances invoked by mortgage arrears and/or possession, although we recognise that the term can also refer to a far wider set of socio-economic processes that undermines the stability and continued growth of the owner-occupied housing market (see Maclennan et al, 1997, for a discussion). Third, we use the term *risk* to refer to situations, events, processes and so on with uncertain or unpredictable variations in outcomes or, as defined in the *Oxford English Dictionary*, as the chance or possibility of danger, loss or other adverse consequence.

The book is organised in the following way. In Chapter One we set the context for the rest of the book by examining something of the recent history of home ownership in Britain, in particular noting how the risks associated with the tenure have changed over time and, briefly, some of the reasons for this. Changes in the owner-occupied sector since about 1979 are detailed and some comparisons are made with other countries. Chapter One also outlines the perspective that has informed much of our thinking about the development, impact and enduring nature of mortgage arrears and possessions, namely what is referred to as the 'risk society' perspective. In Chapter Two we examine a range of statistical materials in order to provide a detailed understanding of the socio-economic distribution of mortgage arrears and possessions over time. We also consider some of the possible causes of the growth of mortgage arrears and possessions. In Chapters Three and Four we move on to examine some of the most significant factors that have invoked changes in the risks associated with home ownership: first, a number of economic developments and, second, the changes in both public and private safety net provision for households with a mortgage. Having explored the distribution and causes of arrears and possessions, in Chapter Five we attempt to assess, in aggregate, some of the wider costs and consequences of the growth of mortgage arrears and possessions for a range of different economic, political and social actors. In Chapter Six we focus on the experience of mortgage arrears and possessions for both adults and children. In Chapter Seven we attempt to locate the experience of mortgage arrears and possessions within the context of debates about public health. In the final chapter we briefly summarise our arguments and make some concluding comments about the analysis.

ONE

The risks of home ownership

Over most of the post-war period home ownership in Britain has been perceived as a relatively 'riskless' undertaking, and this has been one influence on the continuing popularity of owner-occupation as measured by people's stated tenure preferences. For example, home ownership has been portrayed as offering assured and certain financial accumulation compared to the uncertainty of other investments, and as guaranteeing a greater measure of personal control, well-being and ontological security when compared to that experienced by tenants (Saunders, 1990). Of course, there has always been a cyclical component to the owner-occupier housing market, reflecting the economic cycle, and as prices and incomes have lagged and led each other (Hamnett, 1999). However, while for much of the post-war period, and certainly until the early 1980s, these cyclical processes have been unsettling and uncomfortable for home owners, market professionals and the economy, only infrequently did households find their home ownership financially unsustainable.

One of the reasons why the cyclical processes could be weathered and their effects largely accommodated was that the fundamentals necessary to sustainable home ownership remained essentially untouched. For much of the post-war period home owners have been continuously employed in secure jobs with rising incomes. Any employment mobility was likely to be voluntary, the risk of unemployment was limited and, if it did occur, short term. All this was helped by the fact that until the early 1980s the overwhelming majority of mortgagors were professional and white-collar workers who were largely immune from the unemployment experienced by manual workers. These circumstances matched well with the typical financing of home ownership, which is by long-term credit agreement (usually over 25 years), at variable interest rates. A generally upward inflation trend eroded mortgage debt relatively quickly, while after 1948 there was a state safety net for mortgagors who lost all income and had few savings, although, given the socio-economic profile of mortgagors, few claimed on it. The congruence between employment, welfare and owner-occupation made the latter sustainable.

However, as home ownership has 'matured' into the 1990s, it has come to be a tenure more characterised by risk and so with less certain outcomes. For more people it has become *unsustainable*, a situation now recognised by government, albeit signalled obliquely through the discourse of *sustainable* home ownership (DETR/DSS, 2000a). Some simple statistics (discussed in detail in Chapter Two) make the point. Between 1970 and 1980, the number of households who lost their property each year as a result of their lender taking their property into possession ranged between just 3,480 (0.06%) and 4,870 (0.08%). In the early 1990s, possessions rose to in excess of 75,000 (0.77%) at the height of the recession. While they have fallen since then, in 1999 they still totalled 30,000 (0.27%), nearly seven times the 1980 figure. Yet, in 1999, the economy, and particularly the labour market, was regarded as more buoyant than for many years with an increase in the number of jobs and claimant unemployment at its lowest level for 20 years.

It is not only the relationship between the sustainability of home ownership and the health of the wider economy that is subject to a change. There also appears to be a deeper cultural shift in attitudes towards the desirability of owner-occupation. Time series data on attitudes to home ownership suggest a greater questioning of the appropriateness of the tenure. Such equivocation, first seen in the 1990s housing market downturn, has not diminished in the way expected as the housing market recovered in the late 1990s (Ford and Burrows, 1999a). For a number of years the British Social Attitudes Survey (BSAS) has asked people how they would advise a young couple both with steady jobs about buying. Should they 'buy a home as soon as possible, wait a little or not buy at all'? This question has been found to provide a good gauge of respondents' attitudes to home ownership, with those recommending purchase 'as soon as possible' argued to have the most positive attitudes to owner-occupation. Table 1.1 indicates that positive attitudes towards owner-occupation began to fall during the late 1980s, reaching a low point in 1996, and that the proportion of respondents with positive attitudes has subsequently risen (Ford and Burrows, 1999a). However, despite these increases, the level of commitment to owner-occupation remained some 14 percentage points lower in 1999 than it was in 1989 (a comparable point in the economic cycle), despite a more favourable set of circumstances. Thus, over the most recent economic cycle there are indications that as the economy and housing market have 'improved' attitudes have not returned to their previous position, although there are clear cyclical shifts.

The downturn in support for owner-occupation has been most pronounced among younger people. The available evidence points to

Table 1.1: Attitudes to home ownership in Britain: % saying that they would advise a young couple both in secure employment to buy a property 'as soon as possible' (1986-99)

1986	1989	1990	1991	1996	1997	1998	1999
74	78	70	60	54	62	61	64

Source: British Social Attitudes Survey (BSAS) data, 1986-99: authors' own analysis

financial constraints, longer periods in education, student debt and their employment situation as key issues engendering caution (Ford 1999). Young home owners also report a higher level of payment difficulty than older people. However, there is also evidence that in some instances, the retreat from home ownership among younger people is led by a different kind of assessment of non-economic risks. For example, Heath (1999) has reported that among some well-educated young people there is a willingness to delay house purchase, which is associated with their reluctance to 'settle down', live with a long-term partner and accept familial responsibilities, as well as with their satisfaction with shared living whereby friends become the 'new' family.

This book aims to explore the emerging risks to home ownership, principally through a focus on mortgage arrears and possessions which are clear signs of its unsustainability. We suggest that while the housing market has always had (and may continue to have) a cyclical character (Hamnett, 1999), the last two decades have made evident some more fundamental, cross-cutting structural shifts that now shape it and the experience of home ownership as a different kind of venture.

Risk society

The discussion of the emerging risks to home ownership can usefully be located in the context of a broader consideration of the concept of the 'risk society', in particular as articulated by the sociologists Ulrich Beck and Anthony Giddens. Although initially working independently, the theoretical and political conclusions that Beck (1992) and Giddens (1991) came to in the early 1990s concerning the changing dynamics of modern societies, were remarkably similar (although see Lupton, 1999, for a clear explanation of some of the differences between their respective positions). While the conceptual terminology they initially used differed somewhat, the extent of their agreement soon became apparent when they came together with Scott Lash to produce a joint text (Beck et al, 1994). Since this time they, and others, have produced a number of books and essays (Beck and Beck-Gernsheim, 1996; Giddens, 1998; Franklin, 1998; O'Brien et al, 1999) which have elaborated various elements of their approach to understanding contemporary patterns of social change.

We are not uncritical of their approach. In many ways notions of the risk society can simply be read as the latest in a long line of attempts to conceptualise contemporary patterns of socio-economic change. But, whereas other approaches tend to give an analytic priority to either economic and technological change (in the case, for example, of theories of post-Fordism) or cultural factors (in the case, for example, of certain conceptualisations of postmodernism), theories of the risk society have, so far at least, been able to maintain a more agnostic orientation towards patterns of social determinism. Our concern here is not to add to the already large theoretical literature on such matters. Rather, we take the notion of the risk society as a sensitising framework which alerts us to the fact that the empirical materials we present within this book are indicative of a broader set of social processes which have a significance outside of the more narrow sphere of housing policy.

Theories of the risk society attempt to grasp the nature of contemporary social change. Of course all societies experience change, but what characterises the contemporary period is "not only the pace of social change" but also its "scope and ... profoundness" (Giddens, 1991, p 16). Changes in economic life, family life, technology, culture and so on have led many to experience contemporary life as a period full of uncertainty, unpredictability and instability. These experiences add up to more than just *fin-de-millennium* angst; social and economic life *is* more complex and far less clear cut than once it was. While for the major part of the 20th century social traditions combined with economic imperatives meant that the trajectory of many people's lives was relatively predictable, now these are far less certain. Such an observation is not new of course; very crudely this is what debates about the supposed transition between Fordism and post-Fordism have been concerned with (Gilbert et al, 1992; Burrows and Loader, 1994). But theories of the risk society enable us to move from a narrower focus on structural change towards one better able to foreground the role of human agency and identity in processes of change. This is by means of a focus on the ways in which risks of various sorts are generated, interpreted and then acted on.

A distinction can be made between two rather different types of risk – those that are external and those that are manufactured. The former refers to those risks which characterised premodernity and which are largely a function of nature, while the latter refers to those risks which are typical of late modernity and which occur as a consequence of human interventions. Many of these risks have numerous intangibles and are not amenable to actuarial calculation. For example, we cannot assess the levels of risk associated with phenomena such as global warming or with the consumption of genetically modified foods. Furthermore, the 'experts' on these and other subjects cannot agree if there really are risks associated with them either (Lupton, 1999).

Manufactured risk does not only concern nature – or, as Giddens tellingly puts it, 'what used to be nature' – it penetrates into all other areas of life too: relationships; sex; work; and, crucially for our discussion here, housing (Giddens, 1992; Ford, 1998; Nettleton and Burrows, 1998a). It is these types of manufactured risks that primarily concern us in this book. Risks of this sort are, of course, largely a consequence of structural processes such as industrialisation, technological change, urbanisation and, fundamentally, globalisation. However, theories of the risk society are concerned to come to terms with how such risks are inserted both into patterns of human action and into patterns of broader psychosocial and cultural change.

Undoubtedly, globalisation is at the heart of contemporary modernisation processes and so at the heart of the risk society. On one recent definition, globalisation refers to "a new phase in world history in which cross-border flows in goods and services, investment, finance and technology [create] a seamless world market where the law of one price will prevail" (Weiss, 1998, p 167). This new world order, focused on profit, but spatially unconstrained due to the standardisation inherent in mass consumption and innovative communication technologies, drives forward competitive markets in ways that create uncertainty by continually restructuring economic and financial activities over space and time. This threat of economic relocation, and the consequent unemployment, with its associated social, financial and political consequences, exerts a pressure on national states to respond; locally in pursuit of strategies to avoid or minimise the impact of globally generated risk; and at the supra-national level in support of strategies to further the processes of globalisation. In Britain (as in many other countries) a major response has been the deregulation of key structures, principally the labour and financial markets, in order to enhance the ability to compete within the global market. As will be seen in Chapter Three, deregulation of the labour market has enabled employers to develop strategies for using labour 'flexibly' that bring competitive advantages. But at the individual level, flexibility can imply insecurity (Allen and Henry, 1997) and this potentially increases the risk of individuals experiencing variation in income and periods without work.

One of the consequences of the growing pervasiveness of risk is that a distinct feature of modern societies – risk societies – is the way in which risk permeates our psyche, both in terms of how we think about ourselves and how we relate to other people (Nettleton, 1997; Ogden, 1995). Three interrelated conceptualisations, developed by Giddens (1991) capture the key elements of the contemporary experience of risk: *reflexivity of the self*; *lifestyles and life planning*; and *ontological (in)security*. Some of these themes are critically examined in relation to home ownership in Chapters Six and Seven.

For Giddens, a core feature of contemporary risk culture is the constant habit of assessing and making calculations about potential risks that might affect our lives. We seek out, and are continually presented with, information produced by an increasingly diverse array of 'experts' on virtually every aspect of our lives: what we eat; how we sleep; our finances; our intimate relationships; our health; our leisure; and so on (Nettleton, 1997). This means that we are able to work constantly at and negotiate our notions of the self within the context of an increasing array of options. Thus, Giddens argues, we are increasingly required to make lifestyle choices. Such choices may involve decisions about our longer-term life plans such as choosing to buy a particular house, taking out a personal pension, or sending our children to a particular school. This notion of lifestyle choice is, of course, fundamentally related to the availability of resources. Further, while rarely a feature of this theorising, it is important to acknowledge the extent to which reflexivity can be detrimental to self-image and one's biography through a sense of failure (Nettleton and Burrows, 2001). The lifestyle choices and life planning of some individuals and groups can influence and affect positively and negatively not only their life chances but also the life chances of others. This can have a cumulative effect where the social arrangements are such that we are encouraged to make lifestyle choices and life planning decisions that limit the life chances of others. Notions of the contemporary self, then, are constituted by way of an ongoing project in which people are bound to make lifestyle and life planning decisions. Such projects are contingent on the availability of material resources, can have both negative and positive connotations and can often alter and exacerbate social divisions. Giddens links these notions of risk, reflexivity and lifestyle planning to a final, and perhaps more familiar, concept, that of ontological security. Crudely this refers to emotional security and is based on the notion that one's self-identity is linked to one's biography – the narrative that can be told about one's life.

For theorists of the risk society, late modern societies are characterised by greater uncertainty, and this is intensified by a lack of faith in modern science and 'experts'. In their day-to-day lives people seem to be facing a vast array of decisions which are based on probabilities rather than certain outcomes. Hence people are constantly engaged in a process of reflexively organising evidence and information. In turn, this imperative serves to undermine their ontological or emotional security – that is, it permeates their psyche.

In Britain, increasing risk, and individualisation, has also been a consequence of political and ideological decisions about the role of the welfare state. Informed in part by the more limited room for manoeuvre that all states have in a global polity and in part by the reflexive challenge to paternalistic and older order institutions and experts (Taylor-Gooby, 2000a), states nevertheless retain the ability to respond to these processes and their consequences in different ways, giving rise to different structures of welfare provision (Esping-Andersen, 1990). History, political tradition and ideology as well as globalisation inform the responses. In Britain since the late 1970s, ideological support for a limitation of state provision and the belief in individual responsibility and self-provisioning can be seen as chiming with other processes discussed above to support a policy of the transfer of responsibilities for welfare provision from the state to the individual and from the public to the private sector. To the extent that the private sector proves reluctant or unable to 'replace' state provision, the outcomes for individuals are risky as indeed they are solely by virtue of welfare being delivered through the market (Taylor-Gooby, 1999). These issues, as they relate to home owners, are taken up further in Chapter Four.

Home ownership in a risk society

We might think of home ownership as being inserted in the risk society in at least two different ways. The first can be described as 'direct' in so far as the home ownership market itself is subject to the processes of globalisation and its associated uncertainties. For example, developments in the global financial markets create uncertainty in terms of the availability and the ongoing costs of credit. The political alignments that directly serve global processes also, potentially, impact directly on home ownership through supra-national regulation of interest rate policy. Thus, although currently Britain remains outside of the European single currency, concerns have been expressed as to the likely detrimental effect of European Monetary Union on the home ownership market should Britain join (Maclennan and Stephens, 1997). The second insertion of home ownership within the risk society is as a site for the consequences of uncertainties generated by other areas of social and economic life, themselves often structured by globalisation, and so might be thought of as 'indirect'. Here, for example, the risks that emanate from the labour market or from the limitation of state activity with respect to safeguards against key risks can be cited. Thus, as will be seen later, labour market insecurities in the form of unemployment and less secure forms of employment such as self-employment (both products of the drive to maintain a competitive market) are strongly associated with the risks of home ownership (Chapter Three) as is the restructuring of safety nets for home owners (Chapter Four). Further, home ownership is also influenced by the reflexive response to risk in so far as this leads people to question the traditional attributes and benefits available to those who are or might become owner-occupiers.

One consequence of the restructuring of labour market opportunities and of welfare provision, as suggested above, is a shift in the long-standing, mutually reinforcing, and beneficial relationships between home ownership, employment and welfare. Writers have referred to this shift as a 'fracturing' of relationships or the emergence of 'disjunctures' (Ford and Wilcox, 1998) that challenge the fundamental requirements of sustainable owner-occupation (secure, stable and adequate employment – or replacement income – that can support long-term credit). These more permanent realignments are suggestive of a persistent risk to home ownership and a degree of unsustainability.

The key risks to home ownership, and the resulting social distribution of risk, are one of the important concerns of this book, explored primarily in Chapter Two. It is also clear that in discussing the risks to home ownership from social and economic restructuring we are identifying processes that are sometimes also constituted by public policy – for example, housing policy, policy on labour market regulation and social security policy. The potential and actual consequences of these risks are thus public issues, although they are also experienced as personal troubles. Unsustainable home ownership is not therefore personally derived or the result of 'wilful' or 'culpable' mortgagors as has sometimes been suggested. This is not to deny that, in addition to structural change, institutional and personal responses (for example, in the form of the provision of debt counselling or forbearance policies or money management skills) can ameliorate or aggravate the impact of structural factors (Doling et al, 1988), but they should not detract from a recognition of the more fundamental, structural, influences bringing about unsustainable home ownership.

A further, related, issue is explored in this book. This concerns the experience of risk, in particular the experience of mortgage arrears and possessions among individuals and households and the social, economic, social-psychological and health impacts of unsustainable home ownership. These experiences and impacts occur both at an individual level and in aggregate. At the aggregate level this can be considered in terms of the societal 'costs' of mortgage arrears and possessions: for example, the increased demands on the local authority to rehouse homeless mortgagor households; the public expenditure requirements associated with payment of the state safety net to mortgagors; the additional demands on health services from stress related conditions; or the resultant increase in poor households. These issues are examined in Chapter Five.

For individuals, the key questions concern the lived experience of arrears and possessions and the consequential outcomes. There is long-standing evidence that living with mortgage arrears and possession is, in general, associated with stress, social isolation, social exclusion and a loss of social status and valued identity (for example, Ford, 1988; Davis and Dhooge, 1993). However, the detailed nature of the social and emotional experience has less frequently been a focus of attention. Similarly, the consequences that flow from this situation have rarely been explored in detail. Both the social and emotional experience of arrears and possessions, and their highly individualised nature, are discussed in this book, as are the consequences of these experiences for both adults and children. This discussion can be found in Chapter Six and, especially, Chapter Seven.

Before moving to focus in detail on a number of aspects of unsustainable home ownership in subsequent chapters, we turn to a discussion of the recent changes and developments in owner-occupation, in particular the extent and reasons for its rapid growth in the 1980s and the emergence of a set of difficulties in the housing market in the 1990s, including the rapid growth of mortgage arrears and possessions. Initially seen primarily as a product of the recession in both the labour market and the housing market (as to an extent they were), they have increasingly been seen as a manifestation of the 'new' owner-occupation. We also provide a brief descriptive characterisation of owner-occupation at the end of the 1990s.

Finally, some consideration is given to the likely specificity of the development of unsustainable home ownership in Britain.

The rise and stalling of owner-occupation

At the end of the Second World War, most people in Britain were renters. Home ownership accounted for no more than 40% of all households. At the time of writing, 68% of households in Britain are owner-occupiers – 16 million households – 11 million of them buying their property with a mortgage. The growth of home ownership has not occurred at an even rate over this period and the last 20 years have seen particularly rapid growth, in which the socio-economic composition of home owners has changed markedly.

At the point of the election of a Conservative government in 1979, 59% of households were home owners. By 1999, there were a further 4 million. It was evident in the 1970s that there was a long-standing preference for home ownership in the UK, but it was only after a series of policy initiatives that this potential demand was able to be realised. The major initiatives were, first, the mandatory selling of local authority houses at a discounted rate under the Right to Buy (RTB) scheme, which formed part of the 1980 Housing Act and which has resulted in the sale of 1.85 million council homes (Wilcox, 2000, p 114), and, second, a policy that placed restrictions on the use by the local authorities of the capital receipts from the sale of their property for replacement building. Together, these policies resulted in a reduction of good-quality property to rent and led to the residualisation and marginalisation of the local authority sector (Forrest and Murie, 1990; Cole and Furbey, 1993; Burrows, 1999). The government also acted to deregulate the credit market through the 1985 Financial Services Act and the 1986 Building Societies Act, which encouraged new entrant credit providers. A highly competitive market resulted where lenders increasingly offered mortgages to those who had hitherto been regarded as 'riskier' customers.

These initiatives unleashed the mid and late 1980s housing market boom. Tables 1.2 and 1.3 provide an overview of some key changes between 1980 and 1999. There was variation in the number of loans advanced each year as market forces and economic circumstances changed; and despite some years being characterised by a fall in house prices, over the period as a whole there was a very substantial increase.

Table 1.2: Mortgage transactions and lending in Britain (1980-99)

	1980	1985	1990	1995	1999
Number of mortgagors	6,210,000	7,717,000	9,415,000	10,521,000	10,981,000
Number of mortgages advanced	709,000	1,291,000	1,147,000	909,000	1,181,000
Number of mortgages to first-time buyers	318,000	570,000	413,000	419,000	593,000
Average mix-adjusted UK house price (1993=100)	37.7	54.3	108.1	103.7	145.4

Source: Wilcox (2000)

Table 1.3: Mortgage borrowing in Britain (1980-99)

First-time buyers	1980	1985	1990	1995	1997	1998	1999
Average advance as % of dwelling price	73.8	85.3	82.5	89.0	88.0	83.0	80.0
Ratio average advance/ average income	1.67	1.94	2.19	2.26	2.23	2.34	2.27
Average repayment as % average income	19.0	19.9	26.9	18.9	18.2	19.8	18.1
Former owner-occupiers	**1980**	**1985**	**1990**	**1995**	**1997**	**1998**	**1999**
Average advance as % of dwelling price	46.1	59.2	59.3	64.2	64.3	64.1	64.4
Ratio average advance/ average income	1.54	1.83	2.0	1.99	2.04	2.05	2.11
Average repayment as % average income	17.5	18.8	25.5	17.4	16.8	18.3	16.9

Source: Wilcox (2000)

Over the period, the total number of mortgages in force increased by more than 75%. The substantial increase in year-on-year lending in the early and mid-1980s and continuing buoyancy to the end of the 1980s is also clear. The rapid rise in house prices between 1985 and 1990, their subsequent decline and then, at the end of the 1990s, a further surge is also indicated, although throughout 2000 aggregate house price increases levelled out somewhat. Over much of the period, each year, first-time buyers comprised around 44% of all buyers, but dropped to just over a third in 1990 as the rise in house prices and interest rates constrained the affordability of owner-occupation for this group (see Table 1.3). Indeed, the evidence is that in the early 1990s, maintenance of the size of the home ownership sector, and certainly mortgage borrowing, was in large part due to the continuing programme of RTB sales.

Table 1.3 also shows the extent to which financial deregulation and competition resulted in buyers (and particularly first-time buyers) being able to, or having to, stretch their finances in order to enter the tenure. For first-time buyers there was an upward trend in the amount they were borrowing in relation to the price of the property, which lasted until the mid-1990s. One consequence was that these borrowers had less equity in their properties at day one. Only in the last part of the 1990s have first-time borrowers started to provide larger deposits (which may be a result of their caution or that of their lenders). In general, since 1980, first-time borrowers increased the amount borrowed in relation to income. Their average monthly payments as a percentage of average income also increased over the 1980s, peaking in 1990 when the full effect of interest rate increases was felt as the government acted to curb inflation, but falling back thereafter.

Over the 1980s, similar trends characterised the borrowing by former owner-occupiers, but at a lower absolute level. Since the mid-1990s, former owner-occupiers have continued to borrow just under two thirds of the dwelling price while their average advance as a ratio of average income has increased a little. By 1999, former owner-occupiers had slightly lower repayments as a percentage of income than had been the case for most of the 1980s and 1990s.

There was, however, an important regional and local pattern to the demand for owner-occupation, to house prices and patterns of borrowing. Demand, but constrained supply, resulted in the late 1980s in higher prices and more rapid increases in the South, South East and South West of the country than was the case in many other regions. Differences in regional markets resulted in regional disparities in average housing costs

Table 1.4: Socio-economic characteristics of mortgagors in Britain (1980-99) (%)

Age	**1980**	**1990**	**1999**
Under 30	17	16	12
30-44	48	46	46
45-59	33	30	34
60+	2	13	16
Socio-economic status			
Professional	8	10	10
Employer/manager	24	24	25
Intermediate non-manual	11	14	13
Junior non-manual	10	7	9
Skilled manual	34	30	24
Semi-skilled manual	8	7	8
Unskilled manual	1	1	2
Economically inactive	4	7	10
Gross income by tenure (£ per week)	**1980**	**1992**	**1998**
Mortgagors	142	320	401
Outright owners	81	194	220
Local authority	68	110	130
Furnished private renting	*87*	*170*	*250*

Source: Derived from Wilcox (2000)

and mortgage commitments. To take just one example, against the mix-adjusted index of 100 in 1993, average prices in 1989 were 82.3 in the North and 129.4 in the South East. While the gap had closed by 1992 to 97.9 and 104.2 respectively, this was the result of a continuing rise in prices in the North but also a rapid fall in prices in the South East which started in the early 1990s. In 1992, average mortgage repayments in the North were £38.81 per week compared to £75.91 in the South East.

The changes in housing policy and housing finance over the period also resulted in changes in the socio-economic characteristics of home owners as shown in Table 1.4.

While owner-occupation in general, and mortgagors in particular, remain heavily characterised as a middle-class tenure, home ownership has become more diverse, and arguably now constitutes the most diverse tenure in Britain. There has been a reduction in the proportion of younger borrowers and an increase in older mortgagors; a small increase in the proportion of manual worker mortgagors; and a six percentage point increase in economically inactive mortgagors. The gap in gross income between mortgagors and tenants has widened, and (as discussed in Chapter Two) the proportion of low-income home owners and mortgagors has increased. The proportion of households from ethnic minority groups has also increased but not uniformly. As will be shown later, this increasing diversity, a consequence of a number of policy changes that enabled and encouraged the meeting of preferences and unrealised demand for home ownership, has in turn become a source of greater risk to the sector.

Following the liberalisation and expansion of owner-occupation in the 1980s, many writers have chronicled and analysed the subsequent downturn in the overall housing market which also impacted differentially across the regions (Forrest and Murie, 1994; Ford et al, 1995; Clapham, 1996; Hamnett, 1999). The availability of this literature means we do not need to rehearse the arguments in detail, but simply identify a number of key reference points. First, in 1987, there was the announcement of the ending of 'double MIRAS' (mortgage interest relief at source) which had enabled two unrelated adults jointly to purchase a property, each receiving mortgage interest tax relief up to £30,000. However, by providing three months notice of its withdrawal, the Chancellor of the Exchequer further fuelled the ongoing housing boom. Second, in 1989, there was a rapid increase in interest rates designed to cool the housing market. This contributed to the subsequent economic recession that impacted on both blue- and white-collar mortgagors and brought the first post-war experiences of unemployment to many professional and managerial home owners. Third, the decision taken in 1987 to limit the safety net for mortgagors without income contributed to a growth of home owners unable to maintain their mortgage payments. Arrears and possessions also resulted even where households retained one working member (and so lacked any eligibility for safety-net provision) because of the high financial gearing around housing (particularly in the South East) which required a two-income household to service the debt. At the height of the economic recession, in 1991, 75,540 households lost their property either as a result of court action or by giving voluntary possession, while approaching 900,000 households had arrears of at least two months missed payments. Finally, economic difficulties resulted in the fall in house prices, the emergence of negative equity and the reduction in the number of housing market transactions.

Despite frequent claims from 1995 onwards that the housing market was 'recovering', such developments proved to be elusive until well towards the end of the 1990s, and then were concentrated primarily in particular places. The term 'recovery' can also be used to denote different things, for example, house price increases, or an increase in transactions. Tables 1.1, 1.2 and 1.3 above indicate the extent of the recovery which was slower than had been expected with rising house prices not necessarily bringing about increased individual borrowing. On some key indicators, for example, the percentage of loan to value, and average repayment as a percentage of average income, mortgagors (and possibly lenders) appear to be more cautious than they were in the late 1980s. However, despite the steady increase in aggregate house prices since 1995 the increase in transactions failed to mirror this change and were fairly muted until 1999 when they approached 1.45 million.

Again, there are regional and local differences with some areas only slowly regaining momentum while others have been referred to as 'hot spots'. London was among the first of the late 1990s 'hot spots' but that label began to apply more widely in the South East. At the same time there is some evidence that, in some areas of the country – principally in pockets of industrial decline – the demand for owner-occupation may be faltering to such a degree that the fall in house prices is dramatic and part of the blighting of some local markets. Here, mortgagors may be 'trapped' or only able to sell while retaining very substantial debts. For those with arrears or those seeking to trade down in order to limit the risk of arrears this is a very damaging set of circumstances.

Finally, the mid and late 1990s have seen the advent of a low-inflation environment aided by explicit inflation targets. This issue is discussed further in Chapter Three but here it is at least important to note that for owner-occupiers low inflation has a number of disadvantages, principally the lengthening of the period of maximum debt exposure and higher real interest rates than might otherwise be the case, which in turn may constrain affordability.

Looking at mortgagors at the end of the 1990s, there is also evidence that there have been some changes in the way they manage their mortgages. In particular, since 1996 roughly 12% of mortgagors each year have been making higher than required payments. The percentage of borrowers making one-off lump sum repayments, while small, has increased from 2% to 4%. The advent of 'flexible' mortgages, which allow overpayment without penalty as a matter of course (plus other payment facilities such as underpayment, payment holidays and so on), has also proved popular;

flexible mortgages now account for roughly 5% of the mortgage market and 11% of new mortgages and are growing rapidly (Ford and Seavers, 2000). Some of these changes in individual financial behaviour are driven by a wish to reduce costs and increase flexibility in order to manage risk, although the evidence to date suggests that the former predominates, not least because of the current low-inflation environment that prolongs the real value of debt as noted above. Finally, one of the hallmarks of the booming housing market of the 1980s, equity withdrawal, remains relatively low at the end of the 1990s. In 1988, equity withdrawal amounted to 6.3% of disposable household income or £19 billion. In 1999, it was equivalent to just 1.3% or £8.2 billion (Wilcox, 2000), although the evidence for 2000 indicates some increase in the rate of withdrawal.

Overall, housing market behaviour in the late 1990s has some similarities to that seen in the late 1980s. Its characteristics have been described as those of 'cautious expansion' (Ford and Seavers, 2000), but, as noted above, there are also some differences, not least a distinct profile of borrowing and mortgage management. The evidence is that, increasingly, potential borrowers have to make decisions in an environment that is more complex and less certain than has hitherto been the case and that there is a recognition of this complexity and of the potential riskiness now associated with home ownership. The clear factors that might encourage borrowing (for example, growing average income, house price increases and so on) are only one part of the environment which now also includes a higher degree of labour market insecurity, a reduction in state support for mortgagors and an uncertain private market for mortgage protection. The situation amounts to what Taylor-Gooby (2000b) has referred to as the paradox of 'risk amidst affluence'. It is this complexity that in large part gives rise to the likelihood of a persistent level of unsustainable home ownership.

Unsustainable home ownership in comparative perspective

This book does not offer a comparative perspective or analysis of unsustainable home ownership. However, what we have to say about the developments in the UK may be resonant with developments in a number of other countries and an indicative discussion is therefore appropriate. Although the growth in home ownership since the late 1970s has put Britain among the countries with the highest levels of home ownership – and particularly mortgagors – many countries have seen their home ownership sector grow since the early 1980s; for example, Italy, Ireland, Spain, Portugal, the Netherlands and Germany (for further details see the European Mortgage Federation website at www.hypo.org). Some European countries (for example, Ireland, Spain) now match Australia and the United States, which historically have had the highest levels. Further growth is a policy objective in some countries, for example the Netherlands where the proposal is to increase owner-occupation from 52% to 65% by 2010.

The proportion of home owners that are mortgagors (as opposed to outright owners) also varies by country, but all mortgagors face the same objective of seeking to make regular payments over time, for which they require stable secure employment and a means to meet such payments when income is disrupted. Mortgagors seek this certainty, or to manage the risk, in the context of unique market structures and housing finance systems which, directly or indirectly, may be more or less conducive to sustainable home ownership. Some indicative examples of this variation can be noted. There are inter-country differences: in the availability and nature of state-sponsored subsidies to low-income entry; in the extent to which a dwelling is purchased using a succession of short-term loans or a longer-term credit agreement with loans typically made for 10 years in Italy but more than 25 years in Austria and Denmark; in the use of (or balance of) fixed or variable interest rates; in interest rates per se; and in loan to value ratios which average around 50% in Italy and Austria but exceed 80% in France, Spain and Denmark. House price inflation also varies, influencing the period over which the value of the loan decays.

Against an index of 100 in 1990 house prices increased to 190 in Ireland and 181 in the Netherlands but there was only moderate growth in Germany, Sweden and Denmark and a fall in Finland to 91. There are also differences in the degree to which the state in different countries supports home owners without income, and in the extent to which insurance against key events is compulsory or available. Thus, in France, insurance against illness and disability is compulsory, while no such insurance provision exists for this or unemployment in Portugal. In Australia, as in some other countries, insurance is in the form of cover for the lender should foreclosure prove necessary.

These descriptive data are significant as aspects of the housing finance system can in themselves increase risk as in the case of one or more of high loan to value or low inflation or limited safety nets. These structures and processes are also the backdrop against which other changes impact, not least the deregulation and outcomes of economic competition associated with globalisation. Again, indicative evidence suggests that in many countries since 1980 there has been an increase in one or more of the forms of flexible employment – part-time, temporary, or self-employment (White, 1996). As will be elaborated in Chapter Three, such forms of employment potentially jeopardise the requirement of mortgagors for stable, secure and 'appropriately' paid employment. Deregulation of financial services has freed the availability of credit, and established the principle of cross-border credit. Both developments may draw into home ownership those previously regarded as too high a risk, or draw people in with 100% loans. Describing the previous functional 'fit' between labour, (finance) capital and the housing market, Berry et al (1999) say:

> ... over the past 20 years, economic restructuring and social change sweeping though the OECD countries has undercut and, in some cases, obliterated the institutional connections and functional fit described above. 'Globalisation' has released a set of institutional responses that are broadly similar across the OECD member states, though particularly apparent in the Anglo-Democracies.

With respect to Australia, they go on to list the set of institutional and other responses: reform and deregulation of national financial systems; the growth of flexible labour markets; the triumph of neo-liberalism and the reintroduction of market discipline; and seemingly irreversible demographic change and greater housing market volatility; and they note that rising arrears and defaults (possessions) are closely associated with these developments. A not dissimilar analysis is discussed with respect to Finland by Doling and Ruonavaara (1996).

Given the developments outlined above, it is not surprising that the issue of unsustainable owner-occupation is one of significance beyond the UK. Characterised by a measure central to this book – as an increase in, and persistence of, payment difficulties – unsustainable home ownership has been documented in the US (Quercia and Stegman, 1992), Australia (Berry et al, 1999), Finland (Doling and Ruonavaara, 1996), Germany (Potter and Dreverman, 1990) Ireland (Murphey, 1996) and Sweden (Bjork, 1994). The issue is acknowledged in other countries, but sometimes there is a lack of systematic evidence where statistics have not yet been collected and/or not placed in the public domain (for example, in Portugal and France). Beyond the individual country studies there are difficulties in using the statistics on arrears and possessions in a comparative manner because of the lack of common definitions and non-comparable sources of the data, while their interpretation needs to be related not only to the nature of housing finance but to the particular legal systems within which lenders operate.

Despite all these limitations, preliminary discussions (CHP, 2001) indicate the commonality of key influences, but the divergence of national responses as shaped by the history, politics and socio-economic structures of individual societies. The impact of the business cycle is recognised but also the significance of structural changes within the labour market, bringing about a qualitatively different, riskier, housing market structure and experience. Thus an examination of unsustainable home ownership in the UK resonates with and can contribute to an understanding of similar developments elsewhere.

Summary

This chapter has argued that the risks associated with home ownership in Britain have – despite clear cyclical fluctuations – been subject to a secular shift. There are various reasons why this has happened – many of which will be discussed in this book – but most originate from a fundamental breakdown of previously mutually supportive linkages between the spheres of work, welfare and housing. The unsustainability of home ownership is thus emblematic of a set of broader socio-economic transformations that have been conceptualised by social scientists in various ways. In this chapter we took an influential conceptualisation – that of the risk society – as one way of sensitising ourselves to the broader context of change within which our understanding of the causes, costs and consequences of mortgage arrears and possessions might be situated. This chapter also sets out the context for and nature of owner-occupation since 1979, highlighting the late 1980s boom and the subsequent housing market recession. By the end of the 1990s, decisions about home ownership were being made in an environment that was more complex and less certain than had been the case 20 years previously. Further, it was suggested that the growing risk identified with respect to owner-occupation in Britain was also an emerging feature in many other countries throughout the Western world, that were also bound up in and affected by globalisation processes. However, localised circumstances and the specificities of national housing finance systems and policy responses impacted on the nature and extent of unsustainable home ownership in each place.

In the next chapter we flesh out some of the details of both the extent and the socio-economic distribution of the risks of home ownership. We also begin the task of considering the factors that have increased the risks of home ownership.

TWO

The 'epidemiology' and 'aetiology' of mortgage arrears and possession

Until the early 1990s many of the beliefs and assumptions about mortgage arrears, especially those held by lenders (Ford et al, 1995), were based on studies which were not on a large enough scale to control for more than one or two variables at a time. Without much of a systematic evidence base it was easy for the Council of Mortgage Lenders (CML) to assert that the single most important cause of mortgage arrears was relationship breakdown (BSA, 1985; CML, 1991). Further, it was often asserted that the unwillingness of borrowers to pass on to the lender the state safety-net payments (ISMI), which until 1991 were paid directly to borrowers and not lenders, contributed to arrears (Ford and Wilcox, 1992). From this perspective it was the 'private troubles' and personal attributes of individuals which were conceptualised as the main cause of mortgage problems and little consideration was given to deciphering any set of broader structural factors which might be at work. This was despite the efforts of Karn, Doling, Ford and Stafford (Karn et al, 1985; Doling and Stafford, 1986; Doling et al, 1988; Ford, 1988) to demonstrate that, in fact, mortgage arrears and possessions were very much an emerging 'public issue' which had an increasingly clear socio-economic patterning.

Only following the housing crisis of the early 1990s did policy rhetoric begin to move beyond such individualistic explanations. However, now the explanation was often couched in terms of an arrears and possession 'crisis' that had resulted from a contingent set of circumstances. Certainly, as we detailed in Chapter One, towards the end of the 1980s four processes did combine to produce a substantial growth in mortgage arrears and possessions in Britain. To recap, first, as a result of financial deregulation, a highly competitive market and rising property prices, high loan to value mortgages became widely available. Second, mortgage rates rapidly increased from 9.5% in 1988 to peak at 15.4% in February 1990 before slowly decreasing. Third, a deep economic recession led to job losses, underemployment and small business failure. Fourth, and not unrelated, the housing market entered a deep and persistent recession (Forrest and

Murie, 1994). Many highly geared borrowers first faced rising mortgage costs and then often lost income from employment. However, many were denied the possibility of selling their way out of problems due to the housing recession. Consequently, as can be seen in Table 2.1, the number of households with mortgage arrears increased as did the number of mortgage possessions. However, it is the contention of this book that this 'episode' masked the emergence of a set of more enduring secular socio-economic changes which continue to generate a far higher level of risk associated with home ownership than pertained in the 1970s and 1980s.

Table 2.1 shows that in 1970 just 4,171,000 households were buying their homes with a mortgage and of these just 3,760 (0.09%) experienced loss of that home through mortgage possession. Levels of possession were low throughout the 1970s, and by 1980 of the 6,210,000 households with a mortgage just 3,480 (0.06%) experienced possession. As levels of home ownership grew throughout the 1980s there began to emerge a small year-on-year increase in the proportions of households experiencing possession that continued until 1987. In 1987, 8,238,000 households had mortgages – almost twice the number in 1970 – and of these 26,390 (0.32%) experienced possession. Levels of mortgage arrears followed a broadly similar pattern of secular increase. However, during the housing boom of 1988 and 1989 levels of possession decreased, standing at just 0.17% of all households with a mortgage in 1989. At the turn of the decade things changed. In 1990, 43,890 households experienced possession – almost 0.5% of all households with a mortgage. In 1991, the worst year of the housing crisis, 75,540 households were possessed, representing almost 0.8% of all mortgages held in that year. These figures might even understate the real extent of the problem because they represent single year risks of possession. This point has been made forcefully by Alan Holmans, one of the most careful and precise analysts of UK housing statistics. His conclusions are worth quoting at length:

> [I]n 1990-95 the average number of possessions each year was only 0.6 per cent of all mortgages outstanding. This implies that the risk of being dispossessed was still very small, only 1 in 170 (approximately). That, though, is a single year risk, whereas households with mortgages are at risk to mortgage default all the time they have mortgages ... the average length of time that a household has a mortgage appears to be between 30 and 35 years.... With a period at risk of 35 years, an annual risk rate of 0.6 per cent would result in a total risk rate over the whole

Table 2.1: Mortgage possessions and mortgage arrears in Britain (1970-99)

Year	No of mortgages at year end (000s)	No of possessions during year	No of possessions as % of no of mortgages at year end	12+ months arrears	6-12 months arrears	3-6 months arrears	3-5 months arrears	2 months arrears
1970	4,171	3,760	0.090	–	21,140	–	–	–
1975	5,076	4,870	0.096	–	16,760	–	–	–
1980	6,210	3,480	0.056	–	15,530	–	–	–
1981	6,336	4,870	0.077	–	21,540	–	–	–
1982	6,518	6,860	0.105	5,540	27,380	–	–	–
1983	6,846	8,420	0.123	7,530	29,440	–	–	–
1984	7,313	12,400	0.170	9,510	48,270	–	–	–
1985	7,717	19,300	0.250	13,120	57,110	–	97,000	140,000
1986	8,138	24,090	0.296	13,020	52,080	–	125,400	145,200
1987	8,238	26,390	0.320	14,960	55,490	–	121,000	164,400
1988	8,564	18,510	0.216	10,280	42,810	–	124,800	171,600
1989	9,125	15,810	0.173	13,840	66,800	–	122,000	153,900
1990	9,415	43,890	0.466	36,100	123,110	–	206,600	237,500
1991	9,815	75,540	0.770	91,740	183,610	–	305,500	269,800
1992	9,922	68,540	0.691	147,040	205,010	–	275,400	207,800
1993	10,137	58,540	0.577	151,810	164,620	193,660	242,050	198,400
1994	10,410	49,190	0.473	117,110	133,700	169,080	191,590	135,840

Table 2.1: contd.../

Year	No of mortgages at year end (000s)	No of possessions during year	No of possessions as % of no of mortgages at year end	12+ months arrears	6-12 months arrears	3-6 months arrears	3-5 months arrears	2 months arrears
1995	10,521	49,410	0.470	85,200	126,670	177,910	–	119,720
1996	10,637	42,560	0.400	67,020	100,960	139,250	–	148,350
1997	10,738	32,770	0.305	45,200	73,840	117,840	–	112,360
1998	10,821	33,820	0.313	34,880	74,040	129,090	–	122,970
1999	10,981	30,030	0.273	29,520	57,110	96,680	–	–

Notes: Properties taken into possession include those voluntarily surrendered. The CML 3-6, 6-12 and 12+ months' arrears figures are for the end of the year. The Janet Ford survey figures for 2 and 3-5 months' arrears are for the March of the year. Her survey of mortgage arrears figures has now been discontinued from publication following the introduction of the CML 3-6 months' arrears series. Changes in the mortgage rate have the effect of changing monthly repayments and hence the number of months in arrears which a given amount represents.

Sources: Compendium of Housing Finance Statistics & Housing Finance (CML); Janet Ford Survey for *Roof* (figures for 2 and 3-5 months' arrears for 1985 to 1994). Janet Ford *CHP Survey* (figures for 2 months' arrears 1995 to 1998)

> period of 19 per cent, ie a risk of losing the home through mortgage possession at some stage of nearly 1 in 5. This is the grim arithmetic of Bomber Command. (Holmans, 1997, p 191)

As Figure 2.1 illustrates, from this peak in 1991 levels of possession declined throughout the 1990s. Some improvement in economic conditions contributed but a further factor in the early 1990s was the changing relationship between arrears and possessions as lenders sought to limit the latter but as a consequence saw longer-term arrears increase. However, in 1999 – long after the housing crisis had supposedly come to an end – some 30,030 homes were still possessed. This is a figure almost twice that pertaining to a decade earlier in 1989. It is also a figure that means that, on average, over 82 households per day lose their homes in this way. In total in the 1990s, 484,290 households containing over 1.5 million individuals lost their homes.

It is our attempt to understand the causes, costs and consequences of this ongoing 'epidemic' of mortgage indebtedness that provides the main focus for this book. Some might object to such a blatant use of a medical metaphor to describe the phenomenon. However, as we shall discuss in

Figure 2.1: Number of possessions as a percentage of all current mortgages in Britain (1980-99)

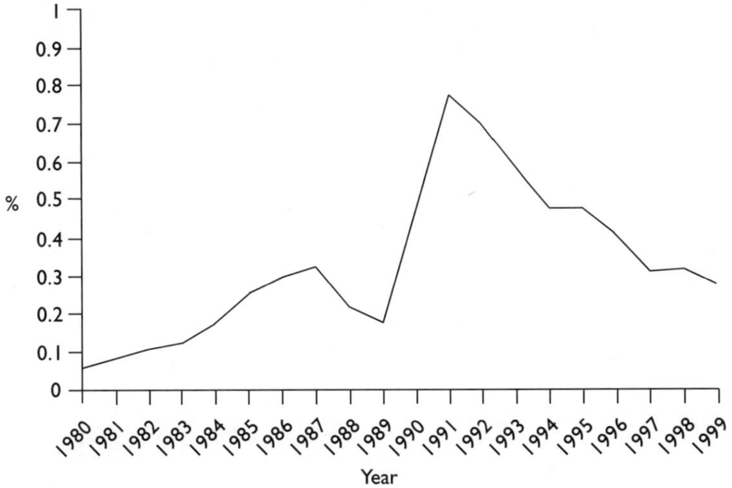

Source: Housing Finance (CML)

Chapters Six and Seven, both qualitative and statistical data from a number of studies suggest that the framing of mortgage indebtedness as an epidemiological variable may be more than just a metaphorical device. There is good evidence to suggest that the experience of mortgage indebtedness is such a stressful life event and is now so common that it could usefully be reconceptualised as a major public health issue (Nettleton, 1998).

In the next section of this chapter we outline what is known about the socio-economic distribution – or 'epidemiology' – of mortgage indebtedness. Not only is an understanding of this social patterning an important topic in its own right but it also gives us some clues as to the generative mechanisms – or the 'aetiology' – which might account for the patterning. We shall consider what 'causal' mechanisms might account for the social distribution of mortgage debt in the final section of the chapter – the details of some of which will provide the focus for subsequent chapters.

The 'epidemiology' of mortgage arrears and mortgage possession

Aggregate data such as those presented in Table 2.1 and Figure 2.1 are useful in that they tell us something about the extent of mortgage arrears and possession and how they have changed over time. However, these are of little use if we want to understand how such risks are socially patterned and how they have changed over time. In order to do this we can examine data from the Survey of English Housing (SEH). The SEH is a continuous government survey that began in April 1993. It is based on interviews with about 20,000 private households in England each year. Details of the sample design, data collection, response rates and so on are detailed in annual reports (Green and Hansbro, 1995; Green et al, 1996, 1997, 1998, 1999; McConaghy et al, 2000). The SEH data can be weighted and grossed in such a way that every single case on the data file for any one year represents 1,000 households. It contains the best available cross-sectional data on housing-related topics in general and the experience of mortgage arrears and possession in particular.

Possessions

In 1998/99 the SEH estimated that a stock of 437,000 households in England (2% of the total) contained someone who had experienced mortgage possession at some time. Of these, 224,000 households (51%) contained both a head of household and a partner who had experienced possession; 163,000 (37%) contained only a head of household who had experienced possession; 35,000 (8%) contained only a partner who had experienced possession; and 16,000 (4%) contained someone else (for example, another family member or a friend) in the household who had experienced possession. Of the 437,000 households containing someone who had experienced possession, 42% had experienced possession in1990 or before and 58% had experienced possession between 1991 and the time of the interview (between April 1998 and the end of March 1999).

Table 2.2 shows some of the socio-demographic characteristics of households containing someone who had previously been possessed in England compared to the characteristics of all other households in England and all other households with a current mortgage in England. The first thing to note is that although households containing someone who has experienced possession are less likely currently to be owner-occupiers than the rest of households in England (70% of the total), nevertheless, 28% are either outright owners or mortgagors. Although the number of cases available for analysis is small, further inspection of the data (analysis not reported here) suggests that as the time since the possession lengthens, the chances of a household moving back to the owner-occupation sector increases (see also McConaghy et al, 2000, pp 39-40). Thus, although such households are over-represented in both the private and social rented sectors, as time goes by many such households find their way back into owner-occupation. However, it is worth noting that of the 98,000 such households currently with a mortgage a full 10% report being in arrears (again) and 29% report having problems making current mortgage payments. Thus a full 39% of such households report either being in arrears or having problems compared to just 16% of all mortgagor households (see Table 2.4 below). This means that households with a mortgage containing someone who has previously experienced possession are over twice as likely to be facing current mortgage payment problems than are other mortgagor households.

Households containing someone who has experienced possession are socio-demographically distinctive in a number of ways. Table 2.2 details a range of these differences. Space considerations preclude a full description of the data but comparisons with households currently buying a property with a mortgage (and not containing someone who has experienced possession) are worth detailing. In particular, 30% of such households are headed by someone who is divorced or separated, compared to just

Table 2.2: Proportion of households in England in 1998/99 containing a member who has experienced possession (%)

Variable	% of all households containing person who has been possessed	% of all households not containing person who has been possessed	% of all households with a mortgage not containing person who has been possessed
N	**437,000 (2% of all households)**	**19,944,000 (98% of all households)**	**8,575,000**
Current tenure			
owned outright	5	27	-
mortgagor	23	43	100
local authority	30	16	-
registered social landlord	14	5	-
private rented sector	28	10	-
Age of head of household (HoH)			
18-24	0	4	2
25-34	21	19	26
35-44	32	20	31
45-54	23	18	26
55-64	16	14	11
65+	8	26	4
Marital status			
not divorced or separated	70	87	89
divorced or separated	30	13	11
Current employment status of the HoH			
employed full time	51	53	86
employed part time	10	6	5
unemployed	7	3	1
retired	9	28	5
unable to work	23	10	5
Type of household structure			
couple, no dependant children	24	36	38
couple, with dependant children	29	22	37
lone parent	20	10	7
large adult household	4	4	3
single male	13	13	10
single female	10	16	6

Table 2.2: contd.../

Variable	% of all households containing person who has been possessed	% of all households not containing person who has been possessed	% of all households with a mortgage not containing person who has been possessed
N	**437,000 (2% of all households)**	**19,944,000 (98% of all households)**	**8,575,000**
Social class of HoH			
I professional-managerial	4	7	10
II intermediate	22	29	37
IIIN skilled non-manual	14	15	13
IIIM skilled manual	34	27	28
IV semiskilled manual	20	15	10
V unskilled manual	7	6	2
Employment situation			
employee	79	87	85
small business owner	4	4	4
self-employed sole trader	20	10	11
Region			
Provinces	68	69	69
South East	12	15	13
Greater London	19	16	18

Source: Survey of English Housing 1998/99: authors' own analysis

11% of households with a current mortgage; 7% are unemployed (compared to 1%); 23% are unable to work (compared to 5%); 20% are headed by a lone parent (compared to 7%); 61% are headed by someone in a manual social class (compared to 40%); and 20% are headed by a self-employed sole trader (compared to 11%).

Arrears

Although data on households containing someone who has experienced possession are of interest they do not really tell us much about the risks of possession at any one point in time. Rather, the data represent a *stock* of households that contain individuals who have been subject to possession at some time in the past. In order to gain an understanding of the risks of possession over time it is perhaps better to consider data on households currently in mortgage arrears, for it is these households which are most likely to face the loss of their homes.

Each year the SEH has asked all heads of household (HoH) with a current mortgage: 'How are you doing with your payments at the moment?', to which they may reply that they are 'up-to-date', or describe how many months they are 'behind'. However, using this measure the estimate of the proportion of households in mortgage arrears in any one year does not coincide with that derived from the regular survey of lenders carried out by the CML (see Table 2.1). Indeed, in general, the CML data estimate levels of arrears almost double that found by the SEH. It is likely that much of the difference is accounted for by a difference in the perception of what constitutes arrears between borrowers and lenders. The SEH questions mortgagors; by contrast the CML collects administrative data which are readily available to lenders, on the basis of a technical definition of arrears. The SEH respondents may well disregard some outstanding arrears if they are up-to-date with their current payments, or if they have fallen behind only temporarily, or, as we shall see in later chapters, they may be unsure of their exact position. If borrowers who are technically in arrears have come to an agreement about repayments with their lender (such as temporarily making reduced payments), or if they regard their arrears as somebody else's responsibility (such as late payment of Income Support Mortgage Interest [ISMI] by the Department of Social Security [DSS]), they may describe themselves as 'up-to-date'. Of course it may also be due to a certain amount of under-reporting by survey respondents due to an understandable unwillingness to admit to indebtedness even if they are clear about their current indebted position. In essence, then, the nationally representative data from borrowers we have available to us may underestimate the overall extent of those in mortgage arrears by about a factor of two compared to a lender definition of arrears.

This measurement problem will be further compounded if the likelihood of it occurring systematically varies across different types of mortgagor household. If it did not vary across household types we could simply double the proportions in arrears for each type of household to get an estimate more in line with lenders' data. However, the available evidence suggests that the level of borrower underestimation of the extent of their arrears is much greater for mortgagor households in receipt of DSS assistance (such as the unemployed, low-income households, lone parents and so on) than it is for households not in receipt of DSS assistance. This means that for households in arrears and in receipt of DSS assistance the 'real' extent of arrears is likely to be greater than double that estimated by the SEH, while for those households in arrears but not in receipt of DSS assistance the 'real' extent of arrears is likely to be less than double that estimated by the SEH.

In addition to this measurement issue there are a number of other important caveats which should be considered when examining data from the SEH on mortgage arrears. First, it is important to remember that the data are cross-sectional in nature and therefore provide only a snapshot of the situation each household is in at the time of interview. As we shall see later in this book, mortgage payment problems often occur for prolonged periods of time and so a single point in time analysis can be misleading. It does not, for instance, reveal how much 'churning' there is in the population. For example, Ford et al (1995) discovered that when data on a sample of households with a mortgage were examined over five years (1991-94) rather than over one year, the proportion experiencing difficulties increased significantly. The analysis revealed that 3% had no current arrears but had previous arrears; 3% were having current payment difficulties and had had arrears previously; 1% were in arrears again, having cleared previous arrears; 1% had been in arrears for the whole of the period under consideration; 3% had fallen into arrears for the first time in the last three years; and 9% had no arrears over the period but had current payment difficulties. In total, over the period, one in five of all mortgagor households had experienced arrears and/or payment difficulties.

Second, the data implicitly infer some sort of temporality between variables, which is not always justifiable. Thus, to take an example discussed further in Chapter Three (see also Burrows and Ford, 1998), we might infer that the risk of arrears is increased if a head of household is a self-employed sole trader *because* s/he is a self-employed sole trader. However, we cannot be certain that the self-employed status was not taken on *after* the onset of the arrears. For example, it might have been the case that unemployment was an initial trigger of the arrears and the self-employed status was only taken on subsequently (Ford, 1989).

Third, much of the data tend to concentrate on the characteristics of the head of each household as a measure of overall household status. There is, however, a valid and well-rehearsed set of critiques of this procedure within the social research literature which demonstrates the importance of the characteristics of other household members, especially female partners, on the overall socio-economic status of the household (Marsh and Arber, 1992).

Fourth, the data are only for England and not for Britain as a whole. Housing markets in Wales, Scotland and Northern Ireland differ and inferences drawn from the English market are not necessarily applicable to them. However, with these not inconsiderable caveats in mind we can examine the SEH data on mortgage arrears.

Table 2.3 shows the proportion of households with a mortgage in England who report being in mortgage arrears *of any sort* in 1993/94, 1994/95, 1995/96, 1996/97, 1997/98 and 1998/99. The figures include households who have a mortgage as part of a shared ownership scheme (some 73,000 households in the 1998/99 SEH). For most of the 1990s percentage arrears among shared owners have been higher than among other mortgagors, and at no time have they been lower. The proportion of households in arrears has fallen by 50% from 6% in 1993/94 to 3% in 1998/99. However, this figure masks some variations in the rate at which levels of arrears have changed over time for different types of household. Table 2.4 shows the proportion of households with a mortgage in England who report being in mortgage arrears of any sort or who are finding current mortgage payment 'difficult' or 'very difficult' for the same years. These figures are important as they reveal something about the depth of the vulnerability that home owners experience and alert us to the possible size of the population who might fall into arrears and/or possession as and when the next economic downturn occurs.

The proportion of households in arrears or facing 'difficulties' has fallen by just 25% from a full one fifth in 1993/94 to 16% in 1998/99. Again, this proportionate decline in households facing 'difficulties' varies across different categories of household. Indeed, in some instances things appear to have improved little over the period. For example, among households where heads of household are unskilled manual workers the proportion facing difficulties has declined from a high of 28% in 1993/94 to an only slightly lower figure of 26% in 1998/99. For households with a mortgage headed by someone unable to work things appear to have actually worsened. In 1993/94, 41% of such households reported difficulties, while in 1998/99 this proportion had increased to 46%. It is worth noting though that arrears and payment difficulties are not just restricted to households currently excluded from the labour market. Although they are at a lower level, 'in-work' arrears and payment difficulties are still a significant problem. Even in 1998/99, 14% of households headed by someone in full-time employment and a full one quarter of households

Table 2.3: Percentage of households in England with a mortgage in arrears of any sort (1993/94, 1994/95, 1995/96, 1996/97, 1997/98 and 1998/99)

Variable	1993/94	1994/95	1995/96	1996/97	1997/98	1998/99
All	**6**	**4**	**4**	**3**	**3**	**3**
Age of head of household (HoH)						
18-24	7	4	0	3	2	4
25-34	7	5	5	4	3	3
35-44	7	5	5	4	3	3
45-54	5	4	4	3	3	3
55-64	3	3	3	2	3	3
65+	3	2	4	1	2	2
Marital status						
not divorced or separated	5	4	3	3	3	2
divorced or separated	11	9	9	7	6	7
Current employment status of the HoH						
employed full time	5	3	3	2	2	2
employed part time	8	9	7	6	6	5
unemployed	24	19	22	19	16	11
retired	3	2	2	1	2	1
unable to work	14	11	15	13	17	15
Type of household structure						
couple, no dependant children	4	3	2	1	2	2
couple, with dependant children	7	5	4	4	3	3
lone parent	13	14	12	10	9	9
large adult household	9	6	7	4	7	2
single male	8	6	5	4	4	4
single female	4	4	3	2	2	2
Social class of HoH						
I professional-managerial	2	2	2	1	2	1
II intermediate	4	3	3	2	2	2
IIIN skilled non-manual	6	5	4	3	4	3
IIIM skilled manual	9	6	5	5	3	4
IV semiskilled manual	8	5	7	6	5	4
V unskilled manual	10	7	9	5	8	7
Employment situation						
employee	4	4	4	3	3	3
small business owner	7	4	3	2	3	2
self-employed sole trader	12	8	6	8	6	4

Table 2.3: contd.../

Variable	1993/94	1994/95	1995/96	1996/97	1997/98	1998/99
All	**6**	**4**	**4**	**3**	**3**	**3**
Region						
Provinces	5	4	4	3	3	3
South East	7	5	4	3	3	3
Greater London	7	5	5	4	4	4
Right to Buy (RTB)						
Not RTB	6	4	4	3	3	3
RTB	8	5	5	5	6	4
Mortgage as % of purchase price						
not 100%	5	4	4	3	3	2
100% mortgage	10	8	8	7	6	6
Year current house purchased						
pre-1987	5	4	4	3	3	3
1987-89	8	7	6	5	4	4
post-1989	5	3	3	3	2	3

Source: Survey of English Housing 1993/94, 1994/95, 1995/96, 1996/97, 1997/98, 1998/99: authors' own analysis

headed by someone in part-time employment reported arrears and/or payment difficulties.

It is interesting to begin to disentangle the main factors that are associated with arrears and to estimate what relative importance should be attached to each. This can be done by using a statistical technique known as logistic regression to model the odds of a household being in arrears. Those familiar with the mathematics of horse racing will recognise the odds of an event to be simply another way of expressing a probability that it will occur. The odds of an event are given by $p/(1-p)$ where p is the probability of an event occurring.

Table 2.5 shows the results of carrying out logistic regression analyses of the chances that a household will be arrears for 1993/94 and 1998/99. Analyses have been carried out for all of the years for which we have data but, as we discussed in Chapter One, these two years represent both ends of a major change in the housing market. In 1993/94 the housing market was still in crisis following the slump of the early 1990s (Forrest and Murie, 1994) and, as we have seen, 6% of households with a mortgage reported that they were in arrears. In 1998/99 the market had recovered somewhat, house prices were rising again and only 3% of households

Table 2.4: Percentage of households in England with a mortgage in arrears of any sort or finding current mortgage payments 'difficult' or 'very difficult' (1993/94, 1994/95, 1995/96, 1996/97, 1997/98 and 1998/99)

Variable	1993/94	1994/95	1995/96	1996/97	1997/98	1998/99
All	**20**	**18**	**17**	**16**	**15**	**16**
Age of head of household (HoH)						
18-24	21	15	11	17	19	19
25-34	19	18	18	15	15	16
35-44	22	19	18	17	16	18
45-54	19	18	17	14	14	15
55-64	18	14	14	15	14	14
65+	17	19	11	14	16	19
Marital status						
not divorced or separated	18	16	15	14	14	15
divorced or separated	33	32	30	28	29	29
Current employment status of the HoH						
employed full time	16	15	14	13	13	14
employed part time	35	31	24	28	32	25
unemployed	57	46	50	52	42	43
retired	14	13	9	12	14	20
unable to work	41	39	42	43	43	46
Type of household structure						
couple, no dependant children	14	12	11	10	10	11
couple, with dependant children	23	19	18	17	16	18
lone parent	38	40	35	35	37	35
large adult household	29	26	25	22	24	17
single male	22	22	20	15	18	16
single female	20	20	17	17	18	20
Social class of HoH						
I professional-managerial	10	9	9	8	8	7
II intermediate	16	14	13	12	11	12
IIIN skilled non-manual	21	20	18	18	18	23
IIIM skilled manual	24	22	20	18	18	19
IV semiskilled manual	24	21	25	24	21	21
V unskilled manual	28	28	26	27	22	26
Employment situation						
employee	16	15	16	14	14	15
small business owner	23	18	17	15	15	17
self-employed sole trader	28	28	24	24	23	22

Table 2.4: contd.../

Variable	1993/94	1994/95	1995/96	1996/97	1997/98	1998/99
All	**20**	**18**	**17**	**16**	**15**	**16**
Region						
Provinces	18	17	17	15	15	16
South East	23	17	15	15	14	15
Greater London	24	24	20	19	20	19
Right to Buy (RTB)						
Not RTB	20	18	16	15	15	16
RTB	22	19	21	20	18	18
Mortgage as % of purchase price						
not 100%	19	17	16	15	15	16
100% mortgage	25	24	24	23	21	22
Year current house purchased						
pre-1987	18	16	14	15	14	14
1987-89	24	22	22	20	19	21
post-1989	19	17	16	14	15	16

Source: Survey of English Housing 1993/94, 1994/95, 1995/96, 1996/97, 1997/98, 1998/99: authors' own analysis

with a mortgage reported being in arrears. Also, and again as we discussed in Chapter One, public attitudes towards home ownership were at something of a low point in the early 1990s while by 1998/99 they had recovered somewhat (Ford and Burrows, 1999a). Consideration of these two years allows us to show, albeit in a very crude way, how patterns of vulnerability among home owners have varied between two significant points in the cycle.

The figures for the unadjusted odds are bivariate logistic regression results and provide little more than a shorthand way of examining associations between two variables. Each individual category of a variable is compared to a selected 'reference' category of the variable, and a measure of the difference between the odds of being in arrears is calculated between the two categories. To take a simple example from Table 2.5, the odds of being in arrears in 1993/94 if the head of household is in social class IIIN is estimated to be 2.9 times greater than if s/he is in social class I; further, this difference is estimated to be statistically significant at better than the 0.05 level. If the head of household is in social class V the model estimates that the household is 5.7 times more likely to be in arrears than if s/he was in social class I, this time at a level of statistical significance better

Table 2.5: Odds ratios and adjusted odds ratios of household being in arrears (1993/94 and 1998/99)

	1993/94		1998/99	
Variable	**Odds ratio**	**Odds ratio adjusted for other variables**	**Odds ratio**	**Odds ratio adjusted for other variables**
Age of head of household (HoH)				
18-24	2.0*	3.4*	1.7	–
25-34	1.2	1.3	1.1	–
35-44	1.3	1.2	1.1	–
45-54	1.0	1.0	1.0	–
55-64	0.6	0.4**	1.0	–
65+	0.7	0.2*	0.5	–
Marital status				
not divorced or separated	1.0	1.0	1.0	1.0
divorced or separated	2.4***	1.8*	3.1***	1.9*
Current employment status of the HoH				
employed full time	1.0	1.0	1.0	1.0
employed part time	2.8	2.9***	2.8***	1.9*
unemployed	9.6***	8.0***	6.8***	5.2***
retired	1.0	3.9*	0.7	0.8
unable to work	3.5***	4.5***	9.0***	7.0***
Type of household structure				
couple, no dependant children	1.0	1.0	1.0	1.0
couple, with dependant children	1.8***	1.6*	2.0***	2.1***
lone parent	3.8***	1.2	6.6***	2.6**
large adult household	2.6***	1.5	1.5	1.4
single male	2.8***	1.9*	2.6***	2.2**
single female	0.9	0.7	1.5	1.4
Social class of HoH				
I professional-managerial	1.0	1.0	1.0	1.0
II intermediate	2.9**	2.5*	2.1	1.7
IIIN skilled non-manual	2.9*	2.0	4.4**	2.6*
IIIM skilled manual	4.4***	3.5**	6.0***	5.0***
IV semiskilled manual	5.4***	3.4**	5.7***	3.5**
V unskilled manual	5.7***	2.8	9.4***	5.4**

Table 2.5: contd.../

	1993/94		1998/99	
Variable	**Odds ratio**	**Odds ratio adjusted for other variables**	**Odds ratio**	**Odds ratio adjusted for other variables**
Employment situation				
employee	1.0	1.0	1.0	–
small business owner	1.5**	1.4*	0.9	–
self-employed sole trader	2.1***	2.0***	1.6**	–
Region				
Provinces	1.0	1.0	1.0	1.0
South East	1.4*	1.6*	1.0	1.3
Greater London	1.5*	1.5	1.4	1.9**
Right to Buy (RTB)				
not RTB	1.0	–	1.0	1.0
RTB	1.8**	–	0.6*	1.8*
Mortgage as % of purchase price				
not 100%	1.0	1.0	1.0	1.0
100% mortgage	2.3***	1.9***	2.8***	2.6***
Year current house purchased				
pre-1987	1.0	1.0	1.0	–
1987-89	1.8***	1.8***	1.4	–
post-1989	1.1	1.2	0.8	–

* significant at $p<0.05$ ** significant at $p<0.01$ *** significant at $p<0.001$
Source: Survey of English Housing 1993/94 and 1998/99: authors' own analysis

than 0.001. The corresponding figures for 1998/99 are 4.4 and 9.4. However, some caution should be exercised when interpreting these figures, and those that follow, in terms of *relative risk*. The odds ratio is similar, but not identical, to relative risk. Further, when the prevalence of an outcome is high, logistic regression models can provide inaccurate estimates. Given this, it is perhaps better to interpret estimates as if they were on an ordinal rather than a cardinal scale. So although we can be confident that a parameter estimate of 5.7 is greater than a parameter estimate of 2.9, we cannot be quite so confident that it is (roughly) twice as great.

These differences may, however, be spurious in that they could simply be artefacts of other factors 'working through' the bivariate association. Indeed, this problem provides a major reason for the necessity of undertaking multivariate analysis. The figures in the columns headed 'adjusted odds' provide estimates of the odds ratios after they have been 'adjusted' to take account of the other associations which pertain in the data. So, for example, when considered on its own the odds of being in arrears in 1998/99 appear to be 3.1 times greater if the head of household is divorced or separated. However, once the influence of the other variables are 'controlled for' the odds ratio is reduced to just 1.9. With these provisos in mind we shall briefly discuss some of the main results emerging from the analysis.

- In 1993/94 the results suggest that even after all the influences of the other variables had been considered, households with heads of household who are young(er) are significantly more likely to be in mortgage arrears than are households with old(er) heads. In 1998/99 this age-related pattern no longer seemed to pertain. It appears then that when arrears are at high(er) levels an age gradient emerges – younger households are more vulnerable. However, when arrears are at low(er) levels no significant age differences in the risk of arrears occur. Patterns of age-related risk may be subject to change over time, however. Those aged between 18 and 35 currently record far lower levels of support for owner-occupation than was the case in the 1980s (Ford and Burrows, 1999a) and this may be due to a perception that the risks of home ownership have been subject to a secular increase for young adults. Indeed, the experience of a protracted entry into the labour market, an increase in the proportion entering higher education, changes in the funding of higher education and so on, all mean that for many young people levels of debt are far greater than they were for previous cohorts and thus the risks associated with home ownership are far greater (Ford, 1999).
- In both 1993/94 and 1998/99 there appears to be an enduring relationship between a household being headed by someone who is divorced and separated and an increase in the chances that the household is in arrears. It appears, then, that the risks of arrears associated with divorce and separation vary little over the cycle.
- In 1993/94 the bivariate association suggests that only those who are unemployed and those who are classified as unable to work are significantly more likely to be in arrears. However, when all the other variables are considered at the same time it is clear that all other employment status categories possess a higher odds of being in arrears than those who are currently employed full time. Those employed part time are almost three times more likely than those employed full time

to be in arrears. Those currently unemployed are almost eight times more likely to be arrears. In this year the unemployment of a head of household has the greatest impact of all factors on the odds of being in arrears. Those who are unable to work are 4.5 times more likely to be in arrears. Surprisingly perhaps, those who are retired are also more likely to be in arrears when all other variables are controlled for. However, because this removes the impact of age (which, as we have seen, decreases the odds of being in arrears) it is likely that this reflects the influence of the 'young retired' who might share some of the characteristics of the unemployed and/or those unable to work. The results for 1998/99 differ somewhat in that (as we have seen) no 'age effect' is included and thus those households headed by someone who is retired do not differ significantly in their odds of being in arrears. When all other variables are controlled for, compared to those households headed by someone who is in full-time employment, those employed part time are almost twice as likely to be in arrears; those currently unemployed are over five times more likely; and those who are unable to work are seven times more likely. In 1998/99 households headed by someone unable to work has the greatest impact of all factors on the odds of being in arrears. Thus, there is some evidence that the nature of employment status-related risk of arrears varies over the cycle. As levels of unemployment decrease overall the arrears risk of those in unemployment declines somewhat as well. However, over the cycle the odds of arrears for households headed by someone unable to work increase.

- In 1993/94 the bivariate association suggests that, compared to couples with no dependent children, all other household types except single females are at greater risk of being in mortgage arrears. However, when all other variables are controlled for, this pattern of association changes. Compared to couples with no dependent children only couples with children and single male households have significantly increased odds of being in arrears. The bivariate results suggest that lone parents have significantly higher odds of being in arrears, but this apparent association is not maintained when all of the other variables are controlled for. In this case it is likely that it is not lone parenthood per se which is associated with mortgage arrears but factors associated with it, such as divorce or separation, unemployment or the inability to work, which account for its lack of independent efficacy on mortgage indebtedness. In 1998/99 the results differ somewhat. When all other variables are controlled for it is the case that, compared to couples with no dependent children, both couples and lone parents with dependent children are significantly more likely to be in arrears, as are single males. In 1998/99 being a lone parent retains an efficacy in addition to marital status and employment circumstances. The data suggest that as other factors associated with arrears improve (for example, as unemployment falls) the efficacy of differences in household type takes on a greater importance.

- In both 1993/94 and 1998/99 the bivariate results suggest a clear social class gradient. As one moves down the class structure the odds of arrears increase significantly. This pattern of association broadly holds in both years when all of the other variables are controlled for. However, in 1993/94 those in social class V do not appear to differ significantly in their odds of being arrears to those from social class I. However, this is likely to be because we have taken out the impact of being unemployed, the chances of which increase significantly as one moves down the class structure. Thus, in this year it is perhaps the case that it is not the impact of being in social class V per se which increases the odds of being in arrears but the greater propensity that people in this social class have of becoming unemployed which is picked up. In 1998/99 this is not the case. The class gradient is far more pronounced, with those in social class V being over five times more likely to be in arrears than those in social class I. The results thus suggest that as aggregate levels of arrears decline, social class differences become more pronounced.
- In 1993/94 the self-employed were significantly more likely to be in arrears than employees. This association was maintained even after controlling for all other variables. In 1998/99 this relationship no longer seems to hold when other factors are controlled for. A fuller analysis (not reported here) over the six years for which we have data, suggests that patterns of vulnerability in relation to mortgage arrears for self-employed sole traders and, to a lesser extent, small business owners, varies significantly over the economic cycle. During periods of relative economic recession levels of arrears are high but as economic fortunes improve generally, patterns of vulnerability for the group decline relative to other socio-economic factors associated with a heightened risk of arrears (that is, social class). This point is elaborated on in Chapter Three when we consider the impact of labour market circumstances on home ownership in more detail.
- In 1993/94 the bivariate results suggest that, compared to the rest of England (the 'provinces'), households in Greater London and the South

East were significantly more likely to be in arrears. However, when all the other variables were controlled for, the impact on the odds of living in Greater London becomes insignificant, while the odds were increased for those living in the South East. In 1998/99 the pattern of association had changed somewhat, with Greater London emerging as the locality with significantly increased odds of arrears. Over the period covered by the data we can observe this 'locality effect' shifting away from the South East and towards Greater London.

- In 1993/94 the bivariate results suggest that those households who purchased their homes from local authorities, new town corporations or housing associations were 1.8 times more likely to be in mortgage arrears compared to those households who purchased their homes from private sellers. However, this association was spurious. When all of the other variables are considered at the same time the association was not maintained. This suggests that in 1993/94 it was the likely employment status and social class characteristics of those who purchased under the 'Right to Buy' (RTB) legislation that accounted for the increased odds in the bivariate association rather than the fact that the accommodation was purchased under conditions per se that increased the odds of being in arrears. In 1998/99 the nature of the relationship has altered. The bivariate results suggest that households who purchased their property under the auspices of a RTB scheme were *less likely* to be in arrears. However, when all of the other variables have been controlled for it is revealed that those who purchased via the RTB are, in fact, significantly more likely to be in arrears. Again, we see that over the cycle, as the extent of arrears has decreased in general, the vulnerability of those who purchased through the RTB has taken on an efficacy independent of other socio-economic factors.
- In 1993/94 the bivariate results suggested that those with a 100% mortgage were over twice as likely to be in arrears as those with a mortgage representing a lower percentage of the purchase price. This association held even when all other variables were controlled for. Those with a 100% mortgage were almost twice as likely to be in arrears. In 1998/99 a similar pattern of association exists. Indeed, over the whole cycle, households taking out a 100% mortgage were vulnerable to arrears with the risks, if anything, increasing over time. It is also worth noting that the data in the SEH on *current* household income/mortgage costs ratios, although by no means a direct measure of what multiple of household income(s) the mortgage represented at the time it was taken out (unfortunately the SEH does not contain this information), are

highly suggestive of a strong association between high initial multiples and an increased odds of being in arrears. Even when currently economically inactive heads of household were excluded from consideration, a very strong and highly significant association between current mortgage costs/income ratios and the odds of being in arrears was maintained over all of the years for which we have data (results not reported here).

- In 1993/94 in the bivariate analysis those households who purchased in 1987-89 were over 1.8 times more likely to be in arrears than were those who purchased pre-1987; however, those who purchased post-1989 did not differ significantly in their odds of being arrears. This relationship holds when all other variables were considered simultaneously. The reasons for this are well rehearsed (Ford et al, 1995; Forrest and Murie, 1994) and do not require extensive elaboration here. As we have already discussed, 1987-89 represented the peak of the housing boom and it was also during this period that many households entered owner-occupation in order to qualify for 'double' mortgage interest relief at source (MIRAS). Notice of three months was given of the changes in MIRAS, pushing many 'unrelated adult households' into owner-occupation ahead of expectation. Many of these households who took out mortgages during this three-month period became especially vulnerable when interest rates increased. Many also fell into default when the households they had 'designed' in order to take advantage of the tax position subsequently revealed themselves to be lacking in any longer-term viability as a social unit. Many of these 'constructed' households were formed of young adults and so some of the impact of this on the odds of being in arrears might also be picked up in the age of the head of household, which has already been discussed. This 'Lawson boom' effect is apparent in the data for much of the period under discussion. Only in 1998/99 does the effect begin to disappear. Thus, the influence of this variable – a product of the conjunction of events that resulted in the housing market collapse of the late 1980s and early 1990s – has faded over time.

Discussion

It is clear, then, that the importance of different factors in explaining variations in the risk of arrears varies over the economic cycle. Patterns of relationship breakdown (and, relatedly, differences in household structure), current employment status, social class differences and responsibility for high percentage mortgages all have enduring influences. However, some other factors only seem to assert a significant influence periodically, and at different points during the cycle. During periods of recession the young appear to be more vulnerable than at other times, as do the self-employed. Only during periods of relative boom does the influence of house purchase through the RTB assert itself. And the influence of particular contingent historical conjunctures – such as occurred between 1987 and 1989 – fade with time. In general then, the data are consistent with a view that sees changes in the risks associated with home ownership as having a strong long-term secular element overlain by shorter-term cyclical movements.

Of course, other variables, not considered here, may well contribute to an understanding of this patterning. In particular, households with low(er) incomes are likely to be more vulnerable. This income effect will be picked up by most of the variables already considered but has not been considered in its own right in the analysis above because the SEH only contains data on current household incomes. For most households in arrears – almost by definition – current incomes are likely to be less than in previous periods due to such contingencies as those picked up by some of the variables already considered: relationship breakdown; unemployment; failed self-employment; and so on. However, and as we shall detail in the next section of this chapter, the growth of low-income home ownership is certainly a factor in the secular change in the risks associated with home ownership.

The 'aetiology' of mortgage arrears and mortgage possession

To restate, the central thesis of this book is that the contingent set of circumstances which generated the housing crisis of the early 1990s masked a set of more enduring socio-economic transformations which have raised the 'normal' (in the Durkheimian sense of this term) level of risk associated with home ownership compared to that which pertained in earlier periods. The 'epidemiology' of mortgage arrears examined in the previous section gives us some strong clues as to the most important factors underpinning the social patterning already described. In addition the SEH also contains valuable data on the reasons that householders themselves give for their arrears. Some householders give more than one reason so the figures presented in Table 2.6 add to more than 100.

We only have data from 1995/96 to 1998/99 using this particular classification of reasons for mortgage arrears. The main reasons given relate to events that lead to a loss of income. In each year we can see that between 61 and 71% of householders cite loss of income as a contributory reason to their mortgage arrears. Within this, in all years, being made redundant or unemployment is stated as the most important cause. In three of the four years this is followed by a reduction in self-employed income. However, in 1998/99, loss of earnings through sickness or injury appears as the second most important factor with self-employed reduced income falling back to third place.

In each year we can see that between 25 and 30% of householders cite household changes of some sort or another as a contributory reason to their mortgage arrears. Within this a spouse or partner leaving the home or dying is the main reason given. In 1998/99, for example, some 23% of all of those in arrears cited this as a contributory factor.

In each year between 23 and 30% of householders cite increases in

Table 2.6: Reasons given for mortgage arrears in England (1995/96, 1996/97, 1997/98 and 1998/99) (%)

Reason	1995/96	1996/97	1997/98	1998/99
Lost earnings through sickness/injury	12	10	16	19
Self-employed income reduced	22	28	20	16
Made redundant/unemployed	38	36	33	32
Lost overtime or reduced hours	11	7	9	8
Worked same hours for less pay	7	2	3	2
All loss of income	*71*	*68*	*68*	*61*
Spouse/partner left/died	14	15	17	23
Other contributor to mortgage left	6	6	2	4
Contributor became pregnant/new baby	8	8	6	5
All household changes	*26*	*27*	*25*	*30*
Increase in mortgage payments	14	11	15	24
Increase in other payments	17	14	15	18
All increase in expenditure	*24*	*23*	*26*	*30*
Other	*18*	*14*	*17*	*16*
Total number of household (000s)	326	268	252	235

Note: Percentages add to more than 100 because some people gave more than one reason.

Source: Survey of English Housing 1995/96, 1996/97, 1997/98 and 1998/99

expenditures as a contributory factor in bringing about arrears while between 14 and 18% cite some other reasons not otherwise covered in the classification.

These 'individual' level reasons for mortgage arrears are, of course, not just the product of disparate 'private troubles' but, rather, are the manifestation of a set of more systematic 'public issues'. Four main factors have routinely been identified which have increased the long-term insecurity of home owners (Ford and Burrows, 1999b; Ford and Wilcox, 1998; Munro, 2000). These are: the expansion of home ownership; demographic transformations; economic transformations; and the restructuring of safety-net provision. In the rest of this chapter we rehearse some of the arguments relating to the impact of the first two of these – the expansion of home ownership and demographic transformations. We then move on to dedicate a chapter each to the impact of economic transformations (Chapter Three) and the restructuring of safety-net provision (Chapter Four).

The expansion of home ownership

The causes of the expansion of home ownership in the post-war period, but especially post-1979, have been briefly noted in Chapter One. As we discussed, this has led to an ever-greater diversity of households within home ownership (Forrest et al, 1990). Nevertheless, no more than 12% of households in owner-occupation are, on a common measure, currently low-income households (Wilcox and Burrows, 2001). However, among those with low incomes, owner-occupiers form the majority. Despite this, the full extent of low-income home ownership is not always appreciated. Studies have tended to focus on specific groups of poor home owners or specific situations that may particularly affect low-income households rather than on the broader picture. However, it is the case that, currently, half the poor are home owners and levels of support for such households are inadequate (Burrows et al, 2000; Burrows and Wilcox, 2000).

As we outlined in Chapter One, this situation is the result of successive post-war governments' actions to promote the growth of home ownership, both through a favourable tax regime and specific policies aimed at encouraging the entry of lower-income households into home ownership. Together, government policy, rising real incomes, widely available mortgage finance, and strong household preferences for home ownership, have seen home ownership in the UK rise to account for 68% of all dwellings. The 'success' of these policies, however, has generated ever-greater numbers of households who, potentially, find home ownership difficult to sustain.

Table 2.7 shows that in 1997/98, a majority (57%) of individuals in the lowest-income decile (taking account of differences in household structure, or 'equivalised' to use the technical term) measured before housing costs (BHC) are owner-occupiers and that more than half of them have a mortgage. Further, home ownership among mortgagors grew by 18 percentage points between 1979 and 1997/8. Measuring incomes after housing costs (AHC) are taken into consideration suggests that home ownership within the lowest-income decile grew from 30% in 1979 to 42% in 1997/98. However, these figures almost certainly underestimate the extent of low-income home ownership as the 'after costs' methodology does not take account of home owners' repair and maintenance costs or the capital payments due on their mortgages.

Despite affordability being such an important concept in policy development for the rented sector, only exceptionally do analyses take into consideration the prevailing housing cost to income ratios for specifically lower-income home buying households (Wilcox, 1999). However, concerns about sustainability suggest that this is an important concept for the home ownership sector too. As can be seen from Table 2.8 the mortgage cost to earnings ratios for lower-income homebuyers are around twice the average level for all homebuying households.

Table 2.7: Tenure of the lowest equivalised income decile of household members in Britain before (BHC) and after (AHC) housing costs (1979, 1990/91 and 1997/98) (%)

	1979		1990/91		1997/98	
	BHC	AHC	BHC	AHC	BHC	AHC
Tenure						
Owned with mortgage	11	13	27	36	29	29
Owned outright	28	17	24	10	28	13
All owned	40	30	51	46	57	42
Rented	60	70	49	54	43	58

Note: The 1979 and 1990/91 figures are based on Family Expenditure Survey (FES) data; the 1997/98 figures are based on Family Resources Survey (FRS) data; the definitions of income are, however, directly comparable.

Sources: Households below average incomes 1979-1990/91, DSS; additional 1997/98 data Analytical Services Division, DSS

Table 2.8: Mortgage as a percentage of gross income

Year	Bottom 20%	Next 20%	Middle 20%	Next 20%	Top 20%	All %
1993/94	36	16	13	12	9	17
1994/95	31	15	12	11	9	15
1995/96	26	14	12	10	9	14
1996/97	24	13	11	10	9	14
1997/98	28	15	13	11	9	15

Notes: Income quintiles are related exclusively to owners buying with a mortgage, and are not 'equivalised' to adjust for variations in household type and size.

Source: Green et al (1999)

In 1997/98, the mortgage cost to income ratio for the lowest quintile of homebuying households in England was 28% (it should be noted, however, that this figure is for the lowest quintile of homebuying households, rather than for the smaller number of homebuyers that fall within the lowest income quintile for all households). Superficially this ratio might be compared with the 25% rent to income ratio set as part of the definition of affordable rents by the National Housing Federation (NHF). However, the NHF ratio is defined in terms of gross rents to net household incomes, while the 28% ratio for home owners relates to mortgage costs only, and excludes any repair costs. It is also based on gross, rather than net, incomes.

However, an analysis of 1996/97 data from the Family Expenditure Survey (FES) shows that homebuyers in the lowest income quintile of all households (unequivalised and before housing costs) have housing costs (mortgage and repair costs) amounting on average to 42% of their net disposable incomes (Wilcox, 1999). This is perhaps a more appropriate measure to set against the NHF affordability guidelines; and on this basis low-income home owners' housing costs can clearly be seen to exceed those guidelines by a substantial margin. Despite this, the current welfare benefit system does not function to supplement the incomes of low-income home owners in the same manner as it does for households living in other tenures. Current policy is not tenure-neutral.

Despite the plethora of low-cost home ownership schemes, low-income home owner households receive very limited government help with their ongoing housing costs, and that assistance has been cut back substantially over the last decade, whether in the form of Income Support for Mortgage Interest (see Chapter Four) or home improvement grants (Burrows and

Wilcox, 2000, ch 2). Means-tested help with housing costs for home owners amounts to less than 10% of the equivalent help provided to low-income tenant households, and this imbalance has been thrown into sharp relief with the final abolition of mortgage interest tax relief in April 2000 (Burrows et al, 2000). There is no assistance with housing costs for in-work, low-income mortgagors.

Demographic changes

Higher rates of household dissolution and instability present further challenges to the ability of households to remain home owners. This is particularly the case for lower-income homebuyers, who are less likely to be able to manage the process of dividing the household assets and incomes to enable either or both parties to continue as home owners. Ford et al (1995) found that some one in eight of a sample of households that had experienced possession gave relationship breakdown as the main reason for the arrears that led to their possession. As we have already seen, Table 2.6 suggests that this proportion may have been growing – in 1998/99 almost one in four households in arrears cited loss of a partner (either through relationship breakdown or death) as a contributory cause of arrears.

More than one in five of all the couples that married between 1970 and 1979 were divorced 15 years later. For couples that had married during the equivalent period 20 years earlier fewer than 1 in 10 were divorced after 15 years (Haskey, 1999). In large measure as a consequence of this rising trend in divorce rates, by the year 2021 it is projected that previously married single people in England and Wales will comprise a fifth of all households; more than twice the proportion in 1996 (Shaw and Haskey, 1999). A comprehensive analysis of the impact of divorce – and subsequent remarriages – and their implications for housing demand in all tenures has recently been completed by Holmans (2000).

Divorces increase the number of 'successor' households, even after allowing for remarriages, and Holmans estimates that during the 1990s this process resulted in a *net* addition of some 45,000 households a year in England and Wales. The parallel process of the dissolution of cohabitation arrangements added further to this increase, but it is more difficult to produce robust estimates of their numerical impact. Homeowner married couples have a lower divorce rate than married couples in other tenures but, because of the dominant size of the home owner sector and the larger proportion of home owners that are married, almost three fifths of all divorces between 1981 and 1991 (for couples married in 1981) involved home owner couples. In the 1990s just over 100,000 home owner couples a year divorced. Of the resulting 200,000(+) divorcees, some 80,000 initially stayed on in the former matrimonial home, about 65,000 moved to other owner-occupied dwellings, 25,000 moved into rented accommodation, and some 35,000 went to live in the household of someone else, in many instances men going to live with their parents.

It is notable then that the process of divorce leads to a 45% increase in the number of owner-occupied households, while at the same time it results in some 30% of former members of home owner married couples moving out, either into rented housing or someone else's household. This 'gross' effect is reduced by subsequent remarriages – some 20,000 remarriages a year involve two previously divorced owner-occupiers.

It is also notable that divorcee households remaining within owner-occupation have lower incomes, occupy dwellings that have lower values and are in poorer condition, have higher mortgage to income ratios and experience greater difficulties meeting their mortgage costs than continuing 'first married' home owner couples. While just 11% of all home owner 'first married' couples had gross weekly incomes below £200 per week, almost three in five of divorced female lone-parent home owners had incomes below that level. This illustrates the importance of relationship breakdown and divorce as factors in the expansion of low-income households within the owner-occupied sector.

Similarly just over half of all 'first married' couples occupied dwellings in the three lowest tax bands – covering dwellings valued below £68,000. In contrast some 70% of the divorced female lone-parent home owners occupied dwellings within those lowest council tax bands. This comparison is an indication of the extent to which 'trading down' is a key element in the capacity of divorcing households to remain within the home owner sector.

However, the adoption of economic policies geared to maintaining low levels of inflation substantially reduces the potential for home owners to 'trade down'. The Holmans' analysis of divorce and remarriage is based on early 1990s data, and the equity holdings of home owner households at that time will have, in the main, reflected the very high level of house price inflation during the 1980s. Given the much lower levels of house price inflation over the 1990s, a subsequent analysis of divorces a decade later could be expected to find a lower proportion of households able to remain in the owner-occupied sector following divorce.

Summary

This chapter has detailed both the extent and the socio-economic distribution of mortgage arrears and possession. We are hopefully left with a clear understanding of the patterning of risk experienced by home owners that pertains over the economic cycle. The chapter has also begun to outline some of the main factors that underpin this risk profile. Factors associated with the expansion of home ownership, especially post-1979, were considered, notably in relation to the growth of low-income home ownership. The impact of demographic changes on unsustainable home ownership, especially divorce and separation, was also noted. However, the main factors that account for both the extent and the socio-economic distribution of mortgage arrears and possessions, are considered in the next two chapters. In Chapter Three we examine the impact of economic transformations of various sorts, while in Chapter Four we consider how these interact with the impact of the restructuring of welfare provision on home owners.

Note

This chapter draws on material previously published in: Burrows (1998a) and Burrows and Ford (1997) which was unfunded research; Burrows (1998b) which was funded by the CML; and Burrows and Wilcox (2000) which was funded by the CML.

THREE

Owner-occupation and the impact of economic transformations

For much of the post-war period, owner-occupation, economic conditions (in particular, the nature of labour market opportunities), and safety-net provision have been mutually supportive and enabled home ownership to be experienced as a secure and sustainable tenure. However, as suggested in Chapter One, a number of key changes have brought about an ongoing restructuring of these traditionally supportive relationships, as a consequence of which home ownership is now a riskier undertaking. In this chapter we consider first the general picture of labour market change and then proceed to a more detailed discussion of the way in which labour market restructuring challenges secure and stable home ownership. Following a review of the available empirical evidence we present three detailed case studies of households having to deal with different aspects of the emerging disjuncture between the vicissitudes of the contemporary labour market and the sustaining of home ownership. In addition, we consider briefly two further areas of economic change that impact on home ownership: the advent of a low inflation economy and the curtailment and removal of some fiscal incentives to home owners.

Labour market restructuring

Labour markets have always been subject to cyclical processes, but, in addition, in the last quarter of the 20th century much structural change in them has been evident. Table 3.1 summarises the direction of some broad trends, showing, for example, the percentage reduction in full-time employment between 1981 and 1996, the rise in part-time employment, and some growth in self-employment in the early 1990s. The projected figures to 2006 are also given and indicate the likelihood of a continuing fall in full-time employment. These changes already have and will continue to have a differential impact at the regional and sub-regional level. In addition, the impact has been greater for some groups in the labour market than others, as for example, can be seen in the reduction of male,

Table 3.1: Composition of employment in Britain (1981, 1991, 1996, 2001 and 2006) (%)

	1981	1991	1996	2001	2006
Full-time employees	71.8	64.2	62.7	60.9	59.1
Part-time employees	19.0	22.7	24.5	26.5	28.6
Self-employed	9.2	13.1	12.8	12.6	12.3
	100.0	100.0	100.0	100.0	100.0

Source: Lindley and Wilson (1998)

manual, full-time employment in the manufacturing sector and the increase in female, part-time, service sector employment (Lindley and Wilson, 1998).

These long-term structural shifts in the labour market reflect a range of influences such as: the impact of technological innovation and change (including the new information and communication technologies) on the production of goods and services; globalisation processes; the deregulation of the labour market; and employers' strategies towards the more flexible use of labour. As will be discussed later, these changes have resulted in an increase in the proportion of jobs with some in-built instability which constitutes a potentially serious challenge to home ownership.

One impact of these changes has been to create uncertainty about the permanence of economic activity in any one place and to heighten the risk of unemployment. This has encouraged governments to respond by developing policies designed to create the conditions conducive to retaining current economic activity and attracting additional investment (Burrows and Loader, 1994). One essential process has been the deregulation of key markets such as that of the UK labour market and the UK financial market during the 1980s. In the UK, through legislation, there was a reduction in the power of the trade unions, the dismantling of the wages councils, and a reduction in the level of employment protection that had to be afforded to permanent employees. That these were courses of action in line with the ideology of the governments of the time made the task more palatable and more readily embraced (Burrows, 1991), but few if any European countries have been free from having to consider how to respond and have done so in a range of ways (see, for example, Esping-Andersen, 1996). The position is nicely summed up by White (1996) who noted that to some extent "a country may to some extent control the distribution or form of risk, but cannot evade that risk altogether" (p 78). The fact that some groups of employees in Britain have regained some employment safeguards, for example the introduction of a minimum wage and better protection for part-time workers, does not alter the commitment of the UK government to enhance competitiveness by providing a highly deregulated labour market.

Labour market flexibility

Within this context of global competition, uncertainty and deregulation, employers have sought strategies to enhance their individual competitiveness. One key theorisation of this process is that of the flexible labour market which identifies a number of forms of flexibility in the use of labour (see, for example, Gilbert et al (1992) for a discussion). Thus, for core activities and core workers, functional flexibility is sought in the form of multiskilling and an end to functional demarcations. More critical for the discussion of unsustainable owner-occupation, is the emphasis placed on forms of employment contract that provide numerical, temporal and pay flexibility. Thus, employers may seek to recruit only in response to a clear need for labour and to retain workers only as long as such demand is sustained, and a reliance on temporary working and hiring and firing has increased. In 1999, over 7% of workers were in temporary employment compared to less than 5% at the end of the 1980s.

In some instances part-time employment also provides flexibility, for example, in sectors with peak flows (such as catering). Part-time employment has, however, also allowed employers to provide reduced employment protection (and so costs), and attract workers such as women who are traditionally low paid and un-unionised. There is, however, a debate around the proportion of part-time employment that is appropriately classified as flexible, and so more precarious employment. Evidence of the stability in some part-time employment is sometimes contrasted with evidence of the clear risks of part-time work where it is only temporary or held by those who would prefer, but cannot obtain, full-time employment. Designating workers as 'nominally' self-employed (even if to all intents and purposes they are employees) has also been implemented as a means of transferring the responsibility for, and costs of, employment protection from employer to employee. Other strategies to increase flexibility have involved the use of agency workers and new forms of home working. Pay flexibility is exemplified in the growth of contracts such as zero hours contracts that only pay when employees work or annualised hours contracts which now characterise 2% of employment contracts, but also by performance-related pay and local pay bargaining.

There is, of course, a lively debate about how thoroughgoing such restructuring is or is likely to prove to be. Notwithstanding this debate, there is a growing consensus that more flexible, and often more precarious forms of employment are now an established feature of the labour market (Beatson, 1995; Dex and McCulloch, 1997). To the extent that this has occurred, it is a potential challenge to sustainable home ownership with its requirement for secure, permanent and stable incomes.

The growth of employment instabilities

While the majority of people in work remain in full-time permanent employment, the overall average job duration is falling, if slowly, with a 14% reduction in median job tenure for employees between 1975 and 1992 (Gregg and Wadsworth, 1995). But job duration varies by type of employment, and forms of flexible employment have shorter durations than full-time permanent employment. Based on data from 1992, permanent part-time employment and full-time self-employment had average durations just over half that of full-time permanent employment (6.2 years). Temporary employment and part-time self-employment each had durations of around a tenth that of full-time permanent jobs. All part-time job durations have fallen since the start of the 1980s, but it is among the part-time self-employed that the fall is most pronounced.

As noted above, recent and predicted employment growth is concentrated among the shorter duration opportunities. As a result, the trend is towards a higher proportion of less secure labour market opportunities than was previously the case, and hence, a growing proportion of households face less secure employment. This trend is particularly clear when based on an examination of 'new' jobs in the labour market rather than the stock of current jobs. Here, between 1992/93 and 1995/96, while 59% of vacancies were permanent, under 10% were for full-time jobs (TUC, 1996). This compares with the stock of jobs in 1992/93 where 60% of the jobs were full time and permanent. Forty-one per cent of 'new' jobs were temporary (compared to under 10% of the stock of jobs) although more than half were full time. Compared to the current stock of jobs where around a third are part time, between 1992/93 and 1995/96, 65% of 'new' jobs were part time (Gregg and Wadsworth, 1995). While the trend towards more vacancies being part time or temporary holds over the 1990s, their prominence varies year on year.

One potential implication of an increase in less secure, shorter duration employment is an increase in employment mobility, from job to job and/or between types of employment or between employment and unemployment. This is so notwithstanding the evidence that the average job duration has fallen only a little, that many people have very long job durations indeed, and that some mobility is voluntary. Many moves will be motivated by the ending of a temporary job, a completed contract or the failure of self-employment which is widely documented as a 'volatile' status (Buck et al, 1994) and each labour market 'change' has the potential to result in a period of unemployment. Further, there is evidence that unemployment increases the likelihood that re-employment will be in one of the more precarious forms of employment.

Analyses of Labour Force Survey (LFS) data (Gregg and Wadsworth, 1994) show that of those unemployed in the first quarter of 1992, just over half were in a full-time job by the first quarter of 1993, but almost two fifths of these jobs were temporary. The rest were almost equally divided between part-time employment and self-employment. Evidence from the British Household Panel Survey (BHPS) (Buck et al, 1994) is comparable. Of those unemployed in 1991, under half were in employment 12 months later, and only one in five obtained a full-time job. White and Forth (1998), focusing on those unemployed in the early 1990s, also reported that three in four unemployed people got jobs that were temporary or part time, or became self-employed. The overwhelming majority of those taking flexible jobs were still in the flexible sector five years on. Temporary employment offered the greatest mobility with over a third of those initially in temporary jobs in permanent employment after five years.

Mortgagors and precarious employment

Given these overall market changes, a key question concerns the extent to which home owners are vulnerable to unemployment and less secure forms of employment. Evidence of the percentage of mortgagors in such circumstances can be obtained from the Labour Force Survey (LFS) (see Ford, 1998) and from the BHPS. The results from the two sources are broadly consistent, with between a fifth and a quarter of mortgagor heads of household in less secure employment (depending on the view taken about part-time work). Table 3.2 indicates the employment status of mortgagor heads of household as shown by the BHPS. The BHPS tracks the same individuals on an annual basis, providing data on their circumstances year on year. Data are now available for eight waves from 1990/91 to 1997/98. The data have been weighted in such a way as to provide cross-sectional estimates.

In 1997/98, 67% of all mortgagor heads of household were in full-time permanent employment (rising to three quarters among those who were economically active). Three per cent were permanent employees but in part-time employment. More than 4% had non-permanent jobs. Over 13% were in self-employment. Excluding *permanent* part-time workers, more than one in six had a form of flexible employment and a further 2% were unemployed. Twelve per cent were retired or economically inactive for other reasons.

Over the period 1990/91 to 1997/98, the percentage with flexible employment has remained relatively stable, although the percentage with both permanent and temporary part-time work has increased a little and full-time employment has fallen by two percentage points. There has been a significant fall in the percentage unemployed (as the economic cycle picked up) while those retired and economically inactive has increased. Altogether, just under a fifth of all mortgagor heads of household (and just under a quarter of those economically active) had

Table 3.2: Employment status of homebuyer household heads in Britain (1991/92, 1993/94, 1995/96 and 1997/98) (%)

	1991/92	1993/94	1995/96	1997/98
Employee, permanent, full-time	67.1	64.9	64.6	67
Employee, permanent, part-time	2.2	3.1	3.1	3.0
Employee, not permanent, full-time	1.7	1.7	2.1	1.6
Employee, not permanent, part-time	0.6	0.6	0.7	1.0
Self-employed, permanent, full-time	12.4	12.4	12.0	11.4
Self-employed, permanent, part-time	0.7	0.6	0.3	0.3
Self-employed, not permanent, full-time	2.1	1.7	2.4	1.5
Self-employed, not permanent, part-time	0.3	0.3	0.6	0.3
Unemployed	4.4	4.1	3.3	1.8
Other	8.5	10.7	11.0	12.0

Note: Not permanent is the terminology used in the British Household Panel Survey (BHPS) for temporary employment.

Source: BHPS: authors' analysis

precarious labour market positions. The figures discussed above, however, are cross-sectional estimates. As such it is possible that they understate the incidence of less secure employment among mortgagors as they do not capture the 'between date' experiences. It is also helpful to compare the position in the 1990s with the position at the start of the 1980s. At that time, 93% of mortgagor heads of household were in work, 92% on a full-time basis (data on temporary working were not available but is likely to have been very limited among home owners). Thus, the major growth in risky employment among mortgagors appears to have occurred in the 1980s with some further growth in the early and mid-1990s, but pulled back a little at the end of the decade as the economic cycle peaked.

Clearly, this national picture will not be replicated to the same extent everywhere in the country, given the particular economic and industrial traditions of different places, but surveys do show that the national trends have significance at a local level. For example, based on a series of surveys in Bristol and Glasgow, Maclennan et al (1997, pp 8-9) noted that among mortgagors "In 1988 94% of respondents classed their jobs as 'permanent'; by 1995, this share had fallen to 85%" and further that "... what has changed, and is of importance for cyclical and *long-run stability* is the certainty of income and employment" [our emphasis].

The discussion above has focused only on heads of mortgagor households. However, in Chapter Two we also noted the extent to which mortgagor households were dual earner households and that such a pattern was often a prerequisite of being able to buy. Given this, the labour market status of additional earners is also significant in understanding the extent of any risk to home ownership. Table 3.3 indicates that additional earners in mortgagor households are less likely to be in permanent, full-time employment than was the case among heads of household.

When we consider *all* employed adults in the household, the percentage of people in each of temporary employment, in permanent part-time work or unemployed rises. There is a small increase in part-time self-employment. Looking at the household as a unit, the proportion of mortgagor households at risk from labour market insecurity is likely to be higher than the nearly one in five noted earlier for heads of household. However, a major difference between heads of household and other adult household members is the percentage of the latter that are economically inactive. Many of these will be women caring for children, or retired women who still have a partner in employment.

Table 3.3: Employment status of adult members of homebuying households in Britain (1997/98) (%)

	Household head	Other adults	All adults
Employee, permanent, full-time	67.0	40.8	52.9
Employee, permanent, part-time	3.0	16.8	10.4
Employee, not permanent, full-time	1.6	2.4	2.0
Employee, not permanent, part-time	1.0	2.6	1.8
Self-employed, permanent, full-time	11.3	2.8	6.7
Self-employed, permanent, part-time	0.3	1.3	0.8
Self-employed, not permanent, full-time	1.5	0.6	1.0
Self-employed, not permanent, part-time	0.3	0.5	0.4
Unemployed	1.8	3.1	2.5
Other	12.0	29.4	21.3
Total	100	100	100
Number of valid cases	1,957	2,274	4,231

Source: BHPS: authors' analysis

Employment continuity and change among mortgagors

As well as identifying the proportion of mortgagors in less secure positions, it is also important to try and assess the extent of labour market disruption, as each disruption is potentially a threat to home ownership. An early analysis of the extent of employment continuity among mortgagors was reported in 1998 (Ford, 1998). This used data from the BHPS but only considered the period 1991 to 1995. The analysis noted that while the majority of mortgagor heads of household had held one employment status continuously over the period, 28% had experienced some change of employment status (employment, self-employment or unemployment/inactive), and in a small number of cases they had experienced all four 'states'. Of those still employed or self-employed in 1995 (that is, taking out all those who had left the labour market over the period), 32% had at least one period of unemployment during the preceding five years. However, this analysis had a number of limitations. For example, it only considered mortgagor heads of household and so failed to capture the extent of instability among other household earners and it did not link the data to the debate on unsustainable owner-occupation by considering any consequential change in tenure following a change of employment status. The analysis is, in any case, now rather dated.

We have therefore undertaken further analysis of the nature and extent of employment continuity for this book. Using BHPS data for two periods, 1990/91 to 1993/94 and again for 1994/95 to 1997/98, the employment status (employed, unemployed, self-employed or other) of all those who were mortgagor heads of household at the beginning of each period were identified at each successive wave. The period 1990-98 has been divided in this way to distinguish, very broadly, the period of recession and housing market difficulty and the period of economic buoyancy and housing market recovery. Table 3.4 identifies both continuity and change in the two periods for mortgagor heads of household. The table also notes the percentage of mortgagor heads of household that were no longer owner-occupiers at the end of the respective periods.

Considering the period 1990/91 to 1993/94, the analysis indicates continuity rather than change in the employment experiences of

Table 3.4: Employment continuity and change for heads of mortgagor households (1991-94 and 1995-98) and tenure at end date (1994, 1998)

	1991-94 All heads of household with a mortgage in 1991		1995-98 All heads of household with a mortgage in 1995	
Employment pattern	1991 %	% not in owner-occupation in 1994	1995 %	% not in owner-occupation in 1998
Employed in all 4 years	58.4	1.9	61.2	1.1
Employed in 3 of 4 years	10.2	7.3	8.3	6.0
Self-employed in all 4 years	8.4	1.3	7.8	0.7
Self-employed in 3 of 4 years	2.8	3.9	2.2	12.5
Unemployed in all 4 years	0.2	33.3	0.2	0.0
Unemployed in 3 of 4 years	0.8	14.3	0.3	0.0
Other in all 4 years*	7.5	4.5	10.5	4.2
Other in 3 of 4 years*	3.1	3.6	2.1	15.8
More complex sequences	8.7	3.3	7.1	8.0
Totals	100.0	3.0	100.0	2.9

*Includes: retired, keeping home, sick, otherwise unable to work.

Source: BHPS: authors' analysis

mortgagor heads. Two thirds of mortgagor heads were either employed or self-employed throughout. Very few were unemployed throughout while over 7.5% were economically inactive throughout. Seventeen per cent experienced one change of economic status, and almost 9% had more than one change as shown by the term 'complex sequences'. In total, over a quarter of the 1991 heads of mortgagor households had experienced some change of status by 1994.

The second column of the table indicates the percentage of those mortgagor heads in 1990/91 that were no longer in owner-occupation in 1994. Overall, 3% had left the tenure. We cannot assume that all those leaving did so because they could no longer pay the mortgage. Some may have left as a result of relationship breakdown, others could be mobile households currently renting before buying again, and some may have moved out of owner-occupation on retirement, seeking supported housing options. However, while we need to be cautious, it is also the case that many may have left because their home ownership was not sustainable, not least because we have already identified the role that employment change and unemployment play in mortgage arrears. A comparison between those with continuity in any particular status, and those with some disruption to that status (for example, employed in all four years compared to employed in three of the four years) suggests that disruption does impact on the likelihood of remaining in the tenure. Under 2% of those employed in all four years had left, whereas over 7% of those with one 'break' from employment had left. A comparison of those with continuous and those with disrupted self-employment shows a similar pattern. While the figures for unemployment look very stark, the very small numbers mean we cannot take the figures at face value. Overall, as indicative evidence, these figures do not undermine the suggestion that disruptions to employment (breaks in employment and changes of employment status) may be conducive to mortgage arrears and potentially the loss of home ownership.

Considering the period 1994/95 to 1997/98, a slightly higher proportion of mortgagor heads of household in 1995 have continuity of employment and a slightly lower proportion were continuously self-employed. The pattern of unemployment was not dissimilar to the earlier period, while the proportion of permanently inactive mortgagors grew a little. Almost 13% experienced one change of economic status and the proportion with two or more changes of employment status fell by just over a percentage point. There are, though, striking differences in the pattern of exits from the tenure, with rather dramatic increases in the percentage of those with disruptions to self-employment leaving home ownership (12.5% compared to 3.9% in 1991-1994), and an increase in the proportion leaving among those with more than two disruptions. It is only possible to speculate about some of the likely reasons for these shifts. In some instances the gradual recovery in house prices and transactions will have allowed some of those with arrears to sell more easily, either from choice or due to lender action. The same conditions will also have helped anyone wishing to leave the sector but previously delayed by a lack of buyers.

Table 3.5 considers a change of employment status by *any* member of a mortgagor household, but otherwise replicates the information given in Table 3.4.

For both periods, there is a lower proportion of households where all members are continuously in employment or self-employment compared to a consideration of just heads of households. Similarly, a higher proportion of households contain people with more than two employment

Table 3.5: Employment continuity and change for all heads of mortgagor households and their partners (if any) (1991-94 and 1995-98) and tenure at end date (1994, 1998)

	1991-94 All heads of household and their partners (if any) with a mortgage in 1991		1995-98 All heads of household and their partners (if any) with a mortgage in 1995	
Employment pattern	**1991 %**	**% not in owner-occupation in 1994**	**1995 %**	**% not in owner-occupation in 1998**
Employed in all 4 years	55.1	2.3	59.2	1.6
Employed in 3 of 4 years	10.1	8.0	9.7	4.9
Self-employed in all 4 years	6.5	1.8	6.8	2.7
Self-employed in 3 of 4 years	2.1	5.5	2.0	10.4
Unemployed in all 4 years	0.3	33.3	0.1	0.0
Unemployed in 3 of 4 years	0.6	14.3	0.4	25.0
Other in all 4 years*	10.2	9.4	10.9	3.5
Other in 3 of 4 years*	4.9	14.1	3.3	8.1
More complex sequences	10.3	8.4	7.7	8.6
Totals	100.0	5.0	100.0	3.2

*Includes: retired, keeping home, sick, otherwise unable to work.

Source: BHPS: authors' analysis

changes than was found for just heads of household, but the gap is narrower in the period 1995-98. Considering the percentages of household members no longer in owner-occupation in either 1994 or 1998, again, a lower percentage of those with continuous employment leave than is the case where there is a change of employment status. Not surprisingly, the household figures show a slightly higher percentage leaving the tenure than is the case for just heads of household.

Home owners and unemployment

Unemployment among mortgagor heads of household grew during the 1980s, reaching 4% in 1993. In England it peaked in 1994 at 5%, and fell back to 1% in 1998/99 (McConaghy et al, 2000). The rise in unemployment in the early 1990s was partly a result of a rising rate of unemployment among professional and other white-collar workers, but also due to much higher rates of unemployment among manual and routine white-collar workers, many of whom took mortgages and entered owner-occupation during the 1980s. The BHPS notes a similar trend for Britain, but reports that unemployment peaked sooner (1991/92) and at 4% before falling to 1.8% in 1997/98 (see Table 3.2). This source also indicates that in 1997/98 unemployment among other adult earners was higher than among heads of mortgagor households, again suggesting that the figures from heads of household underestimate the impact of unemployment on mortgagor households. The figures are also cross-sectional, and so over a period of time, the number of mortgagors at risk will, in all probability, be higher.

While we saw in Chapter Two that unemployment increased the risk of mortgage arrears very considerably, there are important caveats to be entered. Not all unemployment results in mortgage default and so unsustainable owner-occupation. Individual households may have savings, although calculations show that in 1991/92 more than half of all households had financial wealth of under £455, and a proportion of these will be mortgagors (Banks et al, 1994). There may be other household earners who can meet the existing financial commitments, unemployed mortgagors may receive assistance from kin (Ford, 1995), and the availability of safety-net provision, both public and private, may mitigate any financial distress.

The changing structure of employment opportunities and the incidence of unemployment are, however, only two examples of the ways in which labour market change potentially jeopardises home ownership. A third major issue, that of low pay, is explored next.

The growth of low-paid employment

In principle, the growth of low- and lower-paid workers has a number of implications for the housing market. It may preclude some households who have a preference for home ownership from entering on grounds of affordability (McLaverty and Yip, 1994; Kempson, 1994). Equally, low pay may reduce mortgagors' ability to manage upward movements in housing costs, and so jeopardise the sustainability of their owner-occupation. Recent examples of cost increases include: the imposition of tax on insurance policies; the reduction and eventual abolition of MITR; and from the late 1980s, rapid increases in interest rates. Few low-paid workers have the means to meet these variable costs, not least where low pay is associated with part-time employment and where pay settlements in low-paid sectors are often below the rate of inflation.

Although average income is rising in Britain, there is growing evidence of income polarisation (Hills, 1995). The divisions are not only between those in work and those solely reliant on social assistance benefits, but also between those in work. An increasing number of employees are in low-paid employment and a proportion of these workers have incomes from employment that are less than the Income Support subsistence benefit. The extent of low pay for workers *irrespective of tenure* can be measured in a number of different ways. One of these is the number of workers earning below the Council of Europe's 'decency' threshold, which in 1999 was £7.18 gross per hour. In total, over 11 million full-time and pro-rata part-time workers were in this position, almost half of all employees. Using another, 'tighter' measure, in April 1996 approaching one in five of all full-time workers earned no more than £3.99 an hour as did three quarters of part-time workers. Low pay was proportionally more prevalent in the service sector and in part-time jobs (and therefore among women). These are the sectors of the labour market projected to grow in coming years. The impact of these developments for home ownership will depend in part on the extent to which mortgagors are to be found in the low-pay sector.

There are a number of different indications of the extent of low pay among mortgagors. For example, an analysis commissioned by the Social Security Committee from the Institute for Fiscal Studies showed that in 1992 there were close to 1.5 million owner-occupied households not in receipt of Income Support, but with incomes below Income Support levels (Social Security Committee, 1995). Of those, 850,000 were homebuyers with a mortgage. While a proportion of this figure might be low-income pensioners still with a mortgage but unwilling to claim benefits, the majority are likely to be in employment.

A second indication of the extent of low-paid mortgagors comes from an analysis of the 1995 Family Expenditure Survey (FES). This shows 1.12 million homebuyers with gross annual incomes of no more than £234 per week. This encompasses the four lower-income deciles. Excluding mortgagors in receipt of Income Support and so not in employment, there were around 620,000 mortgagor households with incomes from employment well below the Council of Europe low-pay threshold (which was £239 per week in 1995). A third indication comes from a secondary analysis of the 1998/99 Survey of English Housing (SEH) which can be used to identify households with incomes below £5,000 per annum (under £100 a week). Over 220,000 households with a mortgage in England have an annual income of £5,000 or less. Of these, 57,000 are headed by someone who is currently employed and 85,000 are headed by someone who is economically inactive.

Self-employed mortgagor heads of household are also over-represented in the lower-income deciles (where housing costs as a percentage of income are highest). By 1992/93, among households with below half of average income (before housing costs), there were 690,000 mortgagor households headed by a self-employed person, approaching a quarter of all self-employed households. The absolute numbers have increased by 510,000 since 1979 as a result of threshold, size and risk effects (DSS, 1995).

While all these figures are only indicative, low pay is clearly a potential difficulty for a sizeable minority of home owners (depending on the measure of low pay, the figure ranges from 6 to 9%, that is about one in every 17 to about one in every 11 mortgagor households). While the extent of their individual vulnerability to rising costs will vary, depending on the proportion of income devoted to mortgage costs, we have seen in Chapter Two that lower-income borrowers already have a higher percentage of income committed to housing than do those with higher incomes.

Low pay, insecure employment and unemployment

As suggested earlier, low pay, the changing pattern of labour market opportunities and unemployment all interact. This is clear *in general* from a range of analyses of large data sets and the evidence already presented above to the effect that unemployment is often followed by insecure employment. In addition, Buck et al (1994) using the BHPS showed that across all tenures, half of those interviewed at wave two, who had experienced involuntary unemployment in the preceding 12 months, but then been re-employed, faced an average drop of 10% in their income on re-employment.

The same interconnections have also been noted in studies specifically focused on mortgagors. The first national study of mortgage arrears and possessions (Ford et al, 1995), noted that 14% of respondents had recently experienced a drop in earnings as a result of having to take new, lower-paid work. Lower pay was also experienced by those retaining their jobs where the study showed that 6% of mortgagors had suffered a recent reduction in their working hours and 6% had lost overtime. Similar findings come from a study of owner-occupiers in Bristol, Luton and Glasgow (Maclennan, 1994) where between 9% and 19% of respondents had suffered reduced income or lost overtime, or had lost a second job, in the preceding three years. At the time the study was carried out, between 19% and 23% of owner-occupier household members had also lost their jobs since 1989 and would therefore have been vulnerable to the patterns of unemployment and re-employment noted above. Further support for this suggestion comes from Burrows and Wilcox (2000) who detail the evidence showing that more mortgagors *become* poor than start out as poor.

These interconnections carry a range of implications for mortgagor households as they attempt to manage their housing costs. Qualitative studies have shown, for example, that for a minority of unemployed mortgagors the risks and uncertainties of employment, particularly in the context of low wages, deter them from returning to the labour market often because of a fear of mortgage arrears. Here, the complete withdrawal of the state safety-net Income Support Mortgage Interest (ISMI), on a return to work, constitutes a work disincentive (Ford et al, 1996), although there is now a proposal to provide a four-week ISMI run-on for those returning to employment (DETR/DSS, 2000a). Other unemployed mortgagors take a less 'calculative' view. Their commitment to work leads them to manage within the flexible labour market on a return to work at an inadequate wage but this frequently involves one or more of: a second job; exceptionally long hours in order to increase income through overtime; the entry (or re-entry) of partners into the labour market; and an increase in the hours of work of already working partners (Ford et al, 1996; Quilgars and Abbott, 2000; Ford, 2000a).

Some illustrative case studies

The analysis outlined above presents a complex picture and does not easily translate into an understanding of how these processes of labour market change are 'lived'. Below, three detailed case studies are used to illustrate some of the experiences that such labour market restructuring invokes for home owners. They are taken from Ford (1995, 1998).

Contracts and overtime: the price of mortgage payments

The first case study shows the significance *over time* of: changing labour market opportunities; the association of employment and unsustainable home ownership; the nature and implications of a number of different forms of flexible employment; and the impact of permanent but low-paid work. It was completed in 1998, indicating support for our earlier suggestion that unsustainable home ownership is not only associated with cyclical downturns and unemployment but can characterise more buoyant periods in the economy. It also shows how the hangover of the 1990s market continues to constrain the actions of some borrowers.

> Mr and Mrs C, aged 31 and 33, had three children. Both were working when they were interviewed in 1998. Mr C was running his father's plumbing firm as contracts manager. He started this permanent job in September 1997, and will take over the business when his father retires next year. Mrs C was working part time as a courier for a delivery firm. She had been in the job about a year and thought she was classed as self-employed as she did not pay tax or receive holiday or sick pay.
>
> Mr C earned £20,800 per annum gross. He was working 11 hours a day, Monday to Friday, plus occasional Saturday mornings and some evenings. Mrs C was paid per delivery and worked up to 2.5 hours per day. Her earnings varied between £30 and £70 per week.
>
> Mr C has always been in full-time employment and has had seven jobs since entering the labour market at 18. Yet, he was 'very frustrated'. As he noted, he'd never been out of work, always looked for maximum money or 'to get on'. He'd always worked long hours but, at best, they'd ended up mostly just managing and, at worst, not coping and in debt. Aspects of the flexible labour market contributed to this outcome.

They had married in 1986 and bought their first house. Mr C was by then working for his father in his plumbing business. Mrs C had part-time employment (as she has had for the whole of their married life). Money was tight but Mr C's attempt to move and sustain a better-paying job was unsuccessful because it was in a different town and needed them to move which, it turned out, they could not afford to do. He came back to his father's firm as a foreman. His work now involved trips abroad, which he did not like as he now had two young children.

As a result, Mr C looked for another job and in 1989 went as a contract worker at an oil refinery. Although this work was on a contract by contract basis, there was always another contract following on. The work was well paid at the oil refinery, £420 per week net (based on a 10-hour day for seven days). He was not worried about taking on contract work because there was '... loads of work ... there weren't any gaps ...' and he had a specialist type of job so was in demand. There were substantial opportunities for overtime. As a result, the family moved house. They borrowed on the basis of the total earnings from the contract job, but even so thought they had left themselves some room for manoeuvre once the mortgage was paid.

The contract jobs in the refinery lasted for about three years. Then Mr C had the chance of applying for a job as a supervisor with another firm on the same site. He decided to do so, to 'get on', as this was a permanent job, full-time and salaried. However, they did not realise that being 'salaried' meant that there would be very little overtime. As a result they struggled to meet their mortgage payments of £620 per month plus a further £90 for an endowment policy, and arrears mounted. The total mortgage and mortgage-related costs were essentially unaffordable, approaching 40% of net income. Mr C was in this job for about 18 months but then he returned to contract work. The family needed more money and this opened up the opportunity for overtime again. Mr C had also had a disagreement with the company about their health and safety arrangements and knew they were looking to dispense with him.

As there was plenty of work about, Mr C hoped to be able to take time off between contracts to be with his children. His main place of work was back in the refinery, but on separate plants, which had to be overhauled quickly. He worked long hours and made £480 to £500 per week gross and needed to maximise his income to clear their arrears. During these contracts the arrears did come down and following some of them being capitalised Mr and Mrs C were eventually 'free' from them. There were also gaps between contracts, but Mr C was always quick to 'sign on' as soon as he was paid off. This was to ensure that at least some money came in, especially to help with the mortgage, though not all of the payment was met by ISMI.

This work lasted until 1995. Then the company responsible for the refinery began to cut costs and to keep work 'in-house'. When they did use contractors, the amount of overtime was reduced. Mr C decided to move, and in 1996 he went back into plumbing. At first he acted as a foreman which involved going out and about. Then he became the small works manager, based in the office. While he was doing the foreman's job, he was able to work overtime again; once in the office, he was on a set salary, but he did feel that he had taken a step up the ladder. The foreman's job paid £7 per hour and he averaged £300 to £350 per week on a nominally self-employed contract. As small works manager, he earned £19,000 pa gross, about £260 net per week. This was not enough to pay the mortgage, despite falling interest rates at this time, and once again arrears began to mount.

Finally, money problems, an inability to sell their house due to negative equity, parental encouragement, and his own assessment of the long-term prospects of the family business drew Mr C back to his father's firm as contracts manager. This pushed his salary up a little – £291 net per week. He regards the job as for the long term, as stable, and does not intend to move jobs again. Mrs C's part-time employment continues to be important to the family budget. The job gives her flexibility, as deliveries can be made within two days of their receipt and at times of her choosing. The employer also has flexibility, only paying when deliveries are needed and without responsibility for any of the costs of employment (national insurance, pension, sick provision, etc).

However, in 1998, the mortgage continued to be a problem. Mr and Mrs C's income has not increased enough for them to be able to clear the remaining arrears, despite the recent expansion of the family business. They fear that a previously granted suspended possession order might yet be activated. Until recently they had negative equity but selling is now an option. Rehousing options, however, trouble them. If they are deemed intentionally homeless the local authority will not rehouse them and they believe that renting privately will be no cheaper than their current mortgage. Currently, with the help of an advice agency, their strategy is to persuade the local authority to agree to rehouse them following the voluntary sale of their home.

Insecure jobs, confidence in employability and home ownership

The second case study concerns a household who have managed to sustain home ownership while being involved in the flexible labour market. It illustrates some of the important points already made at a more general level earlier in this book. For example: that employers may change the terms and conditions of employment for existing employees as they seek to remain competitive; the likelihood of re-employment in a low-paid job following unemployment; that arrears are not the inevitable outcome of poor employment although this eventuality is often only avoided by accessing overtime or a second job.

Mr and Mrs A have been together for nearly eight years. They are 38 and 40 respectively. Their current home was the first house they had bought together.

Both were working at the time of the interview. Mrs A was an administrator on a contract described as 'permanent subject to funding'. She had been in this job for two years and expected it to continue for at least another two years. Mr A worked as an HGV driver and had just obtained a full-time, permanent contract with one of the major oil companies having previously been working for them on a temporary contract. Although he was due to start the day following our interview, he was concerned that he had not received written confirmation.

Both entered the labour market at 16. Mr A had had 10 jobs in 22 years and Mrs A 12 jobs in 24 years. Their jobs, the length of time they held them and the reasons for leaving them are set out in Table 3.6.

Table 3.6: Job histories

Mr A			Mrs A		
Occupation	**Length and type of employment**	**Reason for leaving**	**Occupation**	**Length and type of employment**	**Reason for leaving**
Butcher	11 years FT	Wanted a change and to avoid Saturday working	Clerk	3 months PT/FT	Left before sacked
Driver	18 months FT/P	Redundancy	Shopwork Cleaning Factory work	Intermittent P/T	
Driver	2 years FT/P	Changes in terms and conditions	Cleaning	2 years P/T	Available for full-time work as children were at school
			School meals supervision		
Car salvage	few months	Had never intended it to be more than a 'stop-gap'	Supermarket worker	5 months	Boring job
Driver	1 year FT/P	Anxiety about health and safety Not having HGV driving skills	Office worker	2 years	Dissatisfied with pay
Refuse collection	3 years – 6 months contract 30 months FT/P	Change in terms and conditions	Service receptionist	9 months	Redundancy
Delivery driver	18 months FT/P	Excessive hours required to make a living	Fleet car administrator	4 years	Management buy out and poor morale
Tanker driver	3+ months FT/P	Injury. Company not prepared to re-employ	Office worker	1 year	Unsettled
Delivery driver	3 months FT/P	Low pay	Office worker	6 weeks FT/P	Disagreement over holiday entitlement
Tanker driver	6 months FT/T	Offer of permanent job with the same company	Agency temping	8 months FT/T	Found permanent work
			Administrator	Initial 7 months contract FT/contract extended twice	

P =Permanent; T = Temporary; FT = Full-time; PT = Part-time

Mr A started with permanent employment, but over time his employment became less secure. By contrast, Mrs A's early years in the labour market were in very casual, unskilled jobs. Experience, training and persistence had enabled her to get 'better' jobs and even though she did not avoid redundancy, and some were still temporary jobs, she suggested that she had made her way relatively successfully through the labour market. The job moves made by Mr and Mrs A came about in a number of different ways. Sometimes they were voluntary; Mr A moved from his first job as a butcher to be a driver because he wanted a change; just prior to meeting Mr A, Mrs A gave up her supermarket work because it was 'really boring' and she wanted better work in an office.

Some moves followed redundancy while others arose from dissatisfaction with the terms and conditions of employment. This typically followed a company takeover or an internal restructuring. For example, in 1990 when Mr A had been with the agency as a driver and full-time permanent employee, the recession led to the company restructuring and putting the drivers on casual contracts. They were paid only when they worked. For Mr A this was a change from certain, familiar work to a situation where he had to sit by the phone at five or six every morning waiting for a call that would tell him if there was work that day and where it was. Mr A left the agency, a decision made all the easier because he wanted to move closer to where Mrs A was living. Mrs A also experienced some of the impact of restructuring when following a takeover she was offered a different job but found herself alongside someone who was being paid considerably more for the same work. When, after six months, her request for an increase in pay was rejected she left. On another occasion, Mr A had to leave because of a back injury. Following an operation the company were not prepared to employ him for fear of future claims from any further injury.

But both Mr and Mrs A also left jobs voluntarily. With a mortgage to pay and talk of the dearth of permanent jobs, this might be seen as perverse. In practice, both of them, but particularly Mrs A, were confident of their employability and believed that there were temporary, casual jobs 'out there' that they could get if necessary. At one point, leaving a job that had promised much but turned out to be rather different, Mrs A signed on with a 'temping' agency while continuing to look for permanent work and applying for around 50 jobs before she found one. Although it was on a seven-month contract, it offered holiday and sick pay straightaway as opposed to the qualifying period of 750 hours that was operated by the agency. The contract was then extended twice.

Another motive for job change was to access jobs with overtime. Mr A, for example, on one occasion took a job with relatively poor basic pay because it did not stipulate weekend or night work but nevertheless provided the opportunity for this work on an overtime basis. The ideal was a higher basic rate of pay than previously and the opportunity for overtime.

The fact that both were able to find work did not prevent their income from varying, nor from them facing some periodic anxieties about how they would pay their mortgage. When they first bought, both were in permanent jobs. When subsequently they experienced redundancy and money became tighter, Mrs A took an evening job in a pub. They did not consider trading down but this would have been an option if their difficulties had persisted.

They had now decided to move home again. They delayed looking for a property until they were more certain that Mr A had the full-time permanent job, although again this was in part because they thought they might not get a mortgage if he was in temporary employment. They also borrowed more cautiously. Mrs A feared that their own belief in their employability (as a safeguard against the growth of precarious jobs) might be challenged by ageism as she hit 40. As a result she had removed ages and dates of schooling from her CV.

Low pay, mortgage payments and the state safety net

The third case study illustrates a case of an apparently affordable mortgage falling foul of unemployment and the subsequent interaction of unemployment, the availability of temporary and /or low-wage jobs and the work disincentive effect of ISMI. It also shows a number of the social and socio-psychological aspects of mortgage arrears and possession that are discussed more fully in Chapters Five and Six.

Mr and Mrs N had two children. They bought their house in 1991 with a mortgage of £47,000 on a property for which they paid £57,000.

When they were interviewed in 1995, they had arrears of £3,000 and substantial negative equity. They had bought close to friends and family in a Midlands village and Mr N had a job in a quarry bringing home around £250 a week after tax while Mrs N had a part-time job that added £31.50 a week. The mortgage payments at that time were £286 a month, and at just under a quarter of their net income was at least on the face of it affordable. Their verbatim account is given below.

"Before I lost my job it was a struggle, but we managed. But when I was unemployed there was no way that we could pay it. Even now that I have a job again we've realised that we still can't manage the house. We are waiting to go to court. Perhaps the house will be sold before then but we want to be rid of it all. I don't know what the arrears are now, but they must be over £3,000. But you see, if we got a cheque for that today and paid them off, we would be back in the same position in a few months.

"I lost my job in the quarry. When that went I got Income Support and the mortgage interest. It went up after a few months [after 16 weeks at 50% mortgage interest] and then we got £234 a fortnight – £114 for living on and £120 for the mortgage. We also got [Mrs N's] money and the Child Benefit. So altogether we had £156 a week. We got it all because the mortgage company were one of those that would not agree to the DSS paying them the interest direct. So we had to try and pass on the £60 a week for the mortgage. On top of that we had to pay them another £11.50 weekly for the endowment and other bits to make it up to the £286 a month. If we had paid them all that we would have had £84.50 a week to live on, to pay everything. We just couldn't do it. We had to use the mortgage money to live and pay them what we could. Sometimes £40, but not always.

"At one point the arrears were more that £2,500 and they kept writing to us. We cashed in the endowment and paid £1,800 off. We got the arrears down to about £600, but then they started to go up again because we still couldn't pass on all the interest they wanted. In the end we took another loan from the Alliance and Leicester for about £1,300 to put towards the arrears. But then we had to pay that one too.

"I started straightaway to look for another job, but it took a year 'till I got this one in 1994. It's selling things. I've had it for just over a year now. I bring home about £140 a week, never less than £136 so far, but I have had £156 on some occasions. There is a basic wage and then some commission. That was quite good at first because I was opening up lots of new accounts, but it's more difficult now to keep that up at the same rate.

"Before this job I went for two or three jobs as a security guard and others, about 15 in all I tried for. The security jobs were 60 hours a week and only paid £3 an hour and there was no commission, but even though I got interviews for some of them I didn't get the jobs. I looked in the paper and signed on with a couple of agencies but nothing came. I also wrote to some places on spec but nothing came back. I went to the jobcentre when I signed on, but the jobs were really low paid and in any case, whenever you saw one it was gone. I don't know whether they leave them up there just to make it look good. When Safeways were building their new shop they wanted hod carriers, so I went there. I only did one day; eight hours work in filthy shit and pouring rain for £21.50. I did do odd jobs on the side when I was on the dole. Cash in hand. But not much.

"We knew that we had to have a job that paid us more than what we were getting on Income Support, so more than £114 a week. And we were still falling further behind with the house then. A hundred and forty pounds a week average is better, but we still can't manage the house. I took the job I've got now because I want to work, but the pay is still not enough to manage. To begin with we've still got to clear some debts to the water and council, but also going back to work costs money. I couldn't go in old trousers and trainers and I had to have a suit. I tried to get the DSS to help pay for those but they said no. In the end a mate down the road lent me the money but that's got to be paid back too. It just goes on and on even now.

"I was desperate for a job. You see, we live in a village and people know. They see you around and then they see you cash the giro. People talk and I won't have them saying I'm a scrounger. I know people do it because I've done it. But having said that, I wasn't going to take anything. I could have had building work but those jobs are £130 for long hours and out in the crap all day. The job I've got now is clean and tidy. Anyway, if I'd stayed on the Safeway's job that would have come to an end soon and then it'd be back to the dole and only half the mortgage interest again to begin with.

"We decided that we would have to give up the house. We realised that it was not worth it, we'd never pay it, and we owed them £2,000 again. It was after they rang and said we should be paying more and threatened to repossess us. Since we've decided to give it up I've not paid the mortgage at all, and as I said we're just waiting for a date to go to court.

"The problem is that you pay one thing by not paying another and you never sort it out. Without mum we would be lost. She shares the cost of the baby every week. She buys all the nappies, as well as the big things like shoes and a coat for the older one. Sometimes she says it's a loan but we all know that it's not really. No one round here knows about the repossession except our family. When we put the house up for sale it just happened at the time when there was a possibility that I might go with this job to another town, so we were able to say to people who asked that we might have to move with the job. It's embarrassing and it's bad for the kids. The little one won't matter but the older one is already upset about perhaps moving schools and keeps asking if we can stay. That's why we want to get a council house here if we can, but it's not easy. We've also got to go to possession because the advice people told us that this council is very tough if you give up by yourself and they wouldn't rehouse us."

Flexible employment and mortgage arrears

Although some mortgagors manage to combine low-paid employment or unemployment with meeting their mortgage payments, we have already seen in Table 2.3 and 2.4 in Chapter Two the extent to which labour market factors do increase the risk of arrears and possessions. Since 1993/94, the trend with respect to arrears has been downwards for every employed group but not necessarily evenly. In 1998/99, arrears were most pronounced among mortgagor heads in part-time employment (5%). Four per cent of self-employed sole traders had arrears. This compares with a figure of 2% for those in permanent employment. Among households where the head of household is unemployed more than one in 10 (11%) had arrears. The evidence indicates not only that those in employment develop arrears, but that it is among those with the riskier forms of employment where the percentage level of arrears is higher. Given that it is the riskier forms of employment that are predicted to grow, this in itself gives grounds for thinking that mortgage arrears are likely to continue. However, as we have seen in Table 2.5 in Chapter Two, different aspects of labour market position interact in complex ways over the cycle in relation to the risk of arrears. Differences in social class and employment status appear to have an enduring impact on the relative risk of arrears, while the risks associated with self-employment ebb and flow with the economic cycle. During times of relative boom a self-employed status does not increase or decrease the risk of arrears. However, during times of economic slump a self-employed status makes one particularly vulnerable to arrears and possession.

Mortgagors, perceptions of risk and housing market responses

Not surprisingly, studies have shown that it is those who have experienced some labour market risk who have the clearest perceptions of the risks to housing and so are the most cautious about home ownership. Doling and Ford (1995) showed that in the early and mid-1990s the fall in support for home ownership was much larger among those who had experienced recent unemployment than for those who remained employed. Ford and Burrows (2000) confirmed the continuation of this particular relationship at the end of the 1990s but noted that the same was not necessarily the case for those in other risky positions, for example, those with fixed-term contracts. Thus, while, overall, perceptions of labour market risk are more widespread than they were, there is a more complex relationship between individuals' labour market experience and individuals' perceptions of risk, particularly outside of the experience of unemployment. Further, as will be shown in Chapter Four, there is not necessarily a direct relationship between either perceptions of, or experiences of, risk, and risk averse behaviour. Thus, those at risk may still trade up, or may decline insurance against unemployment, while those with little if any exposure to risk may nevertheless be cautious in their housing market behaviour (see also Munro, 2000). To this extent, there can be no guarantee that those most in danger of a labour market disruption that challenges their ability to sustain home ownership will be in a position to avert the associated consequences.

Low inflation and reduced fiscal support

A further economic transformation affecting home ownership has been the advent of low inflation. The UK government's commitment to low inflation, underpinned by the independence given to the Bank of England to set base rates at levels designed to keep inflation at around 2.5% per annum, has profound implications for all home owners, and low-income home owners in particular. In the past, high inflation has acted to reduce mortgage to income ratios for homebuyers over the lifetime of their mortgage careers. One of the advantages of relatively high levels of inflation for homebuyers is that it rapidly erodes their mortgage costs as a proportion of their incomes, and makes them less vulnerable over time to the vicissitudes of the labour market, or to other changes in their domestic circumstances.

High levels of inflation in the past have also provided home owners with the opportunity to move 'up market' during the course of their housing careers, without necessarily returning to the higher mortgage to income ratios associated with their first move into home ownership. Mortgage to income ratios in the first year of a new mortgage are typically somewhat lower for existing home owners than those for first-time buyers. In 1998, for example, the average advance to income ratio for first time buyers was 2.24, while for existing owners it was just 2.05. Conversely lower levels of inflation extend the period over which homebuying households have high mortgage to income ratios, and reduce their capacity to 'trade up' over the years. Moreover, low-income homebuyers have far higher mortgage repayment to income ratios than home owners as a whole, and are thus particularly vulnerable to any employment or domestic changes that reduce their incomes.

Low inflation also restricts the scope for 'trading down' as a means for homebuyers to manage any disruption to the income flow needed to sustain their mortgage payments, whether as a result of job loss, relationship breakdown or other reason. While house prices have risen appreciably since 1998, and the phenomenon of 'negative equity' so widespread in the early 1990s has now almost disappeared (Wilcox, 2000), over the whole of the last decade average house prices in the UK rose by just 35%, compared to 290% in the 1980s (Wilcox, 2000).

Fiscal transformations have also changed the risks associated with home ownership. The support available to mortgagors in the form of tax relief on mortgage interest repayments (MITR) has been progressively eroded by successive governments, particularly over the last decade, and was abolished from April 2000. Historically, the importance of MITR grew as, first, Income Tax was extended to apply to the vast majority of all working households and, second, levels of home ownership grew. MITR has been argued to constitute a clear incentive to house purchase, often making such a proposition affordable for low-income households. However, its value to individuals has fallen successively since 1974/75, limited by loan ceilings, a restriction to the standard rate of tax, and, later, reductions in the rate of tax relief. The abolition of MITR fundamentally alters the balance of financial support given to households in different tenures, and puts into sharp relief the limited support the UK government now provides to low-income home owners, relative to low-income households in other tenures. Other taxes such as capital gains and inheritance, while of benefit to home owners in general, by virtue of exemptions or reduced relief, are often less significant for lower- than for higher-income home owners and more significant for those living in the south of the country. Any support to low-income home owners towards maintenance costs has also been eroded as repair and improvement grants have been eliminated in England (but not in Scotland).

Home owners, however, make a substantial contribution to the Exchequer by way of stamp duty, which is levied every time a dwelling is bought or sold. It lacks any underlying economic rationale and is simply a well-established and easily collected form of taxation. In practice, it raises much the same level of taxation from home owners as would be levied if the current exemption from capital gains tax was abolished. In 1998/99, for example, stamp duty on the sale of residential dwellings in the UK raised £1.1 billion. In April 2000, the rate of duty was raised on properties in excess of £250,000. However, dwellings priced below £60,000 are exempt. Depending on the part of the country considered, this sometimes benefits the entry and early mobility of low-income home owners. More frequently, however, it is regarded as a tax on mobility, which bears most heavily on frequently moving households. Home owners also face a tax on any insurance they take to protect their monthly mortgage payments. A distinct, but implicit tax levied on home owners is that associated with means-testing with respect to care costs. They may have to release equity to pay for care, and in extreme circumstances sell outright, with only a low ceiling in operation for protected, non-assessable assets.

Summary

Changes to the labour market in the form of the growth of precarious employment contribute to a riskier home ownership. In excess of a fifth of mortgagor heads of household now face such risks as they involuntarily move jobs and sometimes experience worsening terms and conditions of employment. The percentage of households that contain someone in 'risky' employment is considerably higher. This position is in marked contrast to that of the early 1980s. The growth of low-paid work is a particular difficulty. Unemployment is the employment status most strongly associated with arrears, but self-employed mortgagors and heads of household in part-time employment have considerably higher odds of arrears than those in permanent work. There is a complex relationship between the extent and pattern of risk, the perceptions of risk and the behavioural response of mortgagors to such risks.

The advent of a low-inflation economy, while reducing the costs of borrowing also prolongs the period over which the initial income to debt ratio holds. Typically, borrowers therefore face a longer period of financial strain, with little, if any, equity growth, and hence a longer period over which their finances remain 'stretched'. Borrowers have also seen the fiscal subsidy to borrowers in the form of MITR end in April 2000, and this is reflected in an increase in the real costs of borrowing. Mortgagors are also subject to a further range of taxes – stamp duty, inheritance tax and insurance tax.

Taken together, these economic transformations remove considerable certainty and assistance that was previously available to mortgagors. Labour market restructuring in particular has resulted in a situation where a substantial minority of borrowers potentially fails to access permanently secure employment and a stable income, two of the key requisites for sustainable owner-occupation.

Note

This chapter draws upon material previously published in Ford (1995, 1998) both from projects funded by Shelter, and on unfunded research published by Ford and Wilcox (1998).

FOUR

Unsafe safety nets

The extent to which the contemporary range of risks impact on home owners and give rise to payment problems, mortgage arrears and potentially mortgage possession, is in large part a consequence of the safety-net provision available to mortgagors. The key risks to home owners have been explored in Chapters One, Two and Three and include the deregulation of the labour market, household dissolution as a result of relationship breakdown and housing policy itself through the emphasis placed on facilitating the access of low-income households to owner-occupation. A further risk occurs where either borrowing or lending lack prudence.

Societies have choices about whether, how, and when home ownership will be supported. In Britain, both tax and benefit measures have been used to support home owners, although as noted in Chapter Three, MITR has now been abolished. With respect to benefits, unlike in many other European countries, there is currently no assistance with housing costs to home owners in employment, however low their income. This is in contrast to the assistance available to low-income, in-work tenants who can receive Housing Benefit. For mortgagors who lose all income, who have savings of less than £8,000 and who meet the other eligibility criteria that allow them access to subsistence benefits (Income Support or income-based Jobseeker's Allowance), there is a state safety net that contributes to their mortgage interests costs – Income Support Mortgage Interest (ISMI). In addition, there is a private insurance safety net in the form of Mortgage Payment Protection Insurance (MPPI). As has been indicated earlier, there is a changing balance between these forms of provision with housing and social security policy placing increasing emphasis on the provision of social protection through the private welfare market.

This chapter explores these recent developments in the nature of safety-net provision for home owners. The central theme of the chapter is to focus on the emerging tension between riskier home ownership and the need for effective safety-net cover on the one hand and the limitations of the contemporary safety-net system on the other, which has become less rather than more 'satisfactory'.

Public and private safety-net support: a changing balance

A state safety net was first introduced in Britain in 1948 to cover borrowers claiming National Assistance (and in time Supplementary Benefit, Income Support and Jobseeker's Allowance) who either lost their jobs or became unable to work. This remained unchanged until 1987 when a number of restrictions were introduced (see Ford and Griffith, 1994, for a fuller discussion).

In October 1995, more far reaching changes were introduced to the state safety-net provisions. They were substantially reduced, but differentially restricted, depending on whether a mortgagor claiming Income Support (IS) or income-based Jobseeker's Allowance (JSA) took their loan pre- or post-October 1995. With some exceptions, borrowers with mortgages that pre-date the changes now receive: no assistance for eight weeks; up to 50% of their eligible interest for the next 18 weeks; and then full eligible interest. Borrowers with post-October 1995 mortgages have less generous cover, receiving: no assistance for the first 39 weeks of their claim; and then help with their full eligible interest. Mortgagors aged 60 and over (or who have a partner over 60) are, however, exempt from these waiting periods. In addition, single parents claiming IS because their partner has died or left, or individuals claiming IS as a carer are exempt from the longer waiting period. Other changes were also introduced. Eligible mortgage interest was restricted to loans of up to £100,000; payments are now made at a 'standard' rate of interest; and successive claims are treated as linked (and so not requiring a second wait period of eight or 39 weeks) provided the second ISMI claim starts within 12 weeks of the termination of the first one.

The 1995 changes were explicitly linked with an expectation that mortgagors would take out private MPPI as the initial safety net that would bridge what came to be referred to as the ISMI 'gap' and that lenders and insurers would facilitate this shift through the development of new products and by encouraging take-up. As is discussed later, the latter have been active on both these counts through the development of a benchmark product and a voluntary Mortgage Code.

The development of MPPI

MPPI has been available since the late 1970s, but relatively insignificant. In 1995, the best estimate of take-up was no more than 12 to 16% (Ford et al, 1995). At the time of the ISMI changes, claims were made by the insurance industry and lenders that the total take-up of MPPI would rise from one million or so borrowers to around 3.5 million, although no time frame was associated with this (Williams, 1995).

MPPI is typically offered as part of a block policy (covering all mortgagors who take a policy through a particular lender on the same terms and at the same price as opposed to individually written policies) and sold through mortgage lenders. Mortgage intermediaries (estate agents, mortgage brokers and so on) also sell MPPI. The larger broking organisations increasingly sell via block policies which they negotiate, while other brokers may select the best product from the market for their client (Ford and Quilgars, 2000). There is also a limited move by insurers to offer individually underwritten MPPI 'directly' to the public.

The predominant form of cover is the traditional accident, sickness and unemployment policy, although many insurers allow borrowers to insure for just some of these risks. Most MPPI policies have a 'wait' or 'deferral' period of 30 to 60 days before the policy takes effect and commonly pay out for a period of 12 months. There are a small number of innovative products that mirror more directly the delay in state provision (the ISMI gap) by offering nine months' cover. Policies can cover both the main breadwinner and a second earner and costs additional to the mortgage such as endowment premiums and the MPPI premium. Borrowers insure for a sum of money – which typically reflects their mortgage payments at the time of taking out their policy.

Policy imperatives and assumptions

The reasons for the changes outlined above were several, not least the rising cost of ISMI in the recession of the late 1980s and early 1990s as the number of home owners losing all income rose. The cost was also affected by rising house prices, high interest rates and so rising mortgage interest charges.

The changes have also to be set in the wider context of the restructuring of welfare and the ideological preference of successive governments (both Conservative and now Labour) to limit state welfare in favour of market provision and public/private partnerships. The belief that this approach was appropriate for mortgagor protection was confirmed by the government in 1998 (DSS, 1998) and the reliance on MPPI as the initial safety net was reiterated in the housing Green Paper (DETR/DSS, 2000a) which also endorsed the industry target for take-up of 55% by 2004.

The proposal to restrict ISMI in favour of MPPI as the initial safety net as from October 1995 was met with a wide-ranging critique. This noted that in relation to the theoretical basis of insurance, the characteristics of unemployment are such that the event is inherently uninsurable (Walker et al, 1995). There were doubts about the affordability of the insurance among some mortgagors, evidence that some of those at risk were excluded from the policies and evidence from the early 1990s that insurers could and had changed the terms and conditions of the insurance in periods when claims rose (NACAB, 1995; Ford et al, 1995). Nevertheless, as seen above, with one or two concessions, the changes were implemented, notably against the assessment of the Social Security Advisory Committee. Since then the critique has continued, reinforcing many of the points made above (for example, Burchardt and Hills, 1997) but also focusing on the effectiveness of the new social protection partnership as outlined in detail below.

In addition to the critique noted above, there has developed a more general interest in the nature and validity of the behavioural assumptions that underpin the reform of welfare, namely, those associated with rational choice theory (Le Grand, 1997). This approach stresses that "individual choices are driven by instrumental rationality" whereby individuals "choose[ing] activities according to the extent to which anticipated gains exceed the sacrifices involved" (Taylor-Gooby, 1999, pp 97-9), and notes that individual choice and individual decision making is paramount. In contrast, writers have suggested that the behaviour of 'consumers' in welfare markets is more complex and requires more 'elaborated' or possibly 'alternative' explanatory frameworks. Taylor-Gooby (1998, p 221) has argued, for example, that choices "are strongly influenced by cultural factors. Ideas about obligations within the family, about equity and about the appropriate range of benefits that should be made available to welfare state citizens contribute", while other writers have noted the extent to which choices and decisions reflect personal predispositions and psychosocial factors. Irrespective of why people enter the market, attention has also been paid to the nature of private welfare markets and in particular to the conditions that such markets have to meet if they are to operate effectively. The debate has been about the extent to which, and why, such markets may need a higher level of trust and coordination than other markets, and whether welfare markets are indeed characterised in this way (Taylor-Gooby, 1999; Ford, 2000b). A lack of trust potentially erodes the development of the market by reducing its overall effectiveness.

The policy of increasing reliance on the private market for mortgagors' safety-net provision is one example of the more general policy of welfare restructuring and as such is also framed within the assumptions of rational choice theory. Thus, it is assumed that mortgagors are informed about the range of risks they face and their likely incidence and the limitations of state support. Consequently, self-interest leads to the choices and decisions whereby they can avoid the consequences of the risks they face by insuring against them. It is also assumed that self-interest results in a market characterised by *adverse selection* and *moral hazard*. Adverse selection occurs because individuals at greatest risk will be the most likely to insure while moral hazard refers to the process whereby those making a claim will seek to prolong the claim rather than return to work. Here there is a deliberative assessment of the economic consequences of a return to employment before a claim has run its fullest possible course. As a consequence, the same principle of self-interest that leads those at risk to insure, necessitates a defensive response from insurers who typically seek to pool risks, to use differential pricing to reflect risk and to manage the claims process in a stringent manner (Barr, 1993; Burchardt and Hills, 1997). These rational choice assumptions led government, lenders and insurers to believe that the market for MPPI would increase significantly, aided by a substantial curtailment of ISMI which made starker the risk of not having MPPI.

Since the implementation of the October 1995 changes, research studies have monitored and evaluated the nature and consequences of this safety-net approach to sustainable home ownership. It is both an empirical and theoretical evaluation. The evidence on take-up and effectiveness denotes how far the policy meets its objective of preventing unsustainable home ownership, but, to the extent that this objective is not met, the studies have also assessed the strength of support for a number of the underlying behavioural assumptions. As this chapter will suggest, there remains a considerable disjuncture between the expectations of the government, lenders and the insurers with respect to MPPI and the research evidence on the effectiveness of the policy. Some of the disjuncture may relate to the relatively recent introduction of the policy changes; where, for example, one argument is that take-up is limited because mortgagors' knowledge of the restrictions to ISMI is still poor. The appropriate policy response may therefore be one that gives greater emphasis to 'educating' borrowers. However, there is also evidence of more fundamental problems with current policy, both in terms of the validity of the theoretical assumptions on which it is based as well as with respect to its effectiveness in so far as MPPI may not always prevent arrears.

Evaluating safety-net provision for mortgagors

In order to evaluate the effectiveness of current safety-net provision as a whole, three key areas are considered below. First, the extent to which the design of ISMI and MPPI separately and together can provide adequate cover for those events that typically give rise to mortgage arrears. Second, the extent of take-up of MPPI. Third, the effectiveness of the safety-net provision for mortgagors as the safety nets are currently operated and experienced. These issues are discussed primarily with reference to three linked studies completed over the period between 1996 and 2000 (Ford and Kempson, 1997a; Kempson et al, 1999; and Ford and Quilgars, 2000). The first focuses on assessing the extent of take-up of MPPI and the characteristics of those taking private insurance, the second provides the first national evaluation of the effectiveness of both MPPI and ISMI (post-October 1995) and the third examines the role of financial intermediaries in the MPPI market. The first two studies use sample surveys of mortgagors, MPPI claimants and ISMI claimants, as well as qualitative interviews with mortgagors, lenders and insurers. Where appropriate, other studies are also highlighted (for example, Holmans and Whitehead, 1999; Pryce, 1998; Ford, 2000a).

ISMI and MPPI: the degree of complementarity?

The rhetoric that surrounded the shift from ISMI to MPPI was of the complementarity of these two safety nets; that MPPI 'bridged the gap' to ISMI. In practice, MPPI and ISMI do not provide cover for an identical range of eventualities. Some indication of the lack of complementarity between the public and private safety nets is provided by Table 4.1. The table, which presents data from the first study of safety-net claimants post the October 1995 changes (Kempson et al, 1999), shows the reasons for claiming for three groups: those receiving only IS/JSA, those receiving ISMI and those in receipt of MPPI.

The range of events covered by MPPI is more restricted when compared to ISMI. In particular, MPPI does not cover those who are without income due to separation from a partner, as a result of a household member becoming a carer, following the death of a partner or in circumstances such as a reduction in earnings. Table 4.1 shows that almost four out of 10 ISMI claimants were receiving help with mortgage costs for events that would not have been covered by MPPI, even if they had such a policy. The table also addresses the question of whether the cover available

Table 4.1: Reasons for mortgagors claiming on public or private safety nets, compared with reasons for arrears (%)

	IS/JSA claimants n=506	ISMI claimants n=330	Successful MPPI claimants n=298	*All mortgagors with arrears %
Own redundancy	63	26	41	42
Partners' redundancy	4	4	6	
Own illness/injury	14	28	48	6
Partners' illness/injury	3	6	16	
Separation from partner	5	21	n/a	14
Self or partner becoming a carer	2	4	n/a	38[1]
Death of partner	–	5	n/a	
Other**	10	7	n/a	

Notes: Percentages may add to more than 100 due to rounding and a small number of cases where there was more than one reason for the claim.

* Survey of English Housing (1996/97).

** The category 'other' includes the 16% of households in arrears due to reduction in earnings and 7% of households in arrears as a result of financial overcommitment.

Source: Postal survey of IS and ISMI claimants and postal survey of MPPI claimants

under either safety net relates effectively to those events that give rise to arrears. Information on the reasons for arrears drawn from the Survey of English Housing is shown in the final column of Table 4.1 and indicates that just over half the reasons given for arrears are ones not insurable under MPPI. About a quarter are in arrears for reasons not covered by ISMI. In particular, neither safety net provides cover for reduced earnings from work, even though, as we have seen in Chapters Two and Three as well, this event is a significant contributor to arrears. Overall, the evidence suggests that neither of the two safety nets covers all the events that give rise to arrears and further, they do not even do so in combination. Further, in exploring how 'comprehensive' the cover is, it must be recognised that while MPPI has some exclusions, it is open to the majority of mortgagors who then choose whether or not to take it. ISMI has a more restricted focus, for example, both partners have to loose income before ISMI can be claimed, and those with savings in excess of £8,000 are excluded from making a claim. As will be discussed in more detail later, any successful claim for ISMI involves a wide range of potential deductions as eligibility criteria (for example, non-dependent deductions) operate.

The take-up of MPPI

Despite the growth in the numbers of low-income home owners, as discussed in Chapter Two, mortgagors remain, in general, higher-income households. As a result, although the risks to home owners have grown, a proportion of households may have access to savings or other resources that can be used to pay the mortgage if they lose all income. Thus, potentially, not all mortgagors need MPPI.

The first estimate of the number of mortgagors who 'should' have MPPI dates from 1995 following the policy announcement of the further restrictions to ISMI. Not surprisingly, they were rather mechanistic, typically focused around those mortgagors who would have been eligible for ISMI had it not been restricted. On this basis, around a third of all mortgagors (roughly 3.5 million) would be eligible to claim ISMI if they lost all income and so would need MPPI to cover the ISMI gap (Williams, 1995; Ford and Kempson, 1997a). Since then, the process of estimating 'need' has been gradually refined (for a review see Ford 2000c), with the most comprehensive estimate to date offered by Holmans and Whitehead (1999). Taking into account the availability of alternative insurances to MPPI, and those with a low risk of income loss, they estimated that more than 50% of mortgagors (approximately six million) lacked adequate resources to meet their mortgage payments for at least a six-month period. This figure has been accepted by the lenders and government as the target for take-up by 2004 as outlined in the housing Green Paper published in 2000.

Measuring take-up of MPPI is not straightforward and this process has also been through a series of refinements (Ford, 2000c) designed to reduce double counting and cancellations and to include those instances where borrowers are offered 'free' MPPI for a period of time. Whereas in 1995 take-up stood at between 12 and 16%, by 1999 the best (and much better) estimate, available from the Council of Mortgage Lenders (CML) and the Association of British Insurers (ABI), indicated that 19% of all mortgagors and 25% of 'new' mortgagors had MPPI. Clearly, the rate of growth in take-up is limited and progress towards the target figure is slow. For a variety of reasons (considered in more detail below), take-up is low among those at greatest risk (defined in terms of unemployment, reduced or low wages), and/or those with potential access to ISMI. The survey undertaken by Ford and Kempson (1997a) noted that of the third of those mortgagors likely to have recourse to ISMI should they lose all income due to unemployment, accident or sickness, only a quarter had MPPI, while the survey of IS/JSA recipients completed in 1999 showed that only a quarter had *ever* had a MPPI policy (Kempson et al,1999). Rather, take-up is concentrated among those facing the least risk and having the higher resources (Ford and Kempson, 1997a; Pryce, 1998; Holmans and Whitehead, 1999). Contrary to expectations there is no evidence of adverse selection.

These findings pose some important analytical questions, in particular because they do not chime with what might have been expected if mortgagors had been responding in line with the rational choice assumptions outlined earlier. Given this currently 'disappointing' take-up of MPPI, there are several possible lines of enquiry. One is that the exercise of rational choice is constrained by inadequate knowledge and information, or by other factors such as cost. Addressing these issues will allow the market to function as expected. Another is the possibility that take-up is primarily influenced by non-economic factors and that it is the explanatory model that is flawed or incomplete.

Constraints on rational choice?

Low take-up and the absence of adverse selection do not *necessarily* challenge the validity of rational choice accounts. For example, mortgagors may be making choices through calculative deliberation between alternatives and responding to the incentives of price and opportunity on the basis of self-interest but on the basis of poor information and/or misperceptions of risk. In both cases this will lead to erroneous judgements although the *process* of rational calculation may be intact.

This issue was considered in detail by Ford and Kempson (1997a), and Table 4.2 indicates respondents' knowledge and understanding of the ISMI provision following unemployment or ill health.

Two thirds of borrowers were uncertain about the ISMI provisions following unemployment while 72% were uncertain about the provision available if they were ill or had an accident. Roughly a third in each case believed they knew what was available. Of these, only about 60% had accurate knowledge. Further analysis showed that, in total, only 16% of borrowers had both *full* and *accurate* knowledge of ISMI, 8% had partial knowledge, two thirds had no idea at all while 1 in 10 thought they knew but were, in fact, fundamentally wrong. The range of misunderstanding

Table 4.2: Mortgagors' knowledge of ISMI provisions (%)

	... for job loss (n=815)	... for sickness or accident (n=819)
Beliefs about provision		
I'm not sure	66	72
No help at all	21	19
No help for months, then repayments in full	5	4
Half repayments for 4 months then in full	2	2
No help for 2 months, half for 4 months, then in full	5	4
Accuracy of beliefs		
Not sure	66	72
Correct knowledge	21	18
Incorrect knowledge	13	10

Source: Ford and Kempson (1997a), borrowers' postal survey

and inaccurate knowledge was therefore considerable. Paradoxically, those most likely to know accurately were those who would be *ineligible* for help from ISMI should they lose all income. Of those who would qualify for ISMI (measured on the basis of their savings), only 12% knew their entitlement correctly. Qualitative research by Munro et al (1998) and Forrest et al (1997) has noted broadly similar findings in respect of the poor and inaccurate knowledge about ISMI.

Mortgagors may also be constrained in making 'rational' choices by difficulties in accurately assessing the risks they face as discussed in Chapter Three. Further evidence in support of this comes from Cebulla (1998) who considered individuals' subjective perceptions of risk, first against an actuarial assessment, and then by comparing respondents' current predictions against their position at some later date. In both cases there was only a limited match and indeed, as noted earlier, researchers have raised some fundamental questions about the extent to which unemployment is an insurable risk because it cannot be predicted at the individual level (Walker et al, 1995).

Again, these findings on poor knowledge and poor risk perception do not necessarily refute the rational choice assumptions but do suggest that the conditions for their successful implementation are lacking. As a result, currently, take-up is limited and inappropriately distributed. One conclusion could be that more information (as well as more accurate information) might increase take-up. Other results add weight to this view, not least the evidence that more than one in 10 mortgagors had never thought about taking MPPI (Ford and Kempson, 1997a).

Low take-up may also be constrained by cost. Early research by Burchardt and Hills (1997) noted the high cost of MPPI, and suggested that it was, in part, unjustified. Cost is the outcome of a risk-based premium, commission and profit and it was the last two elements that were regarded as unduly high. Similar conclusions were drawn by Ford and Quilgars (2000) in their study of financial intermediaries where the charges for MPPI ranged from £1.60 per £100 insured (a lender who purchased at £1.40 and sold on at virtually the same price but made MPPI compulsory) to around £6.00 per £100, with commission rates of 25%. Overall, costs have fallen since the early 1990s from an average of around £7.00 per £100 insured to an average in 1996/97 of £5.49 per £100 insured in that year (Ford and Kempson, 1997a). However, the ABI/CML statistics for 1999 report an average cost of £5.56, indicating that costs have changed little since the mid-1990s.

The evidence from the survey of borrowers and of MPPI claimants undertaken by Ford and Kempson (1997a) and Kempson et al (1999) indicates that cost could both prevent people taking out the insurance and also lead to cancellations among those with a policy. This was particularly so among low-income borrowers. In their survey of IS/JSA borrowers, a majority of those who had a policy at some time, cancelled because of cost. However, for others, the issue was not cost per se but value for money (which they doubted), and sometimes a mistrust of insurers who, respondents believed, would look for a reason not to pay at all.

Economic theory predicts that take-up will increase in response to a fall in price. However, econometric analysis by Pryce (1998) estimated that a reduction of 10% in the price of MPPI would result in an increase in sales of only 5%. Pryce's figures refer to the pre-1995 period and Holmans and Whitehead (1999) comment that price elasticities could be expected to be higher in a more mature market, if remaining relatively unresponsive to price changes overall. However, as seen above, the price of MPPI in the second half of the 1990s has been inelastic. One implication of these findings is that price reductions will have to be very substantial indeed if they are to affect take-up. Equally, the evidence concerning the muted impact of a reduction in price, and the suggestion that the insurance is not seen as value for money, imply that other factors may have a role to play in explanations of take-up. This is further reinforced by Pryce's analysis, which shows that neither an increase in unemployment or a further reduction in ISMI or IS are likely to have any significant impact on take-up, with further cuts in ISMI being particularly insignificant.

Non-economic influences on the take-up of MPPI

Earlier in this chapter, there was a suggestion that choices were potentially influenced by non-economic factors either in conjunction with more economically rational processes or as an alternative to them. With respect to MPPI there is evidence that this argument has some force, as attitudes to insurance and attitudes to risk have been shown to be important influences on the decision to take or decline MPPI.

There is considerable evidence that, in general, consumers still believe that the state should be responsible for the provision of welfare, particularly for vulnerable people but also in general, albeit in a context where those who can take responsibility for at least a proportion of their own social protection should do so, but where those who have made contributions have some right to expect at least something back. Many studies have shown a broad consistency of views (Williams et al, 1999; Taylor-Gooby, 1999, 2000b; Skinner and Ford, 2000). These and other studies have also shown some negative attitudes towards insurance and insurers in several areas of welfare provision. The question is, how widespread are these views and do they influence the take-up of MPPI?

In the first of the three studies evaluating aspects of safety net provision for mortgagors (Ford and Kempson, 1997a) we built an attitude to insurance scale from six attitude statements, and then assigned respondents to one of three categories: anti-insurance (15%); pro-insurance (13%); and neither anti- nor pro-insurance (72%). There was also a strong correlation between the views people held of insurance and the likelihood of them having an MPPI policy. Those with pro-insurance attitudes were three times more likely to have MPPI than those who were anti-insurance as is shown in Table 4.3.

There was a tendency among some of those insuring to 'over-insure', sometimes covering the same eventuality more than once, indicating a relationship between insurance and a risk averse stance. Compared to those without MPPI, borrowers who had such a policy were at least twice as likely to also have one or more of Permanent Income, Permanent Health or Critical Illness Insurance.

In-depth interviews were used to examine the nature of risk aversion and the motivations to 'over-insure'. They indicated that for some people, perception of a potential risk (well founded or otherwise), led to the

Table 4.3: Relationship between MPPI take-up and the propensity to insure (%)

Propensity to insure	Has MPPI	Considered MPPI	Not considered
Overall attitude to insurance			
Anti-insurance*	11	21	68
Neither pro- nor anti-	20	26	54
Pro-insurance*	35	12	53
Level of other insurance			
Low (0-1 other policies)	14	18	68
Medium (2-3 policies)	18	23	59
High (4 or more policies)*	31	24	45

* statistically significant.

Source: Ford and Kempson (1997a), borrowers' survey

need for insurance to provide peace of mind. Such people had little knowledge of state provision and typically assumed they would not receive any help. They were also generally rather poorly informed about MPPI (and possibly their other insurances) which suggests the concern was not with specific risks but with security and piece of mind per se. One of the insurers also interviewed as part of this study reported that their research led them to conclude that about 18% of people are risk averse in this way. This figure was higher than the survey estimate given by Ford and Kempson (13%). Thus, there is clearly a pool of people for whom attitudes to risk are a significant factor in their decision to take MPPI, even if the size of the pool is contested.

In a similar manner Cebulla (1999), examining the take-up of a range of insurances among employed people, identified the role of an optimistic or pessimistic outlook in shaping the decision to insure or not. Those defined as possessing an optimistic bias (measured as having a higher perception of job security relative to others and a lower assessment of the risk of an accident relative to others) were associated with a lower propensity to insure while those with a pessimistic attitude had a greater propensity to insure.

Assessing the influences on take-up

When we looked at the range of potential influences on mortgage arrears in Chapter Two, one concern was to identify their relative significance.

There is a similar concern here with respect to the take-up of MPPI; which factors are the most significant in explaining take-up?

Using multivariate analysis, Ford and Kempson (1997a) identified the statistically significant influences on take-up as: being young and/or a single man; having a post-October 1995 mortgage, for between £25,000 and £50,000 over a term of more than 20 years; having a high level of insurance cover; and positive attitudes towards insurance. Household financial circumstances were not significant and nor were any of the labour market risk factors that were considered. An analysis of the factors that influenced the decisions *not* to take insurance indicated five key influences: perceived low risk; ability to cover mortgage payments some other way; the cost; the issue had never been considered; and negative attitudes to insurance. Pryce (1998) has adopted a similar approach, but the range of variables considered is not the same. While he considered a wide range of demographic and financial factors (wider than considered by Ford and Kempson), no attitudinal and experiential variables were included. Further, the data were collected prior to the policy changes in 1995.

Overall, the take-up of MPPI is shown to be a complex process. Mortgagors are poorly informed about ISMI, and their assessments and perceptions of the risk they face are limited. They do not appear to be very responsive to cost and there is evidence that attitudes to insurance – both positive and negative – are significant influences on the take-up of MPPI as are dispositions towards risk. The evidence indicates that choices are influenced by a range of economic, social, cultural and personal factors, the last of which may override the process predicted by rational choice assumptions. While attitudes remain as negative as they are, they will continue to be a constraint on the take-up of MPPI. This is not to say that better information on the restrictions to ISMI and the risks of not having MPPI would lack any impact, or that lower costs would be without any significance, but on their own they are unlikely to increase take-up.

The effectiveness of safety-net provision

The restructuring of safety-net provision for mortgagors had, as one of its aims, the prevention of mortgage arrears and possession in situations where home owners lose all income. It is therefore important to consider the effectiveness of both ISMI and MPPI, singly and as a combined safety net. Below, the effectiveness of MPPI is considered first (as the initial safety net) and then ISMI. Finally, the interface between the two is examined.

MPPI

The effectiveness of MPPI can be measured in a number of ways. Research to date has concentrated on two or three central indicators: the extent to which mortgagors are excluded from the market; the percentage of claims rejected; and the extent to which the receipt of MPPI precludes arrears and possessions.

Early work by Ford et al (1995) assessed borrowers in arrears against the terms and conditions of the policies in force in the early and mid-1990s and concluded that only a minority would have been likely to have been granted a policy had they applied. Exclusions were likely where borrowers were self-employed, in temporary, casual or contract employment or had pre-existing health conditions. They could also occur where borrowers were in industries known to be prone to redundancies. All of these situations were confirmed by NACAB (1995) which drew on its case study evidence of those with debts.

The damaging effect of such exclusions in terms of the objective of sustaining home ownership was recognised by the CML who, in conjunction with the ABI, worked to develop a set of criteria to be incorporated into MPPI policies in 1999 that became known as the 'baseline policy'. Among other things, baseline policies facilitate the access of temporary and contract workers if they can demonstrate consistent employment, albeit on different contracts. They also limit the deferral period before the receipt of payment to 60 days and restrict the number of times that the terms and conditions can be changed. The current extent of exclusions is unknown but likely to be less than in the early 1990s. The buoyant economy at the end of the 1990s may also limit exclusions as continuous employment, even in different jobs, is more likely, allowing more people to qualify on grounds of consecutive contracts.

Since the mid-1990s, studies suggest that between a third and a quarter of MPPI claims have been rejected per year. The number of claims made is clearly a function of the number of policies sold, while the percentage of claims depends, in part, on the economic cycle. By mid-1998 there was some evidence that claims were starting to rise again. In the first assessment of MPPI claims (Kempson et al, 1999) an attempt was made to provide quantitative evidence on rejected claims but the response rate produced a much lower proportion of rejected claimants than the data from the insurers suggested should be the case. There are a number of reasons why this might have happened (see Kempson et al, 1999) but the decision was made to treat the 53 responses that were received as qualitative evidence. Notwithstanding this, the reasons for rejection given by respondents were broadly consistent with information from the insurers.

The most common reasons for rejection were that applicants had been sacked or had left their job voluntarily (rather than being made redundant); that they were claiming for a pre-existing health condition; or that they had been in temporary employment or on a fixed term contract and so ineligible. Others were rejected for attempting to claim for circumstances specifically excluded by the policies (mental health problems or stress-related claims). At first glance many of these claims look surprising and raise the question of why people made them. In practice, many of these cases were complex and contentious.

In-depth interviews with rejected claimants indicated that while some rejections were clearly appropriate in terms of the policy, in many more instances this was not necessarily the case and the complexity of many issues left claims open to interpretation. This is shown in the two cases described below.

> A couple were working for the same company when it was taken over; they had the option of redundancy or a new contract. They preferred a new contract but when they could not agree the terms and conditions they were sacked. They then claimed on the MPPI policy that covered the man. The case was complicated because just prior to leaving the company he had reformatted the hard disk of his office computer to remove all personal information. It was alleged that he had stolen the files and that his dismissal was justified. The insurer therefore rejected his claim. He took his case to an industrial tribunal which resulted in an out of court settlement. Further negotiations with the insurer, including discussions with the previous employer, led to a reconsideration of the claim, where the insurer offered to pay half the payments. When the policy-holder declined and cancelled his policy, full payment was offered.

> A mortgagor claimed due to illness caused by a benign tumour. Prior to taking out his MPPI policy, and in the course of a consultation about another matter, he had asked his doctor to check a bruise. Subsequently this bruise turned out to be related to his tumour, but neither the doctor nor the claimant was aware of this at the time of the consultation. The claim was rejected on the grounds that this was a pre-existing medical condition. The mortgagor's annoyance was heightened as the consultation had taken place when he was transferring

> his mortgage to a new lender. In doing this he had to cancel his existing MPPI and take a new one (policies are not portable between lenders). Had he not made the transfer there would not have been the consultation and the claim would have been accepted.

In nearly a quarter of cases borrowers did not know why they were rejected or had experienced administrative problems.

In total, a majority of those whose applications had been rejected had claimed for things that were judged to be excluded by their policies. Insurers would argue that their decisions were 'correct'. However, most borrowers in this position had not realised their claim was outside their policy. They had not read the small print, but nor had these exclusions been discussed at their mortgage interviews. Rather, there was a widespread trust that mortgage lenders would only sell them a policy on which they could claim. In two cases, claims had been submitted by borrowers following discussions with their lender.

Others claimed because when applying for a policy they had declared particular health conditions that had not prevented them from being granted an MPPI. These people were aggrieved when rejected on health grounds. There were also instances where borrowers did not agree that they had been sacked or had taken voluntary redundancy but rather that they had been unfairly dismissed. On claiming, they expected their insurer to investigate (and share their view of events) and were disappointed when this did not happen. In particular, the evidence from Kempson et al (1999) and Ford et al (1999) highlights the tension between the shift towards a flexible labour market and its associated uncertainties and a safety net that depends on clarity about the terms and conditions of a claimant's employment and why they became unemployed. The following case study shows this clearly.

> A woman worked full time in a care home. She and her partner had an MPPI policy that paid the mortgage on unemployment. After some time the woman was 'laid off' without pay because of a lack of residents. However, her job was not terminated because of the expectation that in a few months the care home would have more residents and she would be required again. On being laid off, she claimed on the MPPI policy but the claim was rejected because she was laid off, not unemployed. Having explained the circumstances to the insurer, they suggested that the care home should make her redundant, but they were unwilling to do so because, she assumed, of cost. She was, however,

> able to claim unemployment benefit. As she said, "As far as the government were concerned I was out of work ... if it's good enough for the government ... then it's good enough for this tiny firm [the insurer]. I had all the proof to say I was out of work, but it wasn't good enough for them". (Ford et al, 1999)

However, the most significant indicator of the effectiveness of MPPI is the extent to which claimants avoid arrears. The survey of successful claimants (Kempson et al, 1999) indicated that 21% of them nevertheless developed arrears, while among the 53 rejected claimants, almost half developed arrears. Thus, a successful claim does not necessarily preclude arrears while an unsuccessful claim does not necessarily lead to arrears. Those most likely to fall into arrears (in both groups) were younger households (those under 35), those likely to be able to claim ISMI in time (because the head of household was unemployed and there were limited other sources of income and household savings of less than £3,000) and those with mortgages over £200 a month. Table 4.4 sets out the reasons for arrears among successful claimants. In some cases, arrears were a result of multiple factors.

A total of 63% of successful claimants had to wait between eight and 26 weeks to receive their first payment; 13% of successful claimants developed arrears during this period. However, analysis shows that it is not the wait period per se that impacts on arrears but the availability of the resources to manage the wait period. Compared to those who did not develop arrears in the wait period, a lower proportion of those who did had access to redundancy money or the wages of another earner. Consequently, a higher proportion of them had to draw on their savings (and this was only successful where the mortgage was relatively small) and/or rely on assistance from family and friends.

One in 12 successful claimants also developed arrears due to the MPPI payments falling short of full mortgage payments. Few, if any, borrowers had altered the sum insured after they took out MPPI yet mortgage costs can vary as interest rates alter. Lenders hardly ever notified borrowers that their MPPI payments were not matching increases in interest rates and so monthly payments. Arrears also developed as a result of the distribution of MPPI cover, where, if the 'wrong' partner needed to claim, usually the higher earner, and if there was a payment shortfall, the gap was too big for the second earner to fill. Finally, a small proportion of successful and unsuccessful claimants developed arrears as a result of administrative delay or error, particularly delays in dealing with complaints

Table 4.4: Reasons for arrears among successful MPPI claimants

	% with arrears
While waiting for payments from the policy	13
Shortfall in payments from MPPI	7
Claim originally rejected	2
When policy ended and no ISMI	3
Gap between MPPI and ISMI	2
Shortfall in payments from ISMI	3
Other reason	2

Source: Kempson et al (1999), Survey of MPPI claimants

or appeals against rejected claims, or faulty payment processes such as where the insurers would not time the payment to coincide with the required date for payment of the mortgage. Delays, and so arrears, also resulted from claimants failing to submit repeat evidence of their ongoing medical condition or continuing job search.

Currently, the evidence shows that a significant minority of those receiving MPPI, nevertheless develop arrears, and identifies the key reasons for this. In association with the evidence that some claimants are rejected, and that rejection can be complex and contested as well as simply the result of a failure to examine the conditions of the policy, there remains some doubt about the overall effectiveness of the private safety net for mortgagors. Rejected claims and the experiences associated with the claiming process suggest that some people's attitudes to insurance may harden, and their degree of trust in the market is likely to be lowered. Both of these outcomes have been observed (Kempson et al, 1999) with the result that the market is in danger of eroding its own standing.

ISMI

Following the introduction of the post-October 1995 ISMI provisions, there is a key question about the impact of the restrictions on unemployed home owners' ability to manage financially, and ultimately to sustain home ownership. In particular, how well can unemployed home owners manage the now extended ISMI 'gap'; what is the extent of any ISMI 'shortfall' once mortgagors start to receive payments and how easily do claimants manage these?

To answer these questions, it is necessary to be clear about the position prior to October 1995. Studies by Ford and Wilcox (1992) and Ford et al (1995) provide an appropriate benchmark, although the question of the ISMI gap received little attention in these studies as, at that time, the 'gap' was relatively limited at 50% for the first two months. Pre-October 1995, once ISMI was payable, about two thirds of ISMI claimants did not receive full interest payments and so had shortfalls (66% and 70% respectively in the two studies). Approximately 20% of all ISMI claimants were in arrears. Clearly, most of those with shortfalls were supplementing ISMI payments from their own resources or those of their kin but, judged by the level of arrears, ISMI constituted a relatively effective safety net.

Currently, one consequence of the low take-up of MPPI, and the lack of adverse selection, is that only 25% of those claiming IS/JSA possess a MPPI policy to bridge the now extended ISMI 'gap' or wait period (Kempson et al, 1999). Most IS/JSA claimants have to manage the wait period unaided by formal provision and where they are not only unemployed or unable to work, but also with limited or no savings. Even those with MPPI face a wait period for insurance, which for pre-October 1995 borrowers is similar to that of ISMI. Currently, for the majority of claimants (both IS/JSA and ISMI), the shorter wait periods apply but this will gradually change as the balance between pre- and post-October 1995 borrowers changes in favour of the latter (Kempson et al, 1999).

The survey of IS/JSA claimants and those currently in receipt of ISMI showed that, on average, during the wait period pre-October 1995 borrowers had to cover £238 per month and post-October borrowers £273. Assuming claimants cannot meet any mortgage payments in the wait period, this could result in average arrears of up to £950 for pre-October 1995 borrowers and £2,453 for post-October 1995 borrowers. In practice, many borrowers turn to family and friends for help with mortgage payments during this period, or use benefit payments (with the consequential reduction in an already subsistence standard of living), or run down savings, but a sizeable proportion do develop arrears as Table 4.5 indicates.

Among those who were still in the wait period at the time of the survey, 33% had already been unable to meet their payments in full, while over two fifths (44%) of those who had experienced the full wait period had not met the payments in full. Only just over one in 10 claimants said that they had paid their mortgage in full, on time and without difficulty. A smaller percentage of post-October 1995 borrowers had been able to pay in full (5%) than had pre-October borrowers (11%). Table 4.5 also

Table 4.5: Meeting mortgage payments in the ISMI wait period (%)

		ISMI recipients		IS/JSA claimants
	*All	Pre-October 1995 borrowers	Post-October 1995 borrowers	
Payments met:				
In full, on time, without difficulty	11	11	5	12
With difficulty	44	43	62	55
Not met in full and on time	44	45	33	33

*Weighted data

Source: Kempson et al (1999), postal survey of ISMI recipients and IS claimants

shows that roughly equal proportions of pre-October 1995 borrowers either defaulted or had problems paying, while among post-October borrowers, proportionately fewer defaulted and proportionately more paid but with difficulty.

The survey also showed that once mortgagor claimants received ISMI, over 80% had to manage a shortfall on their payments. This represents a small but significant increase from the 70% of claimants who experienced a shortfall before the October 1995 changes as noted above. There was little difference between pre- and post-October borrowers with respect to shortfalls. Table 4.6 shows that the main reason for a shortfall was the imposition of the payment of interest at a standard rate that was periodically lower than the actual interest rate being charged to the borrower.

The standard rate of interest is calculated as the average of the basic rate of mortgage interest charged by a number of lenders. A change in the standard rate is triggered by a 0.25% change in this base rate. However, borrowers do not have 'average' but individual rates and where their actual rate exceeds the standard rate, they have to make good the shortfall or experience arrears. This possibility is exacerbated by the delay of up to three months in implementing upward changes to the standard rate. (Claimants can also be beneath the standard rate if, for example, they have a discounted mortgage, and in these circumstances would benefit.) In addition, about one in seven claimants had interest disallowed because their housing costs were too high. In one in 10 cases second loans were excluded from the interest calculations. A small proportion of claimants

Table 4.6: Reasons for ISMI meeting only part of mortgage interest (all with shortfall) (%)

	All	Pre-October 1995 borrowers	Post-October 1995 borrowers
Housing costs too high	13	13	19
Ineligible second loan	11	11	2
Mortgage interest higher than standard rate	44	44	43
Mortgage taken out during IS/JSA claim	6	6	6
Non-dependant deductions	5	5	0
Other reason	22	22	30

Note: Percentages may exceed 100 due to rounding.

Source: Kempson et al (1999), postal survey of ISMI recipients

also experienced shortfalls as they had taken out the mortgage during an IS/JSA claim, and due to non-dependent deductions.

Despite the difficulties faced, in many cases claimants were successful in making full payments drawing on the same range of responses as they had used to manage the ISMI 'gap', with the use of benefits rising in importance. However, over a third of the sample of all ISMI claimants noted that once they started to receive ISMI, the shortfalls resulted in arrears (or further arrears). Considering only the arrears that resulted from shortfall payments, more claimants experienced arrears than was the case pre-1995.

Thus, the evidence indicates that the proportion of claimants with a shortfall has increased since the implementation of the 1995 ISMI changes. There has also been an increase in the proportion of ISMI claimants with arrears from the 20% that pertained in the mid-1990s. Further, a third and more than two fifths of claimants (pre- and post-October 1995 borrowers) already had arrears as a result of the wait period before they received any ISMI payments. Before October 1995 there was only a limited wait period and clearly the impact of extending it in terms of generating arrears has been substantial.

Drawing together the available information on arrears, 52% of pre-October 1995 ISMI recipients and 46% of post-October 1995 recipients had experienced arrears at some point of their claim. Considering those in arrears, Table 4.7 indicates the source of arrears in the wait and/or shortfall periods or at a change of safety net.

Table 4.7: Mortgage arrears among ISMI recipients (all receiving ISMI and in arrears) (%)

Arrears due to	Pre-October 1995 borrowers	Post-October 1995 borrowers
Wait period only	16	25
ISMI shortfall only	23	6
Both wait and shortfall periods	37	37
Problems with the change from MPPI to ISMI	12	14
Other problems	12	20

Note: Percentages may exceed 100 due to rounding.

Source: Kempson et al (1999), postal survey of ISMI recipients

A higher percentage of post-October 1995 borrowers had arrears in the wait period, which is not surprising given its nine-month duration. For claimants who managed the wait period without arrears, many more pre-October 1995 borrowers reported a shortfall in their interest payments. One contributing factor is likely to be a higher level of second loans among those having held their mortgage for longer (and so more likely to have equity to draw down). Newer borrowers have experienced home ownership in a low inflation environment and one where lenders are more cautious about lending. However, the rather different picture seen between the groups currently is likely to change and further equalise as the time from October 1995 increases.

With approximately half of ISMI claimants experiencing arrears at some point, and many more struggling to meet payments, the evidence would seem to suggest strongly that the present state 'safety net' for low-income mortgagors is providing a far from effective support system.

The MPPI/ISMI interface

Finally, there is the issue of the link between MPPI and ISMI for the minority that claim on MPPI and in time become eligible for ISMI. This transition is assumed to be a smooth one. However, Table 4.7 shows that more than one in 10 claimants in arrears developed them at the 'interface' between MPPI and ISMI. This was due either to the lack of an administratively smooth transition from MPPI to ISMI, or where a return to work involved a lower-paying job than previously; and/or a return to work in a temporary job. If in this last situation their job lasted more than 13 weeks they faced a one-year requalification period before they could claim ISMI again. (Even if they had maintained MPPI premium payments they would also face a one-year 'requalification' period.) Some of the disincentives associated with ISMI have now been addressed by the proposals in the housing Green Paper (DETR/DSS, 2000a) to modify the requalification rules so that they do not act as a work disincentive to temporary employment and to provide for the continuation of ISMI payments for four weeks after a return to employment so as to reduce the likelihood of debt.

Summary

Drawing together the evidence on the safety nets for mortgagors, the available evidence indicates that neither public nor private safety net provision is satisfactory. Both can contribute to the development of arrears, but the restructuring of ISMI has been particularly detrimental. Clearly, a higher take-up of MPPI would assist in reducing the impact of the ISMI wait periods, but would not touch the ISMI shortfall problem. But the take-up of MPPI appears to be hindered primarily by negative attitudes to insurance and poor risk assessment. Poor experiences in the MPPI market also dampen the market to some degree. As things stand, the mixed economy of welfare provides only a limited safety net for the growing risk among home owners. The potential further cut to ISMI (to a 14-month wait period) raised for discussion in the 2000 housing Green Paper (DETR/DSS, 2000a) would be highly detrimental if implemented in the absence of a higher take-up of MPPI and without addressing some of the weaknesses in MPPI that this chapter has outlined.

Note

This chapter draws upon material previously published in Ford and Kempson (1997a), Kempson et al (1999) and Ford and Quilgars, (2000) from projects funded by the Joseph Rowntree Foundation. It also draws upon Ford (2000c), which was funded by the CML, and Ford and England (2000), which was funded by the DSS.

FIVE

The costs of mortgage arrears and possessions

This chapter attempts to map out schematically some of the wider implications of high levels of mortgage arrears and possessions and relates these to some broader debates. As we shall detail in subsequent chapters, at an individual level, in most instances arrears and possessions are at best stressful and in some cases traumatic. However, our concern here is not with individual responses to arrears and possessions in and of themselves, but with aggregate meanings and impacts. In order to do this we develop a simple analytic framework that facilitates a systematic consideration of the full range of costs associated with mortgage arrears and possessions. By the term 'costs' we mean the price paid or required for acquiring, producing, maintaining or losing something measured in money, time or physical energy or social involvement. Undertaking such a mapping of the composition, extent, distribution and impact of different types of costs can make a contribution to a number of different substantive questions and debates. An illustrative, rather than exhaustive, list includes the following.

First, an analysis of costs, particularly the extent and distribution of financial costs, but also costs in terms of the physical deterioration of property (Leather and Mackintosh, 1997), or the social costs associated with housing debt and restricted residential mobility (Ford and Seavers, 2000), which contribute to the debate about the growing diversification and fragmentation of owner-occupation and the role of housing in the production and reproduction of social divisions (Anderson and Sim, 2000).

Second, consideration of financial costs that crystallise as outright losses following mortgage possession, to the extent that they are widespread and substantial, and contribute to a critical assessment of the thesis that owner-occupation offers the basis for the accumulation of wealth and so the modification of patterns of social inequality (Burbridge, 2000; Hamnett and Seavers, 1996; Saunders, 1990).

Third, both the direct or indirect knowledge and experience of costs may be important influences contributing to the formation of attitudes and preferences with respect to home ownership (Kempson and Ford, 1995; Ford and Burrows, 1999a).

Fourth, some costs are recoverable, raising questions about the circumstances in which recovery is pursued. Thus, there is a contribution to more generic issues of regulation and consumer protection. Substantive questions pertaining to the role of the civil courts in holding the balance between powerful lenders and relatively powerless borrowers, and the rhetoric and reality of 'access to justice' are also illuminated through a consideration of the costs of mortgage arrears and possessions (Doling et al, 1984; Ford, 1994; Nixon et al, 1996).

Fifth, analyses of the costs of arrears and possessions are also analyses of the interrelationship between housing, employment and social security through, for example, a consideration of the extent to which the structure of benefits for those in arrears constitutes a work disincentive (Ford et al, 1996), or the extent to which one consequence of cost recovery via the courts is to encourage a detachment from the labour market of those with arrears (Caplovitz, 1974; Ford and Wilson, 1993).

Sixth, the implications of the growth of costs associated with arrears and possessions are also significant for considerations of the relationship between the market and the state with respect to sustainable owner-occupation and thus the future shape of housing policy (Holmans, 1997).

Finally, an analysis of costs may also contribute to debates about the development of a risk society and the social consequences of living in 'insecure times' more generally (Wilkinson, 1996; Nettleton and Burrows, 1998a, 1998b). This more general theme is treated in some detail in Chapters Six and Seven.

A typology of costs invoked by mortgage arrears and possessions

Table 5.1 identifies different types of costs, the different groups and institutions affected by them and some examples of the specific forms that they might take. We differentiate between the following sorts of costs: social; social psychological; health-related; administrative; financial; political; and organisational. Such costs may be experienced by the following: borrowers; lenders; insurers; central government; local government; housing market institutions; labour market institutions; and health services.

Table 5.1: Typology of the potential range of costs associated with mortgage arrears and possessions

Type of cost	Examples of costs experienced by							
	Borrowers	Lenders	Insurers	Central government	Local government	Housing market institutions	Labour market institutions	Health services
Social	Social exclusion Insecurity Reduced standard of living	Loss of trust	Loss of trust					
Social psychological	Stigma of debt Relationship difficulties					Reduced confidence		
Health	Mental health and well-being		Increased risk of accident claims				Employee absenteeism	
Administrative		Collection costs		ISMI direct payment	Homelessness provision			Additional demand for services
Financial	Admin charges Residual debt Increased payments Poverty	Technological Investment 'real' losses	MIG pay-out	ISMI 'Mortgage Rescue' schemes Reduced revenue from transactions	Increased homelessness provision Costs of housing advice	Reduced revenue/ transactions		Additional demand for services
Political		'Cooler' relationships with govt		Electoral consequences				
Organisational	Changes in household financial management	Refocusing of activities and culture			Advice provision	Sector restructuring	Adjust to reduced mobility	

Note: The examples given above are indicative, not exhaustive. An empty box does not indicate the absence of costs.

One important contribution of Table 5.1 is to show how embedded unsustainable home ownership becomes within wider society. Once thought of in this way, the long tentacles of arrears and possessions become clear. To emphasise this, we first provide a brief overview of the range of potential costs and then consider one specific cost – the financial cost – for one group of people – borrowers with mortgage arrears – in some detail. Subsequent chapters develop the discussion of a number of these costs further.

Social, social psychological and health costs

Borrowers unable to sustain home ownership are likely to be subject to quite profound processes of – to use the contemporary argot – *social exclusion*. One of the clearest manifestations is homelessness (Ford, 1997). However, the experience of mortgage possession is also likely to have a number of other social, social psychological and/or health consequences for families. Indeed, Ford (1994) in her study of the financial consequences of possession found that for the respondents it was the *social* rather than the *financial* considerations that were often most central. Motivated by this finding, the full range of social consequences for families was examined systematically by Nettleton et al (1999). In a study of 30 families with children, all of whom had been taken into possession and subsequently rehoused in the social rented sector, five main categories of consequences under this broad heading were deciphered, relating to changes in: *quality of life*; *social status and identity*; *personal and family relationships*; *future aspirations*; and *health and well-being*. A summary is provided in Figure 5.1.

Many of the consequences identified in Figure 5.1 are dealt with in detail in Chapters Six and Seven. Here, however, we provide a brief summary of some of the issues to the extent that they impinge on an analysis of social, social psychological and health-related costs.

Changes in the quality of life

A move from being an owner-occupier to being *homeless* may be accompanied by fundamental changes to the quality of people's lives. There may be fairly significant *lifestyle* changes, for instance involving a move to a different type of *neighbourhood, often one not of their choice* and where they sometimes experienced high levels of crime and drugs. There was also often a reduction in *the social activities and social participation* of those who had been repossessed. For many, the experience of possession

Figure 5.1: Some consequences of mortgage possession

		Experience of mortgage possession impacts on		
Quality of life	**Social status and identity**	**Personal and family relationships**	**Future aspirations**	**Health and well-being**
Homelessness	Stigma	Marital breakdown	Financial insecurity	Poor mental health
Loss of lifestyle	Humiliation	Relationship tension	Fear of the future	Poor physical health
Poverty	Embarrassment	Split up household	Fear can't buy again	Depression
Long-term debts	Loss of 'owner' status	Arguments	Lost 'hopes and dreams'	Stress
Insecure tenancy	Sense of failure	Inability to invest trust in relationships	No independence	
Social isolation	Letting family down	Parenting difficulties	Poverty in old age	
Loss of job	Loss of confidence			
Loss of friends	Loss of self-esteem			
Unsuitable accommodation	Sense of regret			
Lack of space	Becoming 'second-class citizens'			
Loss of personal possessions				
No access to credit				
Loss of pets				

is a route to *poverty, substantial debt and social exclusion.* For example, people lacked the money to go out and to be able to participate in local social life, go on holiday or have trips and treats. Often parents, and particularly women, ensured their children and other household members were provided for first, limiting their own consumption and social activities. Many also felt trapped with respect to decisions about work, fearing that if they had an income, lenders would chase them for the debt they owed.

Changes in social status and identity

Another significant consequence concerns learning to live with, or adjust to, a new social status. This often resulted in feelings of *stigma.* Relatedly, for many people the experience impacted on their *confidence* and *self-esteem.* These psychological effects altered some people's ability to relate to members of their family, their friends, and to others in a range of social situations. Socialising became problematic for those who felt that they had failed and/or let their family down. At its most extreme, some people found it very difficult to venture outside of their current home.

Changes in personal and family relationships

The experience also changed people's personal relationships, especially between partners. Of course for some families, relationship breakdown is an antecedent factor that contributed to the possession. But for couples who stayed together the stress, anxiety and worry associated with possession often resulted in significant tensions. There were also consequences for new personal relationships where homes were lost due to relationship breakdown. Some people found it difficult to invest trust in a new relationship.

Some people found the support that they received from their parents and other family members to be invaluable. This variously took the form of emotional, financial and practical support. Others either did not have any family or were not in contact with them. Worse though for some, were the negative and unsupportive attitudes of other family members. There is much 'felt stigma' associated with losing a home through mortgage possession.

Changes in future aspirations

Many people were very anxious about their future. A key legacy of the experience of possession was a sense of insecurity and an enduring fear about what the future held. A further concern about losing a home and becoming a renter was the associated loss of independence. Many people were anxious about their children. Some had chosen to buy their homes in areas that had 'good' schools and 'good' social environments in which to bring up their children. Often one of the main reasons that they had wanted to buy their homes in the first place was to ensure that they would have something that they could pass on to their children. Now that this was not going to be possible their primary concern was to find some other way to ensure that their children would have a good future.

Changes in health and well-being

The impact of the experience of mortgage arrears and possession on health is so profound that we have dedicated the whole of Chapter Seven of this book to the topic. The overwhelming health issue was stress. This was due to the experiences of *uncertainty* and *lack of control*. The most common physical health symptoms were headaches, which people attributed directly to stress. Those who had chronic conditions such as eczema and asthma found that their symptoms got worse. Others experienced more acute health problems.

In summary, the social, social psychological and health-related consequences of mortgage possession are both dramatic and overwhelmingly negative. At a *personal* level people have felt that their social status, identity and sense of self-worth have all been damaged; personal and family relationships have been disrupted and in some cases shattered; physical and mental health has worsened; quality of life has been blighted; and future aspirations have been severely curtailed. Relatedly, at the same time as people have to endure these individual traumas their *structural* positions in society have also worsened; their range of life choices has been restricted; their resources have been diminished; the risks they confront have been increased; and their ability to act to improve their lives has been lessened.

Administrative costs

Increased administrative costs have been experienced in a number of different institutions. Stephens (1996), for example, identifies 15 different types of impacts resulting from increases in mortgage arrears and possessions on insurance companies, building societies, banks and the government. For example, lenders have had either to establish or restructure their debt collection facilities to ensure practices and procedures are consistent with 'mass processing'. In addition, the growth of mortgagors in receipt of ISMI, and the shift to direct payments, has increased the administrative costs for both central government and lenders. Local authorities have faced greater administrative costs in processing households made homeless due to increased levels of possession (Ford, 1997). These administrative burdens also, of course, have a financial counterpart.

Financial costs

Increased financial costs obviously fall on borrowers. In addition to arrears, they may face one or more of: interest on arrears; administrative charges from lenders for correspondence or setting up payment arrangements; court charges; charges for essential maintenance post-possession; estate agency fees; and so on. We will discuss this in more detail below. However, financial costs also accrue to lenders who not only face 'real' financial losses but also have to increase levels of human and capital investment to 'manage' arrears and possessions. Insurers providing Mortgage Indemnity Guarantee (MIG) cover to lenders also face increased levels of 'pay-out'. Other housing market institutions also faced costs due to the decrease in the number of transactions invoked by such high levels of unsustainable home ownership. For instance, a number of estate agents went 'bust' in the early and mid-1990s.

Central government has faced higher levels of ISMI pay-out (hence their attempt to encourage private insurance cover, as discussed in Chapter Four). As Figure 5.2 shows, in 1989, ISMI payments totalled just £353 million. The figure peaked in 1992 when payments totalled some £1,143 million. In 1996 the figure stood at £867 million and in 1999 it had declined further to £527 million – still considerably higher than the costs 10 years earlier, despite the October 1995 changes to eligibility and the encouragement of borrowers to take out MPPI (as discussed in Chapter Four).

Figure 5.2: Mortgage interest taken into account for Income Support and Job Seekers' Allowance (1980-99)

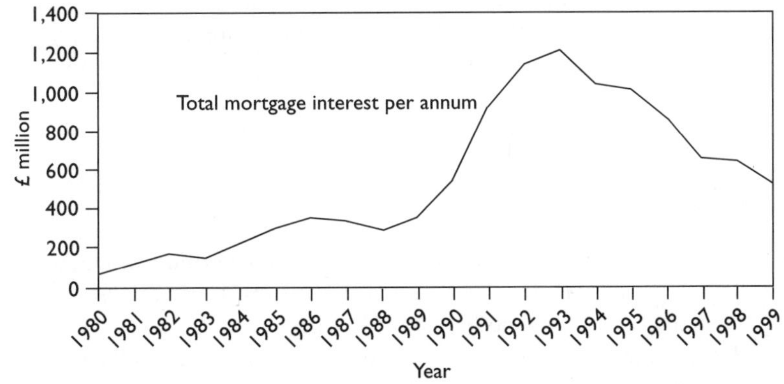

Note: All figures are for the May of the year. Figures to 1990 show mortgage interest liabilities taken into account in calculating eligibility for Income Support, and in earlier years Supplementary Benefit. From 1990 onwards the figures are based on the actual help provided, and are net of non-dependant deductions, etc. The figures from 1997 reflect the introduction of Jobseekers' Allowance. Figures for 1985 are an estimate based on linear interpolation from the 1984 and 1986 figures, as no data is available for this year.

Source: Wilcox (2000, p 209, table 103)

Figure 5.3: Number of local authority homelessness acceptances due to mortgage arrears in England (1990-99)

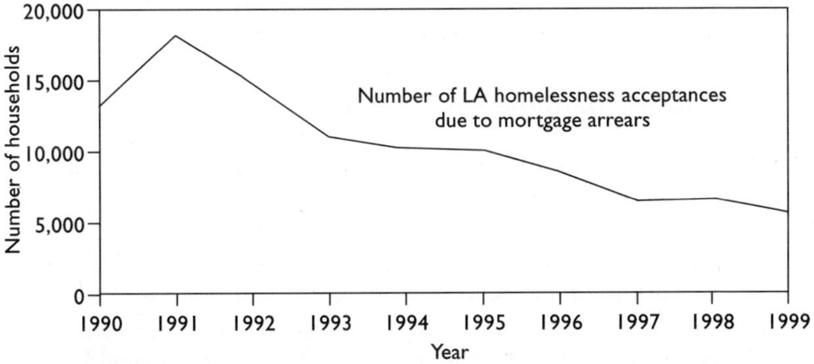

Source: DoE/DETR Homelessness Statistics

Local government obviously faces costs of housing homeless households (Ford, 1997). As Figure 5.3 shows, mortgage arrears account for a significant number of homelessness acceptances in England. At the peak of the housing crisis in 1991 a full 12% of all local authority homelessness acceptances were due to mortgage arrears – some 18,206 households. In 1999 mortgage arrears still accounted for 5% of acceptances, a total of almost 5,600 households.

Political costs

Throughout the 1980s, the expansion of owner-occupation was regarded as an electoral guarantee. The significance of this particular 'positional good' (Hirsch, 1977) was clear in the 1991 intervention by the government and the prime minister's concern to convince people that on the basis of that intervention, the problem of arrears and possessions was 'solved'. Their persistence, particularly coupled with negative and reduced equity and low levels of transactions, could well have contributed to the decline of Conservative popularity (Pattie et al, 1995) and, perhaps, the Labour victory of 1997. The 1997 general election was the first at which the Labour Party won more support than the Conservatives within the owner-occupied sector of the British housing market. Many of those who switched their support to Labour between 1992 and 1997 were in the owner-occupied sector. It is, however, unclear how much housing issues per se contributed to this switch (Dorling et al, 1999).

Without having to detail every instance, it is clear that the growth of mortgage arrears and possessions invokes a potentially wide range of costs to a range of different actors. In the final section of the chapter we focus in more detail on the financial costs to borrowers.

Can housing damage your wealth?

A consideration of the financial costs incurred by borrowers directly addresses questions about the consequences, if any, that the growth of arrears and possessions has for the argument that home ownership provides the means to reshape the social stratification system by radically altering access to wealth and the distribution of wealth. This argument was most clearly articulated by Saunders (1990) but the link between ownership and access to wealth has also been a central aspect of government ideology for many years. However, in considering this issue, there are a series of questions that need to be explored. For example, what impact has the growth of arrears and possessions – in association with other related developments such as the emergence of negative equity (Forrest et al, 1999) – had on capital accumulation? What is the scale of any loss, in terms of numbers affected and size? Are there longer-term financial implications for any households who are so disinvesting?

In working through the financial implications of arrears and possessions for issues of social divisions, there may be a more complex set of outcomes than typically suggested. Potentially, with respect to capital accumulation, those in arrears and possession can be classified into six categories:

Borrowers in arrears may have:

- increasing housing equity, but arrears, leading to a temporary slowdown in capital accumulation;
- no growth in equity, and arrears, leading to the erosion of capital accumulated; and
- negative equity, and arrears, leading to increasing levels of negative equity.

Borrowers in possession may have:

- positive equity, possession with a surplus;
- negative equity, possession with a loss (residual debt), loss written off; or
- negative equity, possession with a loss, residual debt pursued.

In addition, borrowers may be reducing other forms of wealth such as savings, insurance and/or selling goods as they seek to raise income to stem arrears.

Looking at these six possible outcomes, it is clear that not all of them preclude capital accumulation while others moderate rather than deny a gain. Thus in principle, arrears and possession do not necessarily preclude access to wealth or a surplus, albeit at a level lower than might have been the case had arrears not accrued. There is also an important distinction to be made between potential and realised loss paralleling the distinctions drawn in the accumulation debates between a realised and potential gain. So, in order to assess the meaning of arrears and possession for the wider debates outlined above it is necessary to try and obtain some empirical leverage on the point at which any loss or surplus crystallises and particularly the magnitude of any such losses.

The financial costs to borrowers in arrears and possession are made up of several different items and are cumulative. They include missing monthly mortgage payments; interest on arrears; charges for arrears administration;

and charges for court and litigation costs. Once possession is taken, there are additional costs: for example, interest on arrears (accruals); estate agency fees; and essential maintenance to property, such as changing locks.

Table 5.2 provides an example of the way costs accumulate for a hypothetical mortgagor, who bought a house in June 1989 with a £50,000 repayment mortgage, paying without difficulty until December 1990 but then defaulting. The hypothetical lender took possession after only a few months (court actions can be entered after three months' default although the average number of months in arrears at possession is around 12). The property was sold six months after possession.

The hypothetical property was sold for approximately £41,000, and Table 5.3 sets out the borrowers' potential obligations (residual debt) following the sale: the negative equity; arrears; interest on arrears; legal and estate agency fees; and administration costs. This gives a total remaining debt of £16,714.

Table 5.2: Accumulation of financial costs by a hypothetical mortgagor in default

This example assumes a property bought in June 1989, default starting in January 1991, repossession in June 1991 and the sale of the property in December 1991.

Purchase price: £52,632

Mortgage: £50,000 (repayment mortgage)

Sale price: £41,312

		Outstanding debt	Net costs to borrower*	Total costs
Purchase	July 1989	£49,976	£517.90	
	June 1990	£49,743	£576.14	Repayments of £9,983
	Dec 1990	£49,610	£548.32	
Default	Jan 1991	£50,119	£508.83	Arrears of £3,003
Repossession	June 1991	£52,614	£481.65	Admin £125
Sale	Dec 1991	£55,797	£529.65	Interest on arrears £3,184

*Net costs are calculated as follows: gross monthly payment, less MIRAS plus £15 mortgage protection policy. In the calculation the mortgage protection policy is not activated.

Source: Derived from data published by AKG Mortgage Services (1995)

Table 5.3: Residual debt and costs of home ownership period using the same loan/sale details as in Table 5.2

(a) Residual debt		£
(i)	Outstanding mortgage balance after sale (50,000-41,312)	8,688
(ii)	Arrears	3,003
(iii)	Accrued interest	3,184
(iv)	Legal and estate agency fees	1,714
(v)	Administration costs	125
	Total residual debt	16,714
(b) Costs of home ownership for 23 months		£
(i)	Mortgage payments made	9,983
(ii)	Arrears	3,003
(iii)	Deposit (5%)	2,632
	Total cost	15,618
Total costs of entering/experiencing/exiting from home ownership		**29,329**

Outstanding mortgage balance + accrued interest legal and agency fees + administrative charges + costs of home ownership

Table 5.3 also indicates the costs of occupancy incurred by the borrower by providing an indication of what the borrower has spent by entering owner-occupation, spending 23 months in the house and then exiting owner-occupation as a result of possession.

The figures in these tables are only illustrative but show the complex, cumulative make-up of costs. However, while all borrowers in arrears and possession incur financial *costs*, whether they become financial *losses*, and on what scale, depends on several factors, few of which the borrower can control. For example, it depends on the length of time the lenders will forbear before seeking possession, on the speed of sale, the decisions taken about the method of disposal (open market or at auction), the degree of 'trashing' and post-possession vandalism (all of which may have to be rectified before a sale), but also the equity the borrower has in the property and the lender's charging policy. Even where there are absolute losses a lender may decide to write them off from the borrowers' responsibility. At that point they become direct costs to the lender, indirect costs to the investor or shareholder, but no longer a cost to the borrower.

Using a number of empirical studies it is possible to undertake some crude assessments of the financial costs of possessions for borrowers. The most comprehensive data come from a random sample survey of 111 households giving possession between 1991 and 1994 (Ford et al, 1995).

In this study, average arrears for households in possession were £5,600 and the average costs associated with the administration of arrears, litigation and selling were estimated at £2,500, giving total average costs of £8,100. Seventy-two per cent of those giving possession had negative equity. Only three-quarters of properties in possession had been sold at the time of the survey, with approaching 70% sold at an average loss of £6,200. Combining negative equity with arrears and costs indicates an average residual debt of £14,400. The extent of negative equity has decreased since the mid-1990s (Forrest et al, 1999) and so it is likely that post-1995 this figure will have decreased somewhat.

The figures from Ford et al (1995) confirm those available through a series of other studies from the early 1990s. For example, a study of families rehoused by Portsmouth City Council (Evans, 1992) estimated that around 70% were likely to have a residual debt. A similar figure was reported by Ford (1993) in a study of 307 possession cases with one major lender. However, a lower figure (54%) of residual debtors was found in a qualitative study of 16 households rehoused through two local authorities (Ford, 1994). Average arrears in this latter study were £4,328. Given that these were exclusively low-income households, the figure is consistent with the £5,600 reported above and both are broadly consistent with figures of between £4,700 and £5,600 derived from surveys of lenders carried out by Ford between 1994 and 1997. The qualitative study (Ford, 1994), however, noted a rather larger gap between the outstanding loans and the selling price, in all probability the result of the data being collected from two areas characterised by high levels of negative equity.

Using the information above, it is likely that some 70% of the 380,000 households giving possession between 1990 and 1996 – a total of 266,000 households or 2.5% of all mortgagors – did so with an average loss of £14,400. We can be less sure of the figures which relate to the period between 1997 and 1999 when, as we have seen, just under a further 100,000 households gave possession. No systematic research has been carried out during this more recent period that would allow us to estimate a revised average loss figure. Nevertheless, if the postings made by borrowers experiencing arrears and possession to new virtual fora such as the UK Homes Repossessions Page on the website (http://www.home-repo.org/) (see Burrows et al, 2000, for a discussion) are at all indicative, costs continue to be significant.

These borrowers have clearly not shared in any wealth creation process. Even with the calculation based solely on arrears and costs, the total loss to borrowers is £2.1 billion up to 1996. Including the estimate of average negative equity calculated above, the loss equals £3.83 billion up to 1996 and almost certainly well exceeded £4 billion up to the end of 1999.

The majority of mortgage loans that initially exceed 75% of the property valuation have, until very recently, had to have a compulsory, associated insurance – the Mortgage Indemnity Guarantee (MIG). Where there is a loss on sale, the lender can claim on the cover, up to the value of the insured portion, which is usually met in full or in part by the insurers as a payment to lenders. However, having paid the lender, the insurer has the right to recover the whole of the claim from the borrower. They can do this directly or the lender can pursue the debt on the insurers' behalf. In addition, if the loss is greater than the insured portion, lenders will pursue that further shortfall. Insurers and lenders initially have six years in which to commence recovery procedures but that can be extended for a further six years. The decision to pursue borrowers for residual debt is a discretionary decision for insurers and lenders, although the trend is towards pursuing recovery in a greater proportion of cases using debt tracing and debt collection agencies where necessary. Following the publication of NACAB (1999), the Council of Mortgage Lenders (CML) reacted to the 'bad press' that this legal right invoked by issuing guidance to lenders suggesting that they might wish to restrict their use of this right. Some lenders have followed this guidance and now do not pursue outstanding debts for so long. It is likely that the legal basis of this right will be changed by legislation at some time in the future.

Thus, among those giving possession with a loss, two situations emerge. At best, borrowers have lost wealth they had, have no asset, but no debt. At worst, borrowers have lost wealth they had, have no asset but have continuing debt, repayable over the foreseeable future. In a random sample survey in England (Ford et al, 1995), a third of those with residual debt were currently being pursued.

Thus, the majority of the 484,290 households giving possession in the 1990s lost financial resources as a result of their home ownership. Set in the context of the value of owner-occupied housing per se the sums of money may seem insignificant. In the context of a household's finances and the levels of savings among home owners the debt is significant, as is the loss of a potential basis for continuing accumulation. These figures, though, do not exhaust the extent of the financial costs and losses associated with home ownership (Ford and Burrows, 1999b, pp 323-4). In total we calculate that around 4% of home owners have lost or are very likely to lose resources as a result of arrears and possessions in the 1990s; perhaps almost half a million households in total, all of whom face debt recovery procedures for those losses. Again, it is hard to regard these figures as temporary setbacks or irrelevancies on the margin.

But who is likely to lose? We have seen in Chapter Two the relative risks involved in unsustainable home ownership and these risks translate rather predictably in relation to relative financial losses. Borrowers giving possession have considerably lower incomes than borrowers in arrears, who in turn are less advantaged than non-arrears borrowers. For example, in a study conducted in Luton and Bristol in 1993 (of which the in-depth study [Ford, 1994] was a part), average weekly household incomes were £157, £251 and £304 respectively. A similar distribution was found in a later random sample survey of the three groups (Ford et al, 1995). Lower income among those giving possession was associated with greater problems in exercising choice with respect to subsequent housing, housing mobility and temporary housing. A higher proportion of those who had given possession had arrears on other services and commitments than did those with and without arrears. This combination of higher demands on the budget and lower incomes presaged further default. Such households often faced the need for additional resources in order to manage the household's budget, yet their county court judgements precluded them from access to mainstream banking services and credit. At best, this forced them into the high-cost sector of the commercial market or, at worst, paved the way for illegal money lenders (Rowlingson, 1994; Ford and Rowlingson, 1996). In both cases these developments contributed to their growing poverty. And while a small number of those who had given possession (often voluntarily), but with a surplus, had already re-entered owner-occupation, the vast majority in possession believed that they would not easily obtain another mortgage because of credit referencing procedures and the register of county court judgements, or would only do so by paying higher interest costs.

For those managing to re-enter owner-occupation following possession the evidence is, as we have seen in Chapter Two, that they find mortgage payments difficult to maintain the second time around. Households containing someone who has previously experienced possession are twice as likely to be in arrears than are other households with a mortgage. This may be due to their having to pay higher mortgage costs because of their previous possession and/or because the circumstances that pertained originally are enduring (for example, a vulnerable labour market position).

Further, a wide range of other resources would be more expensive, even if access was possible. Thus, issues of unsustainable owner-occupation connect very directly with wider issues of exclusion and poverty. This chapter has concentrated on one potential outcome of arrears and possessions – financial loss and growing disadvantage – and judged that it is a significant and growing issue. The findings presented here at least question the view of owner-occupation as unequivocally associated with wealth accumulation and shared interests, and on the contrary indicate that the extent and distribution of loss cannot be considered as a marginal issue.

Summary

This chapter has suggested that, in principle, a consideration of the costs of mortgage arrears and possessions can contribute to a wide range of substantive issues. It has sought to identify the range of costs to which unsustainable home ownership can give rise, the range of debates to which a consideration of such costs might contribute and to develop the assessment of one set of costs (financial costs to borrowers) in some detail. The analysis forces the conclusion that the costs and losses are substantial both in terms of the numbers affected, the sums of money forgone and the wider individual, social and economic consequences that follow. As the risks to home owners have become more pervasive, so such outcomes are likely to continue to be a feature of our society, their incidence clearly rising and falling in line with the economic cycle, but also becoming more routinely embedded in the experience of owner-occupation. For a significant number of households, their immediate life chances have been affected detrimentally. The expectations of an asset on which to draw in later life or to pass to the next generation have been disappointed. As a group they have become impoverished and caught up in a chain of interconnecting processes which reinforce the initial detriment of losing their home.

Note

This chapter draws upon material previously published in Ford and Burrows (1999b) that was unfunded research and Nettleton et al (1999) which was funded by the Joseph Rowntree Foundation.

SIX

Experiencing mortgage possession

Previous chapters have outlined some of the historical, socio-economic and policy contexts of the emergence of mortgage arrears and mortgage possession as ongoing social problems in contemporary Britain. This chapter shifts the analytic focus somewhat by concentrating less on *structural* factors and more on how mortgage possession is *experienced*. This is an important undertaking because there is a danger that if one concentrates solely on structural factors it is easy to lose sight of "the capacity of people to be creative, reflexive human beings ... active agents in shaping their lives, experiencing, acting upon and reconstituting the outcomes of welfare policies in variable ways" (Williams et al, 1999a, p 2). This chapter thus seeks to understand *how* the whole process of arrears and possession is managed by families and with what consequences.

The material we present derives from a qualitative study of the experiences and perceptions of 30 families with children who had experienced mortgage possession and who had subsequently been rehoused in the social rented sector (Nettleton et al, 1999). Fifty-two households completed and returned a short screening questionnaire and from these 30 were selected for interview in order to mirror as far as possible the known national socio-demographic characteristics of such households (as outlined, for example, in Chapter Two of this book). Semi-structured qualitative interviews were undertaken with 44 adults (some couples being interviewed together) from the 30 families. Twenty of the families lived in the South East and 10 in the North of England. Sixteen of them had experienced mortgage possession in the period 1996 to 1998, 11 between 1993 and 1995 and 3 between 1990 and 1992. In addition, in 10 families, interviews were carried out with children and young people living in a subset of these 30 families. Because in some cases siblings were interviewed together, a total of 17 children, ranging in age from seven to 18 years, were given the opportunity to voice their views. All interviews were tape-recorded and fully transcribed.

The data were analysed in two main ways. First, various substantive issues were explored and described. Such issues included: the stated reasons for getting into mortgage arrears; the events associated with the possession such as contact with the lenders, courts and local authorities; the impact on the children; views on current housing circumstances; and so on. Second, the data were scrutinised with a view to identifying recurrent concerns and themes. In this chapter we focus on how the process of mortgage possession is experienced by both adults and children and with what consequences. In the next chapter we extend the analysis in order to understand some of the consequences of the experience of mortgage arrears and possession for public health. However, first, in order to fully appreciate the experiences of the participants in the study it is worth briefly rehearsing some of the most salient aspects of the process of mortgage possession.

The process of mortgage possession

In England mortgage possession by a lender can either be 'voluntary' or 'compulsory'. In the case of the former the mortgagors either abandon their home, or they return the keys to the lender and sign to confirm they have given up their home voluntarily and that they are liable for any outstanding debt. Compulsory possession involves the lender bringing an action to county court for possession of the property following mortgage default. The case is heard in chambers by a district judge who has a significant degree of discretion. The possible outcomes of the hearing are that the case is either: adjourned; dismissed; a possession order made; or a suspended order granted. If a possession order is made then the mortgagors typically have between 14 and 28 days to leave their home before eviction. A suspended order involves the renegotiation of repayments by the borrower but also gives the lender recourse to possession without a further court hearing, should the borrower default on those payments. While a suspended order may come as a relief for those who want to keep their homes, some fail to sustain their repayments and so they ultimately lose their homes.

As well as the trauma of the process of the possession itself, family members must also decide where they will live in the future. This will of course depend in part on people's preferences, but also on what is available to them. Households experiencing compulsory possession and with dependant children are usually classed as being in 'priority need' by their local authority. Currently, if they are classified as such the local authority is obliged to find them suitable temporary accommodation with a lease of at least two years. They are also added to the waiting list for permanent rehousing. Because in practice such households are in such 'priority need', in many local authorities they will go straight to the top of the waiting list. In contrast, households with dependant children whose homes are possessed voluntarily may be classed as 'intentionally homeless' and so their local authority may or may not accept them as being in 'priority need'. This may also be the case for households who were subject to compulsory possession orders, but who defaulted on payments due to their own mismanagement.

In England, since the start of the 1990s, local authorities have accepted no more than 50% of all households experiencing compulsory possession in any one year and in 1999 the figure was 31%. As a percentage of all possessions in any one year, homelessness acceptances as a result of mortgage arrears have ranged from 19% to 30% in 1991. A considerable percentage of households therefore have to make their own rehousing arrangements. The options are limited. Finding accommodation within the private rented sector can prove difficult for those who are already in debt as deposits and payments in advance are usually required by landlords. Other options include living with family or friends, trying to buy a new home or attempting to secure housing association accommodation. The options will depend on a number of factors such as the reasons for the possession and the structure of the household. It is common for households to experience a number of moves following possession as the initial 'solutions' are often of a temporary nature (Ford et al, 1995).

The experience of possession

Not surprisingly all the participants in the study had found the experience of possession to be very stressful. The following quotations were originally written on the 'opt-in' postal questionnaire and all give an indication of the levels of stress involved:

> "Apart from the death of someone close to us, we found that repossession was the most traumatic experience that we have ever been through. We would not wish this experience on anybody as it is a stigma that will be with us forever." (Couple with dependent children, possessed in 1997)

> "A complete nightmare – stressful. Words cannot say what we felt and went through." (Couple with dependent children, possessed in 1991)

> "A real great upheaval, constant arguments, loads of stress, general worry, plus also when we were put in temporary accommodation we had to

give up our two dogs, which was quite a traumatic time for all the family." (Couple with dependent children, possessed in 1994)

A thematic analysis of the data suggests that there were three main sources of stress: the level of *uncertainty* associated with the processes of possession; the *emotional intensity* of the experience; and a perceived *inability to control* or change the course of events linked to the loss of home. We shall discuss each of these in turn.

Uncertainty

As we can see from the processes of possession described above, every stage of the process is characterised by uncertainty. Families face questions such as: Will the lenders decide to evict us? Will the courts decide in our favour? Will the local authority classify us as homeless? Will we have a home to go to or will we be out on the streets? Often it was not until *the day of the move* itself that the family knew where they would be going. One woman, whose husband left her and refused to pay his share of the mortgage, lost her home because of the significant shortfall that occurred when the Income Support Mortgage Interest (ISMI) payments were much less than her actual mortgage repayments said:

> "There was a person at the council who actually wrote me a letter, who told me that they would fully investigate me, and if their investigations found that I had made myself intentionally homeless, then they would have no legal obligation to rehouse me. And I was really scared, because it was the wording of the letter. And I thought, I could be on the street with my children – cardboard city – you know." (Lone mother, possessed in 1997)

Emotional intensity

As we shall move on to discuss in greater depth later on, losing a home was not only stressful, it was also an intensely *emotional* experience (Nettleton and Burrows, 2000). Everyone interviewed articulated profound emotional responses to their experiences. 'Angry', 'bitter', 'cheated', 'helpless', 'numb', 'resentful', 'hurt', 'heartbroken' were just some of the words people used when talking about their reactions to losing their mortgaged home. Many experience mixed and contradictory emotions. For example when reflecting on leaving her home one woman said:

> "It was like somebody had died that day. I was heartbroken. I felt very angry. I was devastated. It was like my whole world had collapsed around me. I couldn't see any future, I couldn't see anything. All I could see was this dingy little place they'd put me in. And my home was going to be standing empty for I don't know how long. But that was my home. My children – my daughter was born in that house. We went there when my son – he's now 16 – when he was a year old. It was like, everything had happened in that house. That's how I felt. Very lost and alone." (Lone mother, possessed in 1997)

Lack of control

The uncertainties associated with the processes of possession and the emotional intensity of the experience were compounded by the fact that people felt that they had little or *no control* over their situation or their circumstances. This was sometimes due to the fact that they had got into mortgage debt for reasons that were simply beyond their control, factors such as: unanticipated service charges levied by freeholders; job loss due to privatisation; self-employed people not being paid for work they had completed; and so on. Nine out of the 30 families interviewed involved cases where male partners had stopped paying the mortgage and had left the family home. This meant that women who were either 'keeping house' or in low-paid employment were unable to maintain their mortgage payments. For example, one woman whose husband had left her, and unbeknown to her had stopped paying the mortgage sometime earlier, said:

> "I just felt that it was all out of my control you know there was nothing really that I could do. I was just sort of helpless, it's the only way I can describe it and knowing that with just that quick instant decision from the judge I would be on the street ... and ... I suppose it's worse because it wasn't my fault at the end of the day you know." (Lone mother, possessed in 1996)

Lack of control, then, was a critical feature of the experience of mortgage possession. As we shall discuss in more detail in Chapter Seven, the degree of control that one has over one's circumstances has repeatedly been found to be significantly associated with poor mental and physical health (Elstad, 1998). Attempts to regain some control or influence over their circumstances emerged as an important theme in people's accounts of their experience of possession. Thus, while people described feeling immensely frustrated because they had little control over their circumstances they did not passively accept their situation. On the contrary, the interviews revealed that people went to great lengths to try both to save their home and to mitigate the consequences of losing it for themselves and their families. The word 'fight' was commonly used when describing their various efforts.

Strategies to save the family home

Attempts to find solutions to difficult housing circumstances have often been made – for example Forrest and Kennett (1996) have examined how households cope with negative equity and Pickvance and Pickvance (1994) have examined how young people attempt to deal with issues of affordability; and as seen in Chapter Four, Kempson et al (1999) have examined the strategies used by claimant mortgagors to manage the ISMI wait period and ISMI shortfalls. These studies have usefully drawn on the notion of a *coping strategy* in order to make sense of people's responses to their circumstances. This concept highlights the "degree of conscious planning in adverse circumstances" (Forrest and Kennett, 1996, p 373). Certainly the participants in the study reported here articulated a number of ways in which they commonly tried to deal with the problems that confronted them. Attempts to save their home often involved protracted, and in many cases frustrating negotiations with their lenders. Borrowers also tried a range of 'practical solutions' which included trying to sell their home, trying to rent it out, taking companies to court over money that was owed to them, and so on. Women who were left to care for dependent children worked at a further set of solutions such as trying to ensure that men paid their share of the mortgage, trying to get extra work, or trying to 'juggle' benefits. We will examine each of these 'strategies' in turn.

Negotiations with lenders

One response to the problem of mounting mortgage arrears was to make sure that lenders were kept informed about the household circumstances.

This sometimes resulted in mutual agreements between lenders and borrowers about making reduced payments. Lenders have the ability to 'forbear' in a range of ways and for whatever period of time they wish. They may, for example, accept reduced payments or interest-only payments, and under particular circumstances can capitalise the arrears as part of the outstanding mortgage (Ford et al, 1995). However, there are questions and concerns about the extent to which borrowers with similar circumstances receive similar treatment from different lenders. Borrowers, however, were perplexed when lenders seemed to 'suddenly' demand full payments. One family where the father had lost his job due to injury which resulted in him having a chronic physical condition, had kept up with the mortgage payments for two years because he had taken out mortgage payment protection insurance (MPPI). When the policy ran out, because he was still unable to work, he had come to an agreement with the lender that he would make reduced payments. However, after a time the lender demanded that the full payments should resume. The couple explained how they tried to negotiate with them:

> "We kept asking them, 'Look we can't afford the full amount, will you just accept the reduced payments again?'. And they said that it weren't their policy to accept payments after a certain time, 'You got to pay the full amount'." (Couple with dependent children, possessed in 1997)

As well as trying to negotiate reduced payments some borrowers made other suggestions in the hope that the lenders would help them find a way through their difficulties. Suggestions were made to the lender that they should allow the mortgagors to remain in the property and pay rent instead of a mortgage as part of a mortgage rescue scheme (Ford and Wilcox, 1992). In one case the staff in the organisation running the mortgage rescue scheme tried to pursue the lender on behalf of the family but, according to the respondent, the lenders did not want to cooperate. This said, one family in the study did successfully remain in their home and paid rent as the mortgage rescue scheme took over the property.

Among those families who were aware that they were in difficulties, virtually all kept lenders informed about their situation and in many cases they thought creatively and imaginatively about how they might solve their financial problems.

> Wife: "The one thing that we did do from the word go, we kept in touch with everybody, we got in touch with the bank

straightaway, we got in touch with the building society straightaway. We did all the things that they tell you to do. You know they say don't bury your head in the sand, don't throw the letters away and ignore them, get in touch and we did. And we were sitting there, we were coming up with ideas ... we came up with loads of ideas that we could see would solve the problem.... You know we said okay convert it to rent, do this, do that."

Husband: "But we couldn't do that because we was in arrears."

Wife: "Nobody helped us, nobody helped us. No matter what good ideas we came up with. They just pooh-poohed it or ignored it and that was it." (Couple with dependent children, possessed in 1994)

Another man remembered:

> "They just dug my grave until in the end I fell into it. You know telling me that because I was constantly contacting them, telling them about my situation and what I can do, they said to me, 'It's all right, you've got no worries, no worries, no problem, we understand, your things will level out, you will sort it out, don't worry'." (Couple with dependent children, possessed in 1994)

Their situation did not get sorted out and the lender sought possession. The family were rehoused in local authority accommodation which they found to be intolerable, and at the time of interview were living in the private rented sector but were having to find a new home as their contract with the landlord was soon to expire.

Attempts to find practical solutions

All the participants in the study worked hard at trying to find practical solutions to their difficulties. Selling the property and 'trading down' or moving into the private rented sector were often not options for people in the study. This was due to a number of reasons such as: negative equity; lack of buyers; legal battles concerning outstanding service charges; and, in some cases, lenders who would simply not allow them to sell. A further compounding factor was the fear that if they were successful in selling their property they could then be considered 'intentionally homeless' which might mean that their local authority would not have any obligation to rehouse them.

The participants described a whole range of often very imaginative ways in which they tried to keep their homes. Some families gave detailed descriptions of how they had approached their household budgets so that they might make payments that the lenders would find acceptable. One couple with five children who were just £900 in arrears, came to an agreement with their lender that they would pay £50 per month but even this became "completely impossible because of what [they were] given from the social security to live on".

Other solutions included borrowing money from the extended family or friends or, failing this, from 'financial advisors' – moneylenders who offered 'solutions' to their current difficulties by lending them more money but charging them very high rates of interest. For example, one man, now retired, with two children, had been advised to take this route by an 'advisor' who had come to his mortgaged home. This man sold him a number of loans that ultimately compounded his difficulties:

> "I think the first one was for £3,000. Then you've got your interest rate on top of that, which was bigger than what you'd borrowed. And I didn't know all this until it was accumulated altogether. After I'd done that three times, and realised what I'd done, and I thought, oh, crikey, I owe all that much now. And it was – altogether it was £27,000, that my mortgage [loans] became. So that was a lot of money that I couldn't afford to pay." (Couple with dependent children, possessed in 1996)

Where people could find work they tried to work extra hours to supplement their income. Some couples worked shifts so that they would not incur childcare costs. For example, one woman who worked during the day told us how her husband "was doing night work, so that he could have [daughter] during the day so we didn't have the childminding fees".

Other families considered taking in lodgers, but this usually proved impossible due to lack of space. One couple with two children, a girl and a boy, had considered this among other things:

> Husband: "We put the house on the market, we tried all sorts. We were going to try and let rooms, but it meant the two kids sleeping together, and it – well [daughter's] 11 – she's nearly a woman now isn't she – she needs her privacy."

Wife: "We tried to find other ways of getting finances, like looking for jobs and stuff. Looking at whatever for work."

Husband: "And trying to sell things to keep it going, but you can only sell so much before you run down. And the embarrassment of course." (Couple with dependent children, possessed in 1997)

Women coping with mortgage debt and dependent children

Women whose male partners had left the mortgaged home and stopped paying the mortgage also pursued some of these strategies to keep their homes. Some women enlisted the support of the courts or the Child Support Agency (CSA) to try to get their partners or former partners to contribute to the costs of the family home. This was not always easy. In some cases the men simply refused to pay what they were obliged to pay, and still others vanished and could not be traced. In a number of cases women were left not only with the mortgage payments and arrears to manage but also additional debts which their partners had taken out in their joint names, or because their names had been used purely for 'business purposes'. For a detailed analysis of the gendered nature of the experience of mortgage arrears and possession see Christie (2000).

Strategies to try to minimise the consequences of losing the family home

A striking feature of the data was that, having lost the home through possession, all the participants in the study worked hard to to make the best of their new circumstances. Strategies included negotiating with local authorities and attempting to deal with outstanding debt. Another major concern for all those interviewed was how to minimise the consequences for children in the family. We discuss this topic under a separate heading below.

Negotiations with local authorities

None of the families in our study were classified as being 'intentionally homeless' and so their local authorities was obliged to find them accommodation (see our earlier discussion on the processes of mortgage possession). As we have noted, a major source of anxiety for both parents and children was where they might 'end up'. Some families did try to negotiate with the local authorities, and informed them of their needs and circumstances to try to avoid being placed in what they considered to be 'poor' accommodation or 'bad' areas. One family, for example, sought documentation from both their GP and their teenage daughter's schoolteacher to try to prove that moving into a 'rough area' would exacerbate her existing behavioural problems. They finally got the local authority to rescind their initial offer of accommodation that they said was on a 'very rough estate'. As it was, they were not very happy with their final offer but at least they felt that it was not as bad as it could have been.

Other households, frustrated by the responses of their local authorities' Homeless Persons Unit, went to other housing advice agencies and in some cases managed to secure housing association accommodation which they felt was preferable to that which would have been offered by the council. One family who had been placed in accommodation which they considered to be very poor indeed managed to find a home in the private rented sector. It was, however, temporary and at the time of interview they were very anxious about where they were going to live next.

Dealing with outstanding debts

Our findings under this heading strongly support those of the influential NACAB (1999) report on mortgage shortfall debt. People who have lived with long-term arrears and who have subsequently lost their homes through possession almost invariably become poor. They have usually fallen into the situation because of their reduced household income, and at the same time have built up very large debts to mortgage lenders. Some participants said that they had assumed that once their mortgaged home had been taken into possession by the lenders they would no longer be liable for the mortgage payments and costs associated with it. Certainly most were not aware of the extent of the debt and the range of things for which they were actually charged. Where families had worked hard at rebuilding their lives the notification of such debt came as a shock. In fact, when this study was carried out, debt could be pursued by lenders for up to 12 years after the possession (see discussion of recent changes in relation to this in Chapter Five). One family, for example, received a letter five years on from the possession.

Wife: "We didn't realise, we were absolutely shocked when we got this letter.... We thought well that's it. That's everything gone down – our hopes and dreams have just...."

Husband: "Yes, we'd got to five years and we were, you know, we're now pretty much getting back on our feet. We've gone through a horrendous time and all that and we thought 'perhaps we can start rebuilding our future'. And this one comes out and it was 30 thousand and that's it, we're done." (Couple with dependent children, possessed in 1993)

The process of repayment seemed to be negotiable and lenders' practices appeared to many of the participants in the study, to be arbitrary. Indeed, the need to establish equitable treatment for borrowers in similar circumstances but with different lenders is a longstanding issue in research (Ford et al, 1995). For example, while some participants reported how the lenders demanded all the outstanding debts with great tenacity, other people described how the lenders were prepared to accept relatively small pay-offs. For example, one couple who had being paying off their debt of £40,000 following the possession managed to come up with a deal and pay off just 10% of that amount. They recalled their negotiations with a man from the building society thus:

> "He said they had like 10,000 cases to put on this computer. He said, 'and the more cases I can get rid of and not have to put on, the more my manager will be happy', he said, 'so make me an offer'. So we went to my Mum and Dad and said 'can you afford to give us some money?' .... We went back to him, and we said, 'we can give you £2,200 wasn't it' and he said 'no, can we have £2,500?', and I went back and said 'can we meet in the middle?' and he said 'yes, £2,300'. So we paid off the £2,300 – so we paid off about £4,800 I think it was in the end." (Couple with dependent children, possessed in 1993)

When lenders pursue the outstanding debts in cases of marital divorce or separation they were more likely to be able to contact the woman. Women caring for dependent children were, of course, less mobile than their partners. So where men had 'disappeared', it was the women who were being chased for the outstanding debts. Furthermore, in some cases there seemed to be some 'double standards' at work. For example, one couple owed £39,000, the lenders accepted just under £4,000 as payment from the husband, but were still chasing his wife for £19,500 two years on. This woman, who lost the home over two years ago was still, at the time of interview, in negotiations with the lenders. Although she had written many letters to them, they had not offered her any explanation for the apparent 'double standards'.

The consequences for children

Hitherto our discussion has focused on the experiences of adults. In this section of the chapter we shift our attention to the experiences of the children. As far as we know this is the first time that the perspectives of children on the experience of unsustainable home ownership have been analysed.

The children interviewed were those who, having understood the content and aims of the study, agreed to be interviewed themselves (Alderson, 1995; Morrow and Richards,1996). In the event, not all of the children who agreed were interviewed. This occurred for a number of reasons. First, some were too young, or not even born during the possession. Second, in some cases parents did not want their children to be given the opportunity to be interviewed either because they felt that they had already been through enough and the interview would add to their burdens, or because they had not told them the real reasons why they had left the mortgaged home. Finally, some children, having being informed about the study did not want to participate. The following section draws on the interviews with both parents and their children. We discuss the parents' and children's accounts separately, first, because young people sometimes had different concerns to the adults, and second, because the children were in a different situation in relation to the mortgage possession process.

The views of parents

Parents described how they went to some considerable lengths to minimise the impact of losing the family home on their children; their children's happiness, education and future were their main priorities. The range of matters that parents were concerned about in relation to their children included: *whether or not to tell them about the possession; parenting; schools; friends; changes to their lifestyle; behaviour; space*; and *health*.

'To tell' or 'not to tell' the children

Consideration was given to what to tell their children about the possession. Parents seemed to adopt one of two strategies. Most commonly, they felt that it was important to inform their children about what was going on, and to try as best they could to be honest about the reasons for the possession. Less commonly, some parents said that they did not want their children to be burdened with the worry of it all and so did not tell them what had happened, but came up with alternative 'reasons' for the move. This did not appear to be related to the ages of the children.

Not surprisingly mortgage possession was an alarming experience. One mother who decided to explain the circumstances to her children (who were 11 and 15 at the time), said that:

> "They were frightened. They were really quite frightened – what's going to happen, Mum? Where are we going to be? And they were asking quite grown-up questions, and they wanted to know why their Daddy wouldn't pay for the shortfall on the mortgage. Why couldn't the council just rent the house out to us? Why couldn't we pay the council rent? Why couldn't they buy the house? They were asking questions like that. But they understood – I made sure they understood what was going on. I told their schools what was going on – I wrote letters to the schools and explained to the schools, so they had the support of the staff at school as well, 'cos I thought that would probably be better, if they had the support of everybody." (Lone mother, children aged 12 and 16, possessed 1997)

Parenting

Most parents said that the experience did not significantly alter the way they looked after their children. However, during the lead-up to, and the period following, the move, parents did find the demands of parenting to be especially difficult. This was particularly so for those who were dealing with a multiplicity of problems such as job loss, illness, relationship breakdown and so on. One such mother described how she "just couldn't be a Mum, I just couldn't be bothered with them" (Couple with five children, possessed in 1998). Parents were also conscious that the arguments and tensions between them might be upsetting for their children.

Attempts to minimise the impact on children's schooling

A major source of anxiety for both parents and children was the prospect that children might have to change schools when they moved from their mortgaged home. Parents therefore went to considerable lengths to ensure that their children could stay at the same schools, feeling that this would help to minimise the disruption of the loss of home. Children themselves were also keen to stay at the same schools and maintain their network of friends. This often involved ferrying children to and fro on quite long journeys each day.

Where children had to move schools this was very unsettling for parents and children alike. One mother explained how her five-year-old son had 'loved' his old school but hated his new one:

> "I'm really upset, I am gutted to use a phrase. I've had to come to terms with it and I've had to come to terms with it quickly, with my son being upset. I mean he keeps asking for his friends that he used to have and he wants to go back to that school – 'Mummy take me back to my old school'. So I've had to sort of get on with it you know, I've had to put on a front for them and I think I've convinced myself that this is how it is, we've got to get on with it." (Lone mother, possessed in 1998)

Another family had negotiated an agreement from the local authority that they would provide taxis for their two children so that they could remain at the school near their possessed home. Following their move to temporary accommodation and on the day before the autumn term began, the council contacted them and told them that "it wasn't on and so we had to find them another school at the last minute". They had bought the children's school clothes and the children themselves were looking forward to going back. The eight-year-old son had been in the room while his mother was on the telephone and overheard the conversation and she recalled how "he just ran out of the room and tears came into his eyes, and he ran out, and I'd forgotten he was there. He said, 'I don't want to go to a different school'". This same family were still in temporary accommodation at the time of interview and were fearful that their children's schooling would be disrupted again.

Friends

Just as parents were keen to keep their children at the same school they were also anxious that they should maintain their existing friendships. This often proved to be impractical. Some moved a distance away, so it was no longer possible for them to just 'call round' and see their friends who lived in the same street. Now they had to take buses or rely on parents to transport them. Others felt that their children's friends' parents did not like their children coming to visit because they now lived in a 'bad area'.

Changes to lifestyle

The children in some households had become accustomed to regular holidays, money for clothes and treats. Obviously these aspects of life had gone. Other children, however, had been in families that had been struggling for a long time with arrears and the level of poverty was simply intensified.

Behaviour

It is, of course, difficult with children and teenagers to comment on changes in behaviour patterns because they can occur for all sorts of reasons which often remain something of a mystery to parents. However, some parents did say that they felt that their children's behaviour was altered due to the move. They cited examples such as not going to school, not bothering with their schoolwork, becoming more 'difficult'. More often than not, however, this was a temporary change which seemed to improve once they had become more settled in a new home. A small number of parents felt that their children were angry with them and to some extent 'blamed' them for losing the home, and in some cases allowing their marriage to break down as well. This caused tension between them and their children.

Space

Adequate space, and in particular personal space, is very important to children. The parents were very conscious of this and were anxious to try to secure accommodation where children had their own bedrooms.

For younger children space to play outside was also a priority, although sometimes not achieved.

Health

For some children the drawn-out processes associated with possession had an impact on their mental health. This manifested itself in a number of ways. We were told about children becoming more *insecure*, how their *self-confidence* had been affected and how they were less able to *concentrate* on their schoolwork. Parents attributed this to the house move, and explained that their children had become uncertain about what might happen to them and their families in the future.

The loss of home when combined with the marital separation of parents can be especially painful for children. This now lone mother of a 17-year-old son had secured therapy for him. She explained:

> "He's got a lot of anger with his father – when he went to the therapist ... a lot of that came out. More and more is coming out at odd times. He's quite a sensitive person. There's no point in trying to get him to open up until he's actually ready to do that. So you just have to keep an eye on things like that. Watching me worry, watching me struggle – he wrote to his father and told him, and he got a very nasty letter back." (Lone mother, possessed in 1996)

Those children who already lived with chronic conditions such as eczema, asthma or epilepsy were especially vulnerable. In these cases the loss of home and the move affected their conditions sometimes in quite extreme and distressing ways. The move to damp and dismal temporary accommodation also made these conditions much worse. We shall return to these issues in Chapter Seven.

The views of children and young people

Just as the parents were concerned about the impact of the loss of home on their children, the children often worried about their *parents' well-being*. In addition to this, they also articulated concerns about the following issues: the *loss of their 'home'*; *school*; *knowing what is going on*; not being able to *control* the situation; *repeated moves*; *loss of owner status*; *arguments and tension* within the household; *friends*; and *space*.

Parents' well-being

The children interviewed were all concerned about the well-being of their parents. They also recognised, and seemed keen to articulate, how their parents (at least the ones they were still living with) had done their best for them. They described how their parents had put considerable efforts into finding a new home and had often done their utmost to make it welcoming – *to make it into a home*. In circumstances where the father had stopped paying the mortgage some children did feel that they, and their mothers, had been 'let down', and that as a result they would never be able establish a positive relationship with their fathers.

Loss of 'home'

Like their parents some of the children had felt 'sad' to be leaving their mortgaged home. A number pointed out that the home was the one that they had lived in since they were born, or at least it was the only one that they could remember. As one eight-year-old girl put it:

> "I didn't want to move because I had spent my whole life there." (Possessed in 1997)

Two sisters in their early teens (living with mother and father, possessed in 1994) described how they had felt *sad* when they moved out of their mortgaged home because:

Child 1 (13 years):	"We left everything behind."
Interviewer:	"Everything being?"
Child 1:	"The cat was one of them; the people we knew; the house."
Child 2 (15 years):	"The actual house, yes."
Child 1:	"The street even, because we used to play out on the bank and you got used to it, and we were still doing things like that at our age then. And it was just like, 'oh can't go to another street', because it won't be the same. There were silly little things

> like a post at the end of our road that we used to run round and things like that and there were some places being built and they had a little ramp and that which is still there – it was our street."

School

Children had worried about the possibility of changing schools. All the young people interviewed had wanted to stay at their same school, and in fact most had done so, even though this often involved longer journeys. This in turn meant getting up earlier in the morning, and being more restricted in terms of extra curricular activities. On occasion this resulted in hazardous bus journeys because they were 'different' to the other children who lived in their new locality:

> "But then it's dodgy because we get on the bus in the morning and we're like the only two from our school and then the rest of the bus is filled up with [name of school] kids.... And you just feel out of place. And we don't sit at the back of the bus because all of them are there and you don't know what they'll say or do." (Two children living with mother and father, possessed in 1994)

Repeated moves

Worries about the prospect of having to change schools were prolonged for those children who were placed in temporary accommodation. Children who had endured a number of moves following possession did not always fully understand why they were having to move so often. Some children were incredulous at the way their family was being treated by the authorities. A group of three siblings (possessed in 1997) said:

> Child 1 (14 years): "We didn't really understand what the council's been telling my Mum and Dad and everything. So we didn't really know anything about what's happening."

> Child 2 (11 years): "But when we were told we had to move from the flat to [... street], and then [... street] to here, it's like

	why? Why keep moving us? Can't you just put us in one place?"
Child 1:	"And then we might have to move again from here."
Child 3 (7 years):	"If I keep moving I won't even remember a single friend."
Child 1:	"I think that we have a right to know."
Child 2:	"I think that we should have choices. Children have a right to have a say about what's going on."
Child 1:	"I think that the council is out of order."

Having to move more than once could present a further problem. It meant children had to 'explain' these repeated moves to their friends. But while they had been happy to tell their friends that they were moving, they did not want to explain 'why' they kept on having to move. They said that it was *embarrassing*. One lone child aged 15 years said:

> "I told my friends that I was moving, I didn't tell them why I was moving. [Why?] Embarrassment I suppose.... I was worried about what people would think of me at the time." (Possessed in 1997)

Some children said they had not told others the reasons for their move because they felt that it was *shameful*. A number of children had made up other 'reasons' for the move, still others pointed out that it wasn't anybody else's business anyway.

Knowing what is going on

Children appreciated being told about what was going on and found unanswered questions a source of worry. Questions such as: Where might we be moving to? What will it be like? Will we have to change school? Will we lose contact with our friends? However, their parents had not always been able to answer these questions, because very often they did not have answers themselves. One now 17-year-old said that at the time he had been worried that he and his mother might have had to live in temporary accommodation which he thought involved – *living with other families in the same room*. A now 15-year-old said his concerns were made worse because he had seen pictures of terrible housing estates on the television, and this had invoked worrying thoughts about where he and his family might end up. This teenager explained that because his family had not known where they were going to live until very close to the actual moving date he had been:

> "... quite worried really. I knew that the chances of us getting a good house were, well pretty low in relation to actually getting a quite bad house, because it was an emergency sort of thing. We had to have the first house that came available for us ... it was that idea of lucky dip or Russian Roulette ... that was the worry if anything." (Possessed in 1997)

Children with sporting or musical commitments had also worried that they might not be able to carry on with their hobbies.

Lack of control

Out of the 10 sets of interviews with children, four commented that their experiences had been compounded by the fact that they felt that they had *no control* over what was happening to them. This was for two reasons: one, because they felt that no one could have controlled the situation anyway, because that was in the nature of it; and two, because of their position, as dependants, in the household structure. As one 15-year-old boy, whose family had lost their mortgaged home over a year ago, said:

> "I think that the view that other people would have is that it is something that we could have controlled, which at the time I don't think that we could … as ... for me as a child there's relatively little or nothing I can do about it." (Possessed in 1997)

Similarly in one of the households where the husband had stopped paying for the mortgage, a son aged 17 at the time of the interview reflected:

> "I did feel it was being taken away from me and I didn't really have any control over it, and I was ill and there was absolutely nothing that I could do about it. [Can you remember how you felt at the time?] Gutted really. Gutted that my Dad had allowed it to happen."

Later in the interview he expanded on this point, saying:

> "I just wished that there was something, some difference or some way, that I could have helped my Mum to prevent it from happening." (Possessed in 1996)

Loss of 'owner' status

Like their parents some children did not feel comfortable about losing their status as 'home owners'. One group of siblings were pleased to be able to get out of the 'rough' area where they had been living but were not happy about becoming 'renters' rather than 'owners'. Their feelings were described by the middle 13-year-old:

> "Well, I felt quite happy at first I think because we were moving from a bad area, but we knew that it weren't going to be our own house again. It were good to get away from there, but it's not our own house [Right, do you mind that fact that this isn't your own house?] Well it's all right, but all my mates have got their own houses, so I just say that this is mine.... It's all like, my mates are quite posh and it's a bit embarrassing if you're going – 'I don't own my own house'." (Possessed in 1998)

Arguments and tensions in the household

Invariably children said that their parents argued when they were still living in their mortgaged home and (where applicable) when they were in temporary accommodation. In some cases arguments extended beyond the immediate household, and the children witnessed tension with members of their extended family. In one interview, two teenage sisters said that they sometimes felt that they were making everything worse. The problem at the time was that they did not always know what they should be doing or if they were "doing right or doing wrong".

Friends

Because the children interviewed had stayed at the same schools most had maintained contact with their established friends. However, after leaving the mortgaged home they sometimes lived some distance from them. The cost of fares or fuel involved in meeting friends was sometimes prohibitive.

Moving into a different type of area could mean having to establish new types of friendships, especially where families had moved from middle-class suburbia to what were referred to as 'rough' estates. It could take time to acclimatise and two sisters described how the transition involved mixing with local children because they felt it was "safer that way" – better to be "in with the crowd than out" even though it meant getting into trouble.

Space

All the young people interviewed spoke about the importance of having their own 'space'. A bigger house was seen as being desirable and having one's own room was extremely important. For a number of the households interviewed the 'space' situation had much improved following the possession. Two of the 10 interviews were with siblings who, before possession, had been sharing rooms, but who now had rooms to themselves. However, a number of children had also experienced, or were still coping with, very cramped conditions.

Drawing together all the material above provides some insight into the range of concerns and consequences that parents and children have to deal with when they endure mortgage possession. From these accounts we can see the main issues which emerge in relation to the lives of children. First, the loss of a mortgage home was accompanied by a changed *social status*. Second, children endure long periods of *uncertainty*; the loss of the mortgaged home was a significant source of worry for children, especially when they were not certain where they would actually be moving to and when they were placed in temporary accommodation. A third issue articulated very clearly by a number of the children interviewed was that the administrative processes did not take the *views and concerns of the children* into account. Finally, and perhaps most importantly, losing a home through possession invariably occurs due to, or alongside, other major life changes so children were often having to cope not just with a loss of their home, but also the loss of a parent through marital separation, a parent's ill health or job loss. Children are therefore having to deal with a *multiplicity of problems*.

What is clear from the interviews with parents and children is that the loss of the mortgaged home has a significant impact on the lives of the dependent children living in the household; it constitutes a major disruption to their everyday life and can be very disturbing both socially and psychologically. Furthermore, it seems that the *processes* associated with the possession itself (which induced feelings of uncertainty and lack of control) are important in terms of how they affect the children's responses to the experience. Having lost their homes the children then had to adjust to living in new physical and social environments. This was easier for some than others. The ability to cope with such a life event will depend on the individual's circumstances and the degree of support they receive. More generally, it is clear that for both parents and children the experience of mortgage possession has profound consequences for how they come to think about themselves – for their sense of self, or their identity. It is to this issue that we now turn.

Identity

Taylor (1998) has made a useful distinction between what he calls *categorical identity* and *ontological identity*. The former is "where identity is related to the social categories and common experiences of difference". The latter "is the use of identity as a coherent sense of self" (1998, p 340). Participants in the study articulated changes to both of these aspects of their identity. In relation to *categorical identity* a number of people said they had been caught short by the awful realisation that they were now 'homeless'.

> "Yes I wouldn't have thought I was classed, I mean I realise now I'm classed as homeless, wham, but at the time to get a letter from the homeless section is quite a shock because you think of somebody being homeless being laid on a park bench or a lido or whatever." (Lone mother, possessed in 1998)

They had also moved from the social category of 'owner-occupier' to 'council tenant' and had become a 'renter' and not an 'owner'. For example, one couple who had spent their childhood years living on council estates and who had been delighted when they had got on to the 'housing ladder' said:

> "I'd always been brought up to believe – you're somebody if you bought your own home. People look at you in a different way. You fill in forms – the first thing it says is 'home owner', the last thing on the list 'rented/unfurnished/tenant." (Couple with dependent children, possessed in 1993)

For another woman becoming part of the category 'council tenant' had come as a shock:

> "It sounds so snobby but I just, it was just like the thought of my god I'm now a council tenant, I've gone from being a home owner. It was like a culture shock. It was like I never ever thought I'd be in this position, I never ever in a million years dreamt that I'd be living on a council estate." (Lone mother, possessed in 1996)

Placed in this social category people were sensitive to the fact that they were being treated differently:

> "I think it's the social stigma, I knew that when you're indigent you get a certain treatment. You're on legal aid, you're on housing benefit or social, income support or whatever. There's a different attitude. You're treated differently. It's unwritten and it's unspoken, but you can certainly sense the difference that you've failed." (Lone mother, possessed in 1996)

A number of people said that they felt they were now regarded as 'second-class citizens' who were 'dependent' on the state. A few respondents even said that they felt that they would now be classed as part of the 'underclass'. In some cases these notions were reinforced by other people. For example, one lone mother whose husband had left her and who was now in receipt of benefits said how her brother-in-law had told her: "I work my bollocks off for the likes of you".

The social categories in which people found themselves however were not the only sources of their altered identities. People described how the experience had impacted on how they felt about themselves and also what they felt they could and could not do. In particular the experience had far-reaching consequences for some people's self-confidence and self-esteem. In sum, it also altered their *ontological identity*.

The experience of mortgage possession for most people constituted a significant life event. It constituted what Bury (1982) has referred to as a 'biographical disruption' – a concept initially developed in relation to the onset of chronic illness. This suggests that the trajectories of people's lives are altered, which makes them reflect on 'who they are'. For example, one woman described how the events had made her "take a long hard look at myself and to reassess my values" and this had resulted in her "building a brick wall so that no one can hurt me or mine". The re-evaluation of what is important in life was sometimes a positive outcome of an otherwise painful experience. As one man who lost a very well-paid job and his home reflected:

Husband:	"I think my values have changed, I think I was very materialistic wasn't I? Very status orientated, career orientated and all that stuff. I mean the kids say to me I'm a nicer person now than I was then. I'm sure they're right. And I feel a lot happier."
Wife:	"We've had to go through a lot to get there though."
Husband:	"But it was a painful experience." (Couple with dependent children, possessed in 1993)

Discourses of choice, responsibility, uncertainty, risk, and investing in oneself are core themes which transcend many areas of contemporary welfare policy (Nettleton and Burrows, 1998a). Indeed, as we outlined in Chapter One, a number of commentators (Beck, 1992; Giddens, 1991) have highlighted the fact that contemporary society is one where individuals are increasingly encouraged to be enterprising, and to take advice so that they may calculate and negotiate their own risks. Within this reading, people are conceptualised as actively, creatively and *reflexively* participating in *lifestyle planning* in order to shape and invest in their own futures. A distinctive feature of this is the way in which these activities can come to permeate people's psyche, both in terms of how they think about themselves and how they relate to other people (Nettleton, 1997).

A corollary is that the decisions that people make, and especially the decisions relating to their lifestyle and consumption practices, can have a more profound significance than they might have had in the past. Embarking on, and being successful in one's housing career can be an important source of one's self-identity. Conversely, not sustaining such a career can also impact on one's identity (Gurney, 1999). As one father who felt he had let his whole family down said: "I felt like a loser, I felt like I'd failed in life". Similarly another man said: "You feel so little and humiliated. I know the neighbours didn't exactly belittle us ... but, yes it's how you feel. You feel a loser, and angry about everything" (Couple with dependent children, possessed in 1996).

These expressions were linked to normative ideas about housing careers. A number of people articulated how they had expected that once they had moved from the parental home they would rent for a while and then would move on to become home owners. Once in owner-occupation they would move from a smaller to a bigger home. While the notion of a coping strategy implies a short-term response to immediate circumstances, the idea of a housing career implies some longer-term consequences (Forrest and Kennett, 1996). Thus, while people are able to pursue constructive coping strategies in the face of adversity, their more deep-seated notions of self and identity are shaped by the fact that they did not achieve their longer-term goals in their housing careers. This may explain, in part, why so many participants in the study said that, despite everything, they would very much like to become owner-occupiers again in the future.

Summary

We have seen throughout this chapter that the experience of mortgage possession impacts on people's social identity. This in turn impacts on their sense of self and self-confidence. The impact on people's identity is due to two main reasons. First, within the context of British culture there are normative notions of what it means to be a 'home owner' and owner-occupation is regarded as a desirable social status. Second, and from the point of view of our study more importantly, people work hard at both trying to save their homes, and at trying to minimise the detrimental consequences of mortgage possession. This second finding is all the more important given the changing nature of the policy context of owner-occupation. As we argued in earlier chapters in this book, the reasons for the rise in the number of possessions are more often than not factors over which people have no or little control and have been compounded by the privatisation of risk unleashed by various processes of welfare restructuring (Nettleton and Burrows, 1998a). Developing and working at strategies in the face of such changes becomes increasingly difficult and so, if such strategies are not 'successful', it is increasingly likely that people will internalise feelings of 'failure'. It may be, therefore, that the policies which place responsibility for welfare on to individuals not only have the effect of increasing the likelihood that they will be materially disadvantaged, but may also impact on people's psychosocial well-being, and in turn their health (Nettleton and Burrows, 1998b, 2000). It is to this issue that we turn in the next chapter.

Note

This chapter draws on material previously published in Nettleton and Burrows (2001), Nettleton (2001) and Nettleton et al (1999). All of this work was funded by the Joseph Rowntree Foundation.

SEVEN

Mortgage arrears and possession as public health issues

During the last decade there have been some important developments in understanding the social determinants of the distribution of health and illness (Bartley et al, 1998). There has been a shift from presuming that the main link between poverty and ill health is to do with the material conditions of people's lives, to the idea that psychosocial mechanisms may be just as important. This suggestion originally arose from national-level studies that found that increases in wealth did not necessarily lead to improvements in health. In particular, Wilkinson (1996) has shown that the distribution of income and wealth within a nation can influence life expectancy. He suggests that after a certain point of economic development has been reached – what is sometimes termed the 'epidemiological transition' – it is *relative* rather than *absolute* poverty that is critical to overall health status. This means that health status must be associated with things other than *just* absolute material deprivation. Wilkinson suggests that the more unequal the distribution of resources in a society the more likely it is that the social organisation will have health-damaging consequences for individuals. This means that health outcomes must, in some way, be linked to the *experience* of relative poverty.

Attempts to make sense of this have led to the formation of a research agenda which concentrates on "the psychological stress, relative deprivation and psychosocial injuries of inequality structures" (Elstad, 1998, p 40). This agenda has produced growing evidence that variations in certain aspects of psychosocial life – such as sense of control, perceived social status, the strength of social affiliations, self-esteem, feelings of ontological insecurity and so on – lead to variations in health outcomes (Elstad, 1998; Wilkinson, 1996; Wilkinson et al, 1998). Drawing on developments in psychology and physiology it has been suggested that stressors, particularly long-term stress and emotionally charged events, can impact on health both directly (as in the suggestion that there is a link between the nervous system and other bodily systems such as the immune system or hormonal systems) or indirectly (as in the suggestion that stress increases the risk of a person indulging in health-damaging behaviours such as smoking and drinking). What is critical is not just the existence of stressful and/or emotional events themselves but also the availability of resources to 'buffer' their impact and also the extent to which people are able to 'control' the forces that affect their lives. In summary:

> … social inequalities ... not only income inequalities, but also power inequalities ... and status inequalities ... have a fundamental influence on the content of social relations and interactions. The greater the social inequalities ... the more will the quality of social relations suffer. Inequalities will tend to produce anger, frustration, hostility, fear, insecurity, and other negative emotions. Material inequalities will often go together with fear of, or the actual distressing experience of, failures to secure a socially acceptable material standard of living. (Elstad 1998, p 50)

This new research agenda thus incorporates, with varying degrees of commitment, the salience of: the physiological impacts of stress; the importance of meanings, subjective assessment and emotions; and levels of social cohesion.

In this chapter we draw again on the qualitative interview material introduced in Chapter Six in order to argue that the phenomena of high levels of mortgage arrears and possession is not just emblematic of broader social changes associated with the extension of individualisation processes and new patterns of insecurity and risk (as discussed throughout this book) but also that it constitutes a major 'new' public health issue (Nettleton, 1998; Nettleton and Burrows, 1998b, 2000). Having demonstrated some of the mechanisms by which this particular form of acute housing insecurity might invoke ill health at a qualitative level we go on to briefly examine some statistical evidence on the relationship between the onset of mortgage indebtedness and changes in health status.

A stressful episode

We saw in Chapter Six how the experience of mortgage possession can be very stressful. Both direct and indirect dimensions of the impact of stress on health were evident in accounts of the experiences of possession. The loss of home was repeatedly referred to as being a 'complete nightmare'. As one couple said when asked what the 'biggest impact' of the possession had been:

Husband: "I think you're so ground down by it that, you know, I look back on it all and all I remember is being permanently tired, permanently stressed with the phone calls, the letters, the hassle, you know, trying to get a job, it was just a combination."

Wife: "I just thought it was stressful. I'd got like a great big heavy load on my shoulders all the time, it's like a great big heavy weight that was just grinding me down constantly. I just didn't know, you know, which way to turn. It's just I mean I can't describe, stress it was, it was just mainly stress really." (Couple, possessed in 1993)

Some people articulated how the intensity of the stress *directly* affected their health. The experience of the man in the next quote was shared by a number of the people interviewed:

> "I started losing my breath in bed – I was waking up of a night, wasn't I – couldn't catch my breath. And in the end we all went down – we got an ambulance, and they took me to [named] Hospital."

Interviewer: "Did they find anything? What did they say?"

> "No, they said it was just stress and anxiety, what was building up inside me."

Interviewer: "And did you get any medication?"

> "Yes, at the time. I forget what they were but – tablets." (Couple, possessed in 1994)

Another husband and father who was now retired said:

> "It's all worry, inwardly. And it has a lot to do with my health as well. At the moment I'm suffering from a chest complaint which is ... well ... I did go to the doctor once and he told me about this chest and one thing and another, and he asked me if I was worrying, and I said well I have got a bit of worry. And he said, well all this stress and worry can

> cause this on your chest. It can cause you to have this outbreak what you keep getting." (Couple, possessed in 1996)

Another divorced mother who had lost her home because her husband had refused to contribute to the mortgage when he left her had a similar health problem. Five years after the possession she had been contacted about the outstanding debts associated with her mortgaged home. She was being pursued for £60,000. The debts had been 'sold on' to a debt-collecting agency by her building society.

> "I haven't got the same energy that I used to have, it drains you does this. It drains you physically and mentally. All the worry, all the debts, everything.... I mean since [named debt collecting agency] contacted me I've been getting chest pains. And it was when they contacted me, it was just after that I came down with the first bug. Because stress depletes the immune system. It was already down anyway and usually if your immune system's strong, you know, you have a fight." (Lone mother, possessed in 1993)

The idea that the stress associated with the experience of mortgage possession affects one's immune system was shared by a number of people and reflects the findings of research into popular lay perceptions of the immune system more generally (Martin, 1998). Other health problems were often directly attributed to stress, and included loss of hair; heart problems; and the slow(er) recovery from illnesses which had happened prior to the possession. Those people who had chronic conditions such as eczema, asthma and epilepsy described how they had become much worse during the period leading up to the possession and when they were living in temporary accommodation. This was the case for both parents and children.

The *indirect* health effects of stress were also evident in people's accounts when they spoke about 'health-related behaviours' – the 'holy trinity of risks' (as they are referred to in the health literature); smoking, drinking and eating, were especially affected. One woman, for example, took up smoking again having given up nine years prior to the possession. More commonly, existing smokers said that they smoked more. Sleeping was a common problem – with the majority of people saying that they found that they could not sleep well. Some people drank more alcohol and a small minority found that they were drinking excessively. More common were eating problems. Some people said they ate more for comfort, but more often than not people found that they could not manage to eat normally. A number of women still had eating problems some years after their homes had been possessed.

Emotions

A number of authors have argued that the impact that a stressful event might have on one's health is associated with the extent to which it also has an *emotional significance* (Lazarus, 1993; Freund 1990). As we saw in Chapter Six losing a home through mortgage possession was described by most of the participants in the study as an intensely emotional experience – some participants even compared losing their home to losing a loved one, or even losing part of their self.

Feeling lost, isolated and extremely sad, some felt that they had been in desperate need of someone to talk to. One man had rung the Samaritans because he just felt that there was no one else to turn to. One mother with three young children, whose husband had left her with considerable debt and the possession to deal with, said that she had finally dissolved in tears when she was at the health centre talking to the health visitor. She said that although embarrassed at the time, the fact that she had finally spoken to someone about it had actually helped her:

> "I could do with more people to talk to ... somebody to ... not tell you anything in particular, but just somebody perhaps to work it through." (Lone mother, possessed in 1998)

A lone father explained how the anxiety he experienced was intensified by the fact he had no one to talk to:

> "I think that a lot of it was being on my own to face it all. 'Cos I never had no one to turn to. It's sort of you know, you feel like your head is full of it all the time, which is why I used to drink to go to sleep." (Lone father, possessed in 1997)

The experience of mortgage possession is a highly individualised one. It is not something that one shares easily, if at all with one's neighbours or friends. Furthermore, the agencies with whom the families were dealing did not appear to acknowledge the 'emotional side' of the experience. In fact, the emotional intensity of the experience was compounded by the legal and administrative aspects of the possession process itself. We turn now, therefore, to people's accounts of their encounters with the organisational and institutional actors involved in the process of mortgage possession.

Institutional context

The main institutions which the families had contact with were the lenders, the courts, the local authorities and advice agencies. Obviously people's experiences varied between different settings – some having more positive experiences than others. But in general the view expressed was that among the lenders, the courts and the local authorities the administrative procedures compounded the highly negative experience of possession. Two aspects made things worse: the *impersonal nature of the procedures*; and the *uncertainty about their fate and their inability to have any say or control* concerning their future circumstances.

A number of people commented that they felt that they were simply 'figures' on the books – especially where their lenders were concerned. It was felt that there was no scope for acknowledging the social and emotional consequences of the loss of home. As one husband whose family had lost their home over five years previously said:

> "Me, I was angry incredibly angry.... Well, they'd taken the last 15 years of working extremely hard, they had gone overnight – now you had to accept responsibility for buying a home and everything that goes with that. I think I was taken aback at just how black and white and cold it was, I think that really, there was *no human element* in there at all." (Couple, possessed in 1993)

Reflecting on their dealings with building societies, courts, solicitors and housing officers one couple commented that they wished that those working within those settings could go into people's homes and come face to face with the 'human beings' who are being possessed. "If only," they said, "they could see the destruction of the repossession." Especially distressing were those circumstances where lenders had 'sold on' a borrower's debts to debt collectors. This meant that people found themselves in situations where they were being 'hounded' for debts by people with whom they had had no previous contact. Some people told how they were being 'rung up' at all times of the day.

The experience of mortgage possession involves dealing with a whole new set of institutions and social responses with which most people are unfamiliar. A visit to a local authority Homeless Persons Unit is a very different experience from a visit to an estate agent. At the former people were told by those working for the local authority that they would have to accept any accommodation that could be offered, even if they did not like the location or the property itself. Many people found this very alarming and, as we discussed in Chapter Six, had been troubled by questions such as: Would they be living on 'dreadful estates'? Would the family be split up? Would the children have to change schools?

Uncertainty, fear and lack of control

As we have already discussed in Chapter Six, when people in England are in arrears with their mortgage there are no clear-cut procedures and the likelihood of their homes being possessed can depend on a range of factors. These include: the level of arrears; their personal circumstances; the attitude of their particular lender; the state of the housing market; and the decision of a district judge in the county court. The participants in the study therefore had lived with considerable uncertainty for some time. Would the lender 'manage' their arrears and let them continue making partial payments or would they try to evict them? If a notice of eviction was served would the courts decide to suspend their eviction and demand that the lenders allow them to arrange more manageable payments? It is only after a notice of eviction has been served that the local authority is obliged to rehouse a family and for most of the households this uncertainty about if and where was one of the most difficult practical issues to deal with. One lone mother of three described the worries thus:

> "The worry of: What is going to happen to me? When I go into court are they going to suspend it again, are they not going to suspend it again? If they don't what am I going to do? Where am I going to go? Am I going to end up on the street? Am I going to come back from somewhere and find my furniture in the garden? You know – what's going to happen? The fear of the unknown." (Lone mother, possessed in 1998)

Another couple who lost their home four years previously said:

> "I think the main concern was when we originally went to the council, they said they can't do anything until we've received the actual notice of repossession.... And that seemed to take quite a long time to happen,

I think that's what turned me a bit nutty. It was being in limbo, we knew we were losing the house but we didn't know what we were going to." (Couple, possessed in 1994)

Again, as we discussed in Chapter Six, children in the households shared these concerns and, like their parents, found the unanswered questions worrying. Where might we be moving to? What will it be like? Will we have to change school? Will we lose contact with our friends? Their parents had not always been able to answer these questions for them, because, as we have seen, very often they did not have answers themselves. The children in one family who had known that they were going to have to move "because we couldn't afford it" any more explained how:

"At first it were a worry, because we didn't know whether we were going to be moved out into another rough area.... Because I know people and they've been in, like, hotels and stuff." (Child living with both parents, possessed in 1998)

Not only were people uncertain about what was to become of them, but they could not very often actually influence what was going to happen to them. As we have shown in Chapter Six, all the participants in the study made efforts to find solutions to their difficulties both when they were in arrears and once they had lost their homes to try and secure the best accommodation for their families. The feeling of not being in control left some people with an emotional legacy of enduring insecurity. In response to the question, 'If you had to say what was the biggest impact of losing your home what would it be?', one couple answered:

Husband: "Security."

Interviewer: "In what way?"

Husband: "The loss of it in terms of being out of control where you are going to live."

Wife: "I feel very insecure, that's one thing I do feel, it's the one thing that's affected me more than anything else."

Interviewer: "It may sound a daft question but what does it feel like when you say you feel insecure?"

Wife: "I feel frightened, it frightens me."

Interviewer: "Yes."

Wife: "Yes. I can wake up at two o'clock in the morning and feel really frightened that I'm going to end up with absolutely nothing, it's just, I can't explain what it feels like to me, it just feels awful." (Couple, possessed in 1993)

Changes in social status and issues of stigma and shame

Again, as we discussed in Chapter Six, changes in categorical and ontological identity invoked by the experience of mortgage possession led many participants in the study to lose self-confidence and self-esteem. In addition, for many, social isolation was intensified by both felt and enacted stigma. Many participants in the study found it very hard to talk to anyone about what they were going through. Those people who did talk about their situation often found that other people did not want to know. Some reported that people whom they had considered to be friends lost contact with them after the possession. For some, the experience undermined relationships with family as well as friends, especially where people had definite ideas about the 'deserving and undeserving poor'. One couple reported how they still felt shame and embarrassment some four and a half years after the actual possession:

Wife: "I know it sounds probably weird, but the only word that seems to fit in a way is *shame*. I felt awful that I had made an agreement and that I wasn't able to keep to that agreement, I hate owing money to anybody. So once I'd become bankrupt, I knew that I wasn't actually going to pay this money and that made me feel in some ways, it made me feel really bad to think, it was almost like I'd had money under false pretences."

Husband: "Yes, well it did feel degrading. Yes, because you're put in the position where they're in control, yes, I'm not in control any more."

Wife: "And like for me to go and like you know I'm quite a proud person and to go to the Homeless Unit and say I need to be rehoused, I was like really gutted." (Couple, possessed in 1994)

As we saw in Chapter Six, such feelings of embarrassment were also talked about by children and young people. They had not wanted to tell their friends why they had moved house because it was 'embarrassing'. Furthermore, they found the 'renter' rather than 'owner-occupier' status something to be ashamed of.

The vast majority of the participants in the study felt that they had lost self-confidence and self-esteem. The majority also said they had been severely depressed, many receiving medication for it. While on the one hand most people recognised that in practice the loss of home was due to factors that were beyond their control (such as redundancy, illness, additional caring responsibilities and so on), as we have seen they also still felt that they had somehow failed personally. The lack of confidence and lowered self-esteem had some very 'real' effects in that in a number of cases it prevented people from either looking for work or not taking up jobs that they were offered. This was because they did not feel that they would be able to do the work. Some people found that they could not easily go out of the house, others found that they stopped taking part in any social activities. This was the case for one woman who was a qualified nurse and had worked in a variety of jobs throughout her life. She wanted to work to supplement the household income but could not:

> "Well like I said I don't want to go out, I mean I want to get a job but I just haven't got the confidence to actually go out and get a job and I desperately want a job, it would help us a lot but I'm just so lacking in self-esteem as well I suppose that I just, I wish I could get over it, I wish there was something I could do to get over the way I feel." (Couple, possessed in 1997)

Another man found that it affected his ability to do his job:

> "Yes, I mean I'd certainly gone from being fearless about anything ... but ... suddenly I couldn't even make a sales call. I used to make a lot of presentations, 500, 1,000 people, it didn't bother me, I couldn't stand in front of five people at that time." (Couple, possessed in 1993)

A loss of emotional capital?

We have seen from the analysis of these accounts that losing a home through mortgage possession involves more than just losing a property. Of course the material aspects of losing a mortgaged home are very important. As we saw in Chapter Five, buying a property constitutes a capital investment and an important financial asset (Ford and Burrows, 1999b); something to ensure financial security in old age and something to 'pass on' to the children. But losing a home in this way means more than that to most people. The possession of a property constitutes a significant loss of a home that is invested with meaning and memories. Not only that but, as we saw in Chapter Six, the bureaucratic procedures associated with the administrative processes of possession mean that people have to endure long periods of *insecurity* and *uncertainty*. A whole set of events is set in train that is *out of their control*. As we noted in the introduction to this chapter, according to the psychosocial literature on the social determinants of health it is these experiences (uncertainty and lack of control) that are coming to be regarded as among the most crucial determinants of poor health in contemporary societies.

The extent to which such experiences impact on health is contingent on their *emotional intensity*. As we have seen, the experience of mortgage possession is not only very stressful, but it is also an intensely emotional life event that has somatic consequences. The suggestion that social events and circumstances can have bodily correlates is central to current developments within the sociology of emotions – a literature that offers insights into contemporary debates concerned with the psychosocial mechanisms by which variations in health are generated. As one of the main proponents of this view argues it is likely "that people might express, somatically, the conditions of their existence" (Freund, 1990, p 463). Interestingly, using a somatic example that was experienced by a number of the participants in our study, he argues that:

> Subjectivity, social activity and social structural contexts interpenetrate. It is this relationship that comes to be physically embodied in many ways. Irregularity in breathing may accompany muscular tension and experiences of ontological insecurity and the anger, anxiety or fear that is part of this insecurity. (Freund, 1990, pp 461-2)

The likelihood of enduring negative emotional experiences that have detrimental physical effects is greater for those who are in socially disadvantaged positions. In particular it is argued those who are low(er) down in a social hierarchy and so are in less powerful positions are more likely to experience 'unpleasant emotionality of modes of being'. Those who are in less powerful positions are less likely to have their feelings acknowledged, validated, and so on, because the feelings of a person of a lower status may not be given the same weight as those of a higher status.

> In general, the threats to ontological security are greater for those in dependent, subordinate positions. The lack of resources to protect oneself or to legitimate oneself further contributes to status led insecurity. Less powerful people face a structurally built-in handicap in managing social and emotional information and this handicap may contribute to existential fear and anxiety. (Freund, 1990, pp 466-7)

When talking about 'less powerful' here Freund is referring to those disadvantaged by virtue of social divisions such as gender, ethnicity, class and age. However, as we have seen in this study people are often 'disadvantaged' in terms of more situationally specific contexts and are disempowered in relation to their experiences with institutions. In other words, mortgage possession deprives people of an important source of social status; they perceive themselves and are perceived by others to have slipped down the housing ladder. They have suffered a biographical disruption that demands a reassessment of their sense of self. Furthermore, they are relatively disempowered when they come to deal with lenders and local authorities. An altered social status when dealing with family, friends and bureaucracies can engender what Freund, drawing on the ideas of Goffman, calls *dramaturgical stress*. How one presents oneself and plays out one's social roles can itself be stressful. For example, participants pointed to the value of being able 'to talk' about their experiences. Recounting one's story to someone who is genuinely concerned to help can be a source of support. However, having to present the same story in another more impersonal setting, to an official for example, was said by the participants in the study to be 'humiliating'. In the case of the former one's feelings are validated, in the case of the latter they are not.

So not only do people lose out on their capital investment (Ford and Burrows, 1999b), the experience of mortgage possession also takes a toll on what Williams (1998), building on Bourdieu's ideas on different forms of social capital, has called their *emotional capital*. Using this notion he argues that:

> ... emotional exchange involves an intricate 'balance sheet' of profit and losses, debts and investments, including 'economies' of gratitude and resentment, and feelings of pride and shame, which mesh more or less closely with broader patterns of power, prestige and social (dis)advantage. (Williams, 1998, p 128)

Williams argues that what is critical here is that the differential emotional experiences or 'modes of being' involve "different felt ways of feeling *empowered* or *disempowered*: feelings which are very much linked to people's material as well as their psychosocial conditions of existence throughout their embodied biographies" (Williams, 1998, p 128).

By drawing on qualitative data from a study of the experience and meanings of mortgage possession, we have argued that there are a number of features associated with the experience that negatively affect people's health. The stressful nature and emotional intensity of the experience can affect health both directly (through physiological changes) and indirectly (through invoking 'unhealthy' behaviours). In terms of the processes associated with possession itself this is compounded by the protracted and uncertain procedures of local authorities, lenders and the courts.

Our aim has been to demonstrate that unsustainable owner-occupation in Britain has consequences for those with an interest in the sociology of health inequalities. For too long health policy analysts have implicitly regarded home ownership as simply the domain of the contented middle classes and have concentrated their efforts on the health-damaging consequences of the often poor material environments of housing in the other tenures. This, of course, remains an important task. However, there is now also an urgent need to recognise that for significant numbers of people the costs of home ownership in a society marked by increasing levels of individualisation, insecurity and risk can be very great indeed, not just in terms of their wealth, but also in relation to their health.

Statistical evidence

Following the old Weberian dictum that good sociological explanations should seek to be adequate at both the level of *meaning* and of *cause* we now move on to consider briefly some statistical evidence on the relationship between the experience of problematic home ownership and health. By necessity, this involves making some rather crude conceptual and operational assumptions about the workings of what is, as we have seen, a complex social mechanism. Here we present just the main findings of an earlier analysis. Readers interested in the statistical and methodological details should consult Nettleton and Burrows (1998b).

In order to investigate the pattern of association between the onset of mortgage indebtedness and health a sample of individuals was drawn from the British Household Panel Survey (BHPS); a data set first introduced in Chapter Three of this book. The BHPS is suited to analyses investigating the relationship between housing and health because it is one of the few sources of data that brings together variables covering these two domains. In addition its panel design has certain advantages over cross-sectional designs in which we always have to infer the impact of change in some independent variable 'x' on changes in some dependent variable 'y' based solely on inter-unit variations at one point in time.

We examined the impact of the onset of mortgage problems on changes in mental health, as measured by a common subjective well-being scale, and use of primary healthcare services, as measured by the annual number of GP visits in two different 'transition periods' – between 1991 and 1992 and again between 1994 and 1995. The first represents the period in which the housing recession was at its deepest and the second represents the 'beginning of the end' of the same housing recession. For each period we constructed a (suitably weighted) sample of *individuals* made up of all heads of household and, if applicable, their partners (married or cohabiting), living in households with a mortgage, who reported in the first year of each 'transition' that they had no problems paying their mortgage. In the first 'transition' between 1991 and 1992 among our sample of over 3,700 individuals over 15% either fell into arrears or were having problems paying their mortgage. This proportion fell year on year to under 10% of a sample of 3,500 individuals in the period between 1994 and 1995.

As we seen, the onset of mortgage problems can be the product of a complex set of factors, many of which may themselves be related to a change in health status and/or subjective well-being. Our task, then, was to begin to disentangle the independent impact, if any, that the onset of mortgage problems has on subjective well-being.

A measure of change in subjective well-being was constructed for each individual in the sample. This was based on the General Health Questionnaire 12 (GHQ12) – a set of 12 questions the responses to which are taken to be a robust measure of current subjective well-being. The questions that make up the scale ask about: current ability to concentrate; ability to sleep; whether the person feels they are playing a useful role; whether the person feels capable of making decisions; whether the person constantly feels under strain; whether the person has any problems overcoming difficulties; whether the person enjoys day-to-day activities; whether the person feels able to face problems; whether the person feels unhappy or depressed; whether the person feels they are losing confidence; belief in self-worth; and general happiness. Each question can be responded to using a four-point scale (0-3). The measure compared GHQ12 scores, calculated from 0 (excellent) to 36 (very poor), in the second year of the 'transition' compared to GHQ12 scores in the first year. So, for example, if an individual scored 10 in the first year and 20 in the second their change over the two years would be +10. Thus this variable score can logically take on any whole number value between -36 and +36, with negative values indicating an improvement in subjective well-being and positive values indicating a worsening in subjective well-being.

The simple bivariate relationship between the onset of mortgage problems and changes in subjective well-being shows a clear and highly significant pattern of association at both 'transitions'. However, our interest is in whether this relationship is maintained when we control for other factors which on a priori grounds we might suspect impact on a worsening of subjective well-being. In order to examine this a series of other variables was examined alongside mortgage indebtedness using multiple regression. These variables were income and income changes; physical health problems and changes in physical health problems; employment and changes in employment; and age. Analyses were undertaken separately for men and women.

The results suggest that for men in the first period between 1991 and 1992, after controlling for other significant variables in the model, the onset of mortgage problems led to a statistically significant 1.6 increase in the GHQ12 change score, while for women the increase was even greater at 2.5. In the second transition period between 1994 and 1995 the relationship was not so strong. In the multiple regression analysis the impact of the onset of mortgage problems on subjective well-being is not statistically significant for men and is only just significant for women.

It is also possible to decipher the extent to which the impact of mortgage problems leads to an increased use of primary healthcare services. In the first period between 1991 and 1992 a significant increase in GP visits related to the onset of mortgage problems was possible to decipher for men but not for women. In the second period between 1994 and 1995 although both men and women with mortgage problems were more likely to have increased the number of visits they made to their GP, the increases were not statistically significant.

The first transition (1991-92) period represents the peak in the number of mortgage possessions and the number of people who were experiencing difficulties with their payments. This implies that in times when more people are experiencing difficulties the health effects may be greater. It may be that when there are high levels of arrears those who would not normally be at high risk of debt are more exposed to it. The problem may touch a wider diversity of people and may include those who are less likely to have experience of debt and financial hardship. Studies on the impact of financial debt more generally have found that those people who have little experience of this type of 'life event' find it more difficult to cope with (Kempson, 1996, pp 10-16). One might speculate further that at times of greater economic insecurity the qualitative experience of mortgage indebtedness may be different than during times of greater economic security. As we have seen, while there may be greater numbers of people in arrears it is not a life event which is experienced collectively, and its antecedents and consequences are likely to be intensely personal.

Summary

This chapter has drawn on both intensive forms of qualitative research and extensive forms of statistical analysis in order to understand the generative mechanisms by which the experience of mortgage arrears and possession necessarily translate into poor subjective well-being and, more often than not, ill health. As such the chapter tries to make a case for reconceptualising unsustainable home ownership as a new public health issue.

Note

This chapter draws on material previously published in Nettleton and Burrows (1998b) which was unfunded and Nettleton et al (1999) and Nettleton and Burrows (2000) both of which were funded by the Joseph Rowntree Foundation.

EIGHT

Summary and conclusions

In this book we have been concerned to draw together a body of research that has addressed aspects of what has come to be referred to as either *problematic* home ownership or, more typically, *unsustainable* home ownership. The specific aspect of unsustainability considered has been the emergence and persistence of mortgage arrears and possessions. An important concern has been to show the trend with respect to arrears and possession as well as their cyclical nature and to indicate that the issues are not just passing ones – important but nevertheless merely temporary manifestations of short-term economic crisis such as occurred at the end of the 1980s. Rather, unsustainable home ownership, and particularly arrears and possessions, is the consequence of a number of more fundamental shifts in the structures that have historically benefited and underpinned owner-occupation; centrally, the labour market and social security provision. Both of these structures have become 'less predictable' or 'less certain'. This is the result of restructuring that sought to bring about a less regulated, more flexible labour market as well as the growth of more low-paid jobs and policies to shift the responsibility for social protection away from the state and towards private sector provision. The certainties of regular, secure, well-paid employment and a state safety net that had been available to owner-occupiers for much of the post-war period have been eroded and continue to be so, creating risks for a significant proportion of mortgagors.

As outlined in Chapter One, the growing uncertainty that currently characterises the environment in which individuals hold and manage their home ownership is the consequence of its embeddedness within a set of structures and processes influenced by the impact of technological change, urbanisation and, critically, globalisation. It is this latter process, in particular, that is pivotal in the generation of economic and labour market uncertainty and which as a consequence, also informs the continuing necessity for social protection. In addition, aspects of housing policy and social security policy may exacerbate the risks, for example through the implementation of policies designed to widen access to the sector which drew in more marginal households with high exposure to the uncertainties of the labour market or through the failure to provide 'in-work' assistance with housing costs for low-income borrowers.

To the extent that societies continue to be shaped by these macro, global processes, and the insecurities they generate, their effects will continue to impact. It is in this respect that we argue that the current incidence of unsustainable home ownership is not 'pathological' or short-lived but rather has become 'normal' and enduring.

While arrears and possessions are currently much lower than they were at the height of the last recession in the early 1990s, the CML figures show that they have 'plateaued' at a much higher level than was the case in the 1970s and early 1980s. In 1999, 30,000 households lost their property through possession, a further 183,000 owed three or more months' payments, and based on figures for 1998 we can estimate that around a further 100,000 mortgagor households owed two months' payments. These are figures that pertain in very favourable economic circumstances. In addition, approximately one in every seven mortgagors in England reports that they are finding it difficult to meet their mortgage payments. Economic cycles will, of course, periodically amplify the incidence of arrears and possessions, but over the 1980s and 1990s, each 'retreat' from a 'high' recessionary figure has bottomed out at a figure higher than on the previously 'low' occasion as arrears and possessions slowly ratchet upwards. However, this pattern is not immutable; attempts can be made to contain the trend by the introduction of policy measures designed to limit the risks of unsustainable home ownership (for example, the proposed ISMI run-on when people return to work, or an 'in-work' housing allowance that would assist where people had to take low-income work), but this is all within the context of a more risky home ownership than has previously been the case due to fundamental structural change.

In the face of these macro processes and the social and economic change they engender, there have been a number of different conceptualisations that attempt to encapsulate the nature of contemporary life. Reflecting on these, we found the conceptualisation of the risk society as associated with writers such and Beck and Giddens a helpful sensitising framework, in large part because central to its approach are both structural and experiential dimensions of contemporary life, and a focus on the interconnectedness of the two. The former emphasises the extent and nature of the pervasive insecurity and uncertainty associated with contemporary structures while the latter indicates the significance of reflexivity, lifestyle choice and the importance of ontological security in individuals' making and experiencing their biographies in an uncertain world. Thus, one is sensitised to examine both the fundamental underpinnings of, in this instance, home ownership but also home ownership as a lived experience to which people respond. There was, however, no intention to 'test' or 'assess' the risk society framework in any systematic manner. Rather, it is the context within which we thought about the development, patterning, impact and consequences of mortgage arrears and possessions. In particular, we came to understand the development and significance of owner-occupation as a feature of contemporary society, as well as an issue within the field of housing policy.

Against this background of the risk society and the enduring nature of mortgage arrears and possessions, we have sought to indicate the scale of unsustainable home ownership, the characteristics of those with these problems and the ways in which the nature of the risk changes over time and as both social and economic circumstances and the form of social protection change. Thus, for example, we showed that while, overall, self-employment is conducive to arrears, it is particularly during recessionary conditions that self-employed people run the highest risk. We also showed that the changes in the state safety net had a clear impact on arrears as the numbers facing a shortfall in their interest payments rose after the introduction of payment at a standard interest rate in October 1995. Equally, the inadequacies of the private safety net were shown to contribute to payment difficulties and arrears.

Considerable attention was also paid to the costs and consequences of unsustainable home ownership at both the aggregate and individual level. There are implications for a wide range of actors from the more obvious ones of mortgagors and lenders to central and local government and to organisations such as those providing health services or employment opportunities. In that sense there is a 'long arm' to arrears and possessions, only some aspects of which have as yet been explored systematically. Our emphasis was placed on detailing the social, socio-psychological, health and financial 'costs and consequences' of arrears and possessions to borrowers. This examination shows the clear connection between the process and experience of unsustainable home ownership and the development (and interconnection) of both social marginalisation and poverty. It also indicates the implications of unsustainable home ownership for individuals' emotional well-being and sense of security.

Increasing the risks to home ownership

There is little evidence that the risks to home ownership will abate, indeed the enduring nature of the current risks is one of the central arguments set out here. Rather, in trying to discern the future, it is possible to suggest a number of factors that potentially increase further the risks to mortgagors. There are both cyclical factors and ones associated with longer-term trends. By its very nature, discerning the future is a hazardous undertaking, but a number of issues are considered in brief below. We have touched on some of them *en passant* in earlier chapters, but it is useful to draw them together here by considering the further risk associated with economic trends, from prevalent ideologies, from housing policy and from trends in the provision of social protection.

Economic trends

Recent structural change has ensured that arrears and possessions remain significant despite a buoyant economy. There is, however, considerable discussion of the timing and nature of the next economic slowdown that will, *other things being equal*, bring in its wake an increase in households unable to pay their mortgages and experiencing arrears and possession. One of the interesting findings noted earlier from the Survey of English Housing is the year on year consistency in the percentage of home owners who have difficulties paying, but currently are still managing to do so. At a steady 12 or 13% since 1995 this is a sizeable pool of mortgagors vulnerable to any deterioration in their economic circumstances. Labour market changes are a major, but not the only cause of such a deterioration. Further, the low-inflation environment characteristic of the UK since the mid-1990s will limit some more recent borrowers' flexibility with respect to trading down if confronted with arrears because of the limited erosion to their initial debt.

The structural trends in the labour market are also predicted to continue to be characterised by a decline in full-time manufacturing jobs and an increase in part-time, lower-paid jobs (see Table 3.1) and this too will impact on the opportunities available to any mortgagors who experience unemployment either due to restructuring or recessionary processes. Throughout our discussions we have stressed that these eventualities are unlikely to characterise the majority of mortgagors and that full-time, well-paid, permanent work remains the norm. Nevertheless, the recession will impact on a profile of mortgagor households more than a quarter of whom already have one or more people in these forms of more flexible, typically precarious forms of employment. This is a rather different profile of mortgagors to the one that pertained immediately prior to the recession of the early 1990s. In any future recession, employers will also face fewer obstacles to retrenchment where they have such workers, and these will in all probability be joined by others where more permanent jobs are lost.

Housing ideologies and housing policy

Notwithstanding the development and persistence of unsustainable home ownership, it continues to be accorded a central role in British society. Although more people are equivocal about the wisdom of becoming home owners than a decade ago, the majority of those questioned in surveys still express a long-term preference for the tenure and in 1999 almost 70% still expressed a positive attitude towards the tenure (Ford and Burrows, 2000). There remains a well-entrenched culture that views home ownership as an important route to wealth accumulation, and in particular, as conferring status, independence and security. The strength of all these perceptions is underlined by the material we presented earlier that noted just how much those experiencing unsustainable home ownership felt they lost status, independence, security and autonomy when they lost their homes.

These beliefs and perceptions cannot be disassociated from the nature of other available housing options in Britain. The limited availability of good-quality social housing in some areas and particularly its currently residualised nature, in part also informs the preference for home ownership. We have not in this book discussed this issue in any detail or systematic manner, other than to note the detrimental impact on social housing provision (and particularly the local authority sector) of the Right to Buy legislation, the inability to pursue new build via the capital receipts from sales, and the extent to which social housing has been residualised and marginalised over the 1980s and 1990s. However, the current nature of social housing is clearly one factor supporting home ownership, even where such ownership is recognised as 'risky'. This situation also helps to explain why many of those taken into possession in time return to owner-occupation, a move that for them is also 'risky'.

The most recent policy statements on housing from government, both the Green Paper itself (DETR/DSS, 2000a) and the government's response to the consultation on the Green Paper (DETR/DSS, 2000b) show no retreat from the expectation that at least three quarters of households will be home owners. Further, as discussed below, current policy has an explicit commitment to assisting lower-income households into home ownership via a series of low-cost home ownership initiatives. Thus, at a very fundamental level, housing policy itself is continuing to increase the riskiness of home ownership.

Facilitating access to owner-occupation

Housing policy is committed to facilitating access to home ownership for groups who have traditionally found access more difficult. Right to Buy continues, but its impact is of a much lower order than in the 1980s and early 1990s. Low-cost home ownership is an important part of current initiatives with forms of shared ownership (flexible tenure) continuing to receive encouragement. Homebuy is the most recent of a number of approaches that have been adopted in the wake of Do-it-Yourself Shared Ownership (DIYSO) and the Tenants Incentive Scheme (TIS), schemes available to assist in open market home ownership. We have, however, presented evidence that indicates that over a run of years shared owners have a higher risk of arrears than do 'full' owners. Whether or not this will prove to be the case with other forms of low-cost housing (for example, Homebuy) remains to be seen. But these concerns are well founded given the likelihood of a higher risk of unemployment among such buyers by virtue of their socio-economic characteristics and the relatively high percentage commitment of income to housing costs. Thus, again, policy itself is continuing to support and further a risky environment.

There is also a current initiative to assist key, typically public sector workers (teachers, nurses and local authority workers) into owner-occupation in areas where the price of housing is a deterrent to them taking employment, as for example in areas of the South East. The details of the scheme(s) that will be offered are not yet clear. Leaving aside a range of questions about the equity of the schemes as between occupational groups, potentially they may offer a level of support that still results in relatively heavily geared borrowers vulnerable to fluctuating interest rates, low public sector pay settlements, unexpected demands on income and so mortgage default.

The limitations of safety-net provision

The commitment to the privatisation of key areas of welfare provision has recently been reaffirmed in general (DSS, 1998) and, in particular, for owner-occupiers (DETR/DSS, 2000a). Even without further moves to curtail the state safety net (ISMI), the risks to mortgagors as a whole will increase as the proportion of post-October 1995 borrowers in the mortgagor population increases and they have to face the nine-month wait period. Even if the proportion developing arrears remains the same (currently about half), the absolute numbers with arrears will increase. However, as noted earlier, the recent housing Green Paper (DETR/DSS, 2000a) put forward for discussion the further curtailment of ISMI to 14 months. It is hard to see how under current circumstances this could result in anything other than an increase in arrears, and particularly possessions, not least because of the evidence of the increasingly unsatisfactory protection offered by ISMI once it is paid. Lenders asked to forbear for 14 months, only to find arrears mounting further once there was access to ISMI, are unlikely to see merit in any forbearance.

A significant influence on the future trajectory of risk for mortgagors depends on success in improving the take-up and performance of the private safety-net MPPI. As things stand currently, the product itself (defined as its cover and associated processes) is a risk to *a minority* of home owners. However, if the emphasis is placed on achieving higher take-up without offering an improved product, this will only exacerbate the number of mortgagors at risk of arrears and will amplify the problem in any economic downturn. At the time of writing, while there is a target for take-up of 55% by 2004 there has been no evident attempt to address a number of well-researched detriments to the product. Admittedly, not all of these (such as negative attitudes to insurers, a lack of trust in the market) are easily addressed by institutions in the short run, but there has also been little change in aspects such as cost, transparency, the claiming process, and procedures to encourage updating of cover as interest rates change, all of which currently create risks for mortgagors and can deter the take-up and retention of MPPI.

One response to low take-up but evident risk is to make MPPI compulsory. Focusing on an improved product rather than take-up per se is critical if the debate about compulsory insurance is to develop helpfully, as compulsion to take a poor product would be very damaging. Compulsion is not an approach currently favoured by government, although it was recommended as a component of a 'combined' approach by the recent Social Security Select Committee Inquiry into Housing Benefit (House of Common Social Security Committee, 2000).

Unsustainable home ownership: some outstanding issues

Research on unsustainable home ownership has developed significantly since the 1980s and particularly in the 1990s. Both our work and that of others has contributed to the provision of information and analysis of an issue that, as we have stressed, in a number of different ways has affected more than a million households. There remain many unexplored issues however, and this final section notes a number of outstanding questions.

The housing careers of households with arrears and possessions

As noted earlier, there is some evidence that an experience of arrears or possession may increase the likelihood of a further episode of arrears and possibly further possession. This is not surprising given the relationship between arrears, possession, the development of poverty and in some cases persistent indebtedness, on the one hand, and the range of issues that increase the likelihood of a return to owner-occupation on the other (such as the availability of alternative accommodation). Equally it is clear that this is not always the case and that arrears can be a one-off occurrence whether it involves possession or not. But the balance between these sets of outcomes, and the factors that influence these outcomes is not yet understood. Currently there exists no systematic longitudinal analysis of the housing careers of those experiencing arrears and/or possession. It is therefore not possible to be certain of the extent to which, *over time*, the problem of arrears and possessions is primarily one of 'churning' or one affecting home ownership more widely. Such an analysis is of interest in its own right as an aspect of understanding the dynamics of unsustainable owner-occupation, and the interplay between different housing markets, but also has policy implications in terms of considering appropriate interventions to limit the incidence of arrears and possessions.

Does place matter?

Another outstanding issue is the uneven knowledge about arrears and possessions within the UK and indeed on a more widely drawn comparative basis. There exist far better data for England than is the case for Scotland, Wales or Northern Ireland, although some information is available for Scotland (Wilcox, 1998). This situation is largely a result of the availability of the Survey of English Housing and the absence of comparable surveys in the other countries. While the British Household Panel Survey and the Family Resources Survey (FRS) have a wider geographical coverage, the number surveyed in the former does not assist in geographical disaggregation, while neither survey has a detailed coverage of arrears and possessions, and this is particularly limited in the FRS.

Similarly, within England, there is no systematic analysis of arrears by region, although there are regional county court figures on applications for possession and possession orders made (which are not the same thing as possessions) that have been used to offer some discussion of the likely regional patterns (Muelbauer, 1997). Given the local nature of both housing and labour markets, the differential impact of economic restructuring and the different timing of the economic cycle, the different legislative structures in Scotland and Northern Ireland and the different traditions of home ownership, it is unwise to be too confident in any 'read off' of the causes and consequences of arrears and possessions in these places from an understanding of the situation in England or, indeed, in the South East. That said, the key issues of labour market change and safety-net provision are likely to remain prominent. But, rehousing issues and so housing careers post-possession, as well as the options provided by the possession process to 'recover' arrears, may differ significantly, particularly in Scotland, and research supported by the Scottish Executive is now taking place to illuminate these and other issues.

Assistance for low-paid mortgagors

The outstanding issue here is not the inadequacy of the research base, but the slow development of any policy response. We have presented a number of estimates of low-paid mortgagors, and shown that they are the group with the highest percentage of income committed to housing costs and are therefore particularly vulnerable to any further reduction in income or increase in (any) costs. There is considerable evidence to support a link between low pay and mortgage arrears and possessions. However, unlike renters, in-work mortgagors receive no help with their housing costs and the case for the implementation of a tenure-neutral housing allowance has been made repeatedly since the early 1990s (Wilcox and Webb, 1991; Burrows and Wilcox, 2000). The argument is made on several grounds, including equity; removing a work disincentive; limiting the incidence of arrears and possessions; and cost – to the extent that the absence of such support creates housing outcomes (for example, rehousing as tenants) that have to be met by Housing Benefit. This anomaly, the adjustment of which has continually faltered on the grounds that, unlike tenants, owners have access to a capital asset, remains a significant contributory factor to unsustainable home ownership. However, while not addressed directly in terms of an all-tenure housing allowance, the implementation in April 2000 of the Working Families Tax Credit, available to owner-occupiers, will go some way to raising the incomes of low-paid workers and so assist them in meeting housing costs.

Lenders' responses to unsustainable home ownership

Finally, and perhaps crucially, there has been relatively little research on the nature of lenders' perspectives on unsustainable home ownership (but see Ford and Kempson, 1997a; Oldman and Kemp, 1996; Maclennan et al, 1997). Where it has been considered, the focus has tended to be both specific (for example, on lenders' responses to the 1995 ISMI cuts, or their approach to lending after the housing market recession, or estimates of MPPI take-up), and based on studies of a rather small number of lenders. The broader questions of how they perceive and assess the current and future structural trends, and their implications for lending and the housing market and the range of responses that are being made, is not widely discussed.

Journalistic accounts and a small number of presentations by lenders suggest that there is a range of assessments. Preliminary indications also suggest that there are lenders implementing policies aimed at divesting themselves of risk (either via a tightening of the terms of the lending or through stringent screening of the characteristics of borrowers and property). But there are other lenders with different strategic priorities for whom shorter-term competitive considerations are paramount and who accept that arrears management is now an integral part of their activities, with any future economic downturn simply having to be managed. Other lenders are seeking greater exposure as 'niche' lenders to those wishing to return to owner-occupation after possession. But the costs of the finance offered are high while those seeking such finance typically have limited resources.

The extent of risk to owner-occupation will depend particularly on the response of these lenders (who seek to routinise structural risk) when there is a cyclical downturn and hence a rapid increase in the number of borrowers in the nine-month ISMI period. There are similar issues, already noted above, about insurers' management of MPPI in an economic downturn.

One response from lenders and the government has been to suggest that new forms of mortgage products have the capacity to manage the risks to home ownership. In particular, 'flexible' mortgages have been developed that provide borrowers with the means to overpay in times of prosperity and to underpay or have 'payment holidays' when they are without employment. The most sophisticated of these products are such that borrowers run their mortgage and current accounts as one, and draw down equity (often to a capped amount) as they wish. Two early views on these products recognised some possible advantages but also expressed some reservations, first about the number of people who might be able to avoid unsustainable home ownership by these means (Ford and Kempson, 1997b), in part because those most needing to do so had the least ability to accumulate sufficient overpayments; and second because, without fairly sophisticated financial management skills, these products could encourage further indebtedness and so contribute to the problem they were designed to address (Dudleston, 2001). Systematic research on flexible mortgages to illuminate these and other issues is now being undertaken (Munro et al, 2001: forthcoming).

For borrowers, as well as for policy makers, lenders' strategic approach to growing risk and its management is an important issue, impacting on many aspects of home ownership, yet not much researched. Among many things it raises questions about the terms of entry to home ownership and so the ability of government to sustain its housing policy objectives to facilitate access. It raises questions about the commitment of lenders to borrowers in any economic downturn and it raises questions about the extent to which 'product design' offers a means to manage irregular and unstable payment patterns and so preclude unsustainable owner-occupation.

Thus, the study of unsustainable home ownership has developed significantly over the last two decades but there remain some central unanswered questions and outstanding issues. The risks to the sector continue and are likely to grow further while the consequences will be both individual and systemic. Britain *may* have moved away from the boom and bust conditions of the 1980s and 1990s, or at least limited the amplitude of the cycles, but the trend and the dangers remain clear. Homeownership in a risk society may well require a policy response very different to that which was appropriate under different socio-economic and cultural circumstances.

Bibliography

AKG Mortgage Report (1995) *Repayment with interest*, AKG Services Ltd.

Alderson, P. (1995) *Listening to children: Children, ethics and social research*, London: Barnardo's.

Allen, J. and Henry, N. (1997) 'Ulrich Becks's *Risk society* at work: labour and employment in the contract service industries', *Transactions of the Institute of British Geographers*, vol 22, no 2, pp 180-96.

Anderson, I. and Sim, D. (eds) (2000) *Social exclusion and housing: Context and challenges*, Coventry: Chartered Institute of Housing/Housing Studies Association.

Banks, J., Dilnot, A. and Low, H. (1994) *The distribution of wealth in the UK*, Commentary No 45, London: Institute for Fiscal Studies.

Barr, N. (1993) *The economics of welfare*, Oxford: Oxford University Press.

Bartley, M., Blane, D. and Davey-Smith, G. (eds) (1998) *The sociology of health inequalities*, Oxford: Blackwells.

Beatson, M. (1995) *Labour market flexibility*, Research Report No 48, London: Employment Department.

Beck, U. (1992) *Risk society*, London: Sage Publications.

Beck, U. and Beck-Gernsheim, E. (1996) 'Individualization and precarious freedoms', in P. Heelas, S. Lash and P. Morris (eds) *Detraditionalization*, Oxford: Blackwells.

Beck, U., Giddens, A. and Lash, S. (1994) *Reflexive modernization*, Cambridge: Polity Press.

Berry, M., Dalton, T., Engles, B. and Whiting, K. (1999) *Falling out of home ownership: Mortgage arrears and defaults in Australia*, Brisbane, Australia: University of Queensland Press.

Bjork, M. (1994) 'Investigating the experiences of repossession: a Swedish example', *Housing Studies*, vol 9, no 4, pp 511-29.

BSA (Building Societies Association) (1985) *Mortgage payment difficulties*, London: BSA.

Buck, N., Gershuny, J., Rose, D. and Scott, A. (eds) (1994) *Changing households: The British Household Panel Survey 1990-1992*, Essex: ESRC Research Centre on Micro-Social Change, University of Essex.

Burbridge, A. (2000) 'Capital gains, home ownership and economic inequality', *Housing Studies*, vol 15, no 2, pp 259-80.

Burchardt, T. and Hills, J. (1997) *Pushing at the boundaries: Private welfare insurance and social security*, York: Joseph Rowntree Foundation.

Burrows, R. (ed) (1991) *Deciphering the enterprise culture*, London: Routledge.

Burrows, R. (1998a) 'Mortgage indebtedness in England: an "Epidemiology"', *Housing Studies*, vol 13, no 4, pp 5-22.

Burrows, R. (1998b) *The dynamics of the owner occupied market*, London: Council of Mortgage Lenders.

Burrows, R. (1999) 'Residential mobility and residualisation in social housing in England', *Journal of Social Policy*, vol 28, no 1, pp 27-52.

Burrows R. and Ford, J. (1997) 'Who needs a safety net? The social distribution of mortgage arrears', *Housing Finance*, no 34, pp 17-24.

Burrows R. and Ford, J. (1998) 'Self-employment and home ownership after the enterprise culture', *Work, Employment and Society*, vol 12, no 1, pp 97-119.

Burrows, R. and Loader, B. (eds) (1994) *Towards a post Fordist welfare state?*, London: Routledge.

Burrows, R. and Wilcox, S. (2000) *Half the poor: Low income home owners*, London: Council of Mortgage Lenders.

Burrows, R., Ford, J. and Wilcox, S. (2000) 'Half the poor? Policy responses to low income home ownership', in S. Wilcox (ed) *Housing Finance Review 2000/2001*, York: Chartered Institute of Housing, Council of Mortgage Lenders and Joseph Rowntree Foundation.

Burrows, R., Nettleton, S., Pleace, N., Loader, B. and Muncer, S. (2000) 'Virtual community care? Social policy and the emergence of computer mediated social support', *Information, Communication and Society*, vol 3, no 1, pp 95-121.

Bury, M. (1982) 'Chronic illness as a biographical disruption', *Sociology of Health and Illness*, vol 4, no 2, pp 167-82.

Caplovitz, D. (1974) *Consumers in trouble: A study of debtors in default*, New York, NY: The Free Press.

Cebulla, A. (1998) 'A geography of insurance exclusion – perceptions of unemployment risk and actuarial risk assessment', *Area*, vol 31, no 2, pp 111-21.

Cebulla, A. (1999) 'Government plans and individuals' intentions: the case of unemployment insurance', *Benefits*, vol 26, pp 16-21.

CHP (Centre for Housing Policy) (2001) 'Home ownership, employment and welfare in comparative perspective', Papers presented to an international workshop, Centre for Housing Policy Discussion Paper Series, York: Centre for Housing Policy, University of York.

Christie, H. (2000) 'Mortgage arrears and gender inequalities', *Housing Studies*, vol 15, no 6, pp 877-905.

Clapham, D. (1996) 'Housing and the economy: broadening comparative housing research', *Urban Studies*, vol 33, nos 4/5, pp 631-47.

CML (Council of Mortgage Lenders) (1991) *The handling of mortgage arrears: The practice of mortgage lenders*, Circular, February.

Cole, I. and Furbey, R. (1993) *The eclipse of council housing*, London: Routledge.

Davis, R. and Dhooge, Y. (1993) *Living with mortgage arrears*, London: London Research Centre Housing and Social Research, HMSO.

DETR (Department of the Environment, Transport and the Regions)/ DSS (Department of Social Security) (2000a) *Quality and choice: A decent home for all*, London: The Stationery Office.

DETR/DSS (2000b) *Quality and choice: A decent home for all. The way forward for housing*, London: The Stationery Office.

Dex, S. and McCulloch, A. (1997) *Flexible employment: The future of Britain's jobs*, Basingstoke: Macmillan.

Doling, J. and Ford, J. (1995) 'The new home ownership: the impact of labour market developments on attitudes to owning your own home', *Environment and Planning A*, vol 28, no 1, pp 157-72.

Doling, J. and Ruonavaara, H. (1996) 'Home ownership undermined: an analysis of the Finnish case in the light of the British experience', *Netherlands Journal of Housing and the Built Environment*, vol 11, no 1, pp 31-46.

Doling, J. and Stafford, B. (1986) 'Calculating the arrears odds', *Building Societies Gazette*, December, pp 62-3.

Doling, J., Ford, J. and Stafford, B. (eds) (1988) *The property owing democracy*, Aldershot: Avebury.

Doling, J., Karn, V. and Stafford, B. (1984) *Mortgage arrears and variability in county court decisions*, Working Paper No 95, Birmingham: Centre for Urban and Regional Research, University of Birmingham.

Dorling, D., Pattie, C. and Johnston, R. (1999) 'Voting and the housing market: the impact of New Labour', *Housing Finance*, no 43, pp 33-43.

DSS (1995) *Households with below half of average incomes*, London: HMSO.

DSS (1997) *A new contract for welfare*, London: The Stationery Office.

Dudleston, D, (2001) 'The flexible mortgage: a risk reducing product?', *Housing Studies*, vol 16, no 2, pp 163-77.

Elstad, J.I. (1998) 'The psycho-social perspective on social inequalities in health', in M. Bartley, D. Blane and G. Davey-Smith (eds) *The sociology of health inequality*, Oxford: Blackwells, pp 731-53.

Esping-Andersen, G. (1990) *The three worlds of welfare capitalism*, Cambridge: Polity Press.

Esping-Andersen, G. (ed) (1996) *Welfare states in transition*, London: Sage Publications.

Evans, D. (1992) *The mortgage repossession crisis*, Portsmouth: Housing Services, Portsmouth City Council.

Ford, J. (1988) *The indebted society*, London: Routledge.

Ford, J. (1989) 'Casual work and owner occupation', *Work, Employment and Society*, vol 3, no 1, pp 29-48.

Ford, J. (1993) 'Mortgage possession', *Housing Studies*, vol 8, no 4, pp 227-40.

Ford, J. (1994) *Problematic home ownership: The management, experience and consequences of arrears and possession in a depressed housing market*, York/ Loughborough: Joseph Rowntree Foundation/Loughborough University.

Ford, J. (1995) *Which way out? Borrowers in long term mortgage arrears*, London: Shelter.

Ford, J. (1997) 'Mortgage arrears, mortgage possessions and homelessness', in R. Burrows, N. Pleace and D. Quilgars (eds) *Homelessness and social policy*, London: Routledge.

Ford, J. (1998) *Risks: Home ownership and job insecurity*, London: Shelter.

Ford, J. (1999) 'Young adults and owner occupation: a changing goal?', in J. Rugg (ed) *Young people, housing and social policy*, London: Routledge.

Ford, J. (2000a) 'Housing and the flexible labour market: responding to risk', in P. Taylor-Gooby (ed) *Risk, trust and welfare*, Basingstoke: Macmillan.

Ford, J. (2000b) 'Risk and trust: home owners and private mortgage insurance', *Policy & Politics*, vol 28, no 4, pp 527-40.

Ford, J. (2000c) *MPPI take up and retention: Evidence from existing research*, London: Council of Mortgage Lenders.

Ford, J. and Burrows, R. (1999a) 'To buy or not to buy? A home of one's own', in R. Jowell, J. Curtice, A. Park and K. Thomson (eds) *British Social Attitudes: The 16th report: Who shares New Labour values?*, Aldershot: Ashgate.

Ford, J. and Burrows, R. (1999b) 'The costs of unsustainable home ownership in Britain', *Journal of Social Policy*, vol 28, no 2, pp 305-30.

Ford, J. and Burrows, R. (2000) *Labour market influences on attitudes to home ownership*, A report to the DETR, Centre for Housing Policy Discussion Paper, York: University of York.

Ford, J. and England, J (2000) *Data and literature on mortgage interest: State provision and private insurance – An evaluation report and source book*, London: DSS.

Ford, J. and Griffith, A. (1994) 'Preventing mortgage arrears: a shrinking safety net', *Benefits*, vol 10, pp 15-19.

Ford, J. and Kempson, E. (1997a) *Bridging the gap? Safety-nets for mortgage borrowers*, York: Centre for Housing Policy, University of York.

Ford, J and Kempson, E. (1997b) 'Safety-nets: MPPI and flexible mortgages', *Housing Finance*, no 36, pp 23-30.

Ford, J. and Quilgars, D. (2000) *Financial intermediaries and MPPI*, York: Centre for Housing Policy, University of York.

Ford, J. and Rowlingson, K. (1996) 'Producing consumption: women and the making of credit markets', in S. Edgell, K. Hetherington and A. Warde (eds) *Consumption matters*, Oxford: Blackwell.

Ford, J. and Seavers, J. (2000) *Attitudes to moving and debt: Household behaviour in the 1990s*, London: Council of Mortgage Lenders.

Ford, J. and Wilcox, S. (1992) *Reducing mortgage arrears and possessions: An evaluation of initiatives*, York: Joseph Rowntree Foundation.

Ford, J. and Wilcox, S. (1998) 'Owner occupation, employment and welfare: the impact of changing relations on sustainable home ownership', *Housing Studies*, vol 13, no 5, pp 623-38.

Ford, J. and Wilson, M. (1993) 'Employers, employees and debt', *Employee Relations*, vol 15, no 6, pp 21-36.

Ford, J., Kempson, E. and England, J. (1996) *Into work? The impact of housing costs and the benefit system on people's decision to work*, York: York Publishing Services.

Ford, J., Kempson, E. and Wilson, M. (1995) *Mortgage arrears and possession: Perspectives from borrowers, lenders and the courts*, London: HMSO.

Ford, J., Quilgars, D., Walker, R., Cebulla, A. and Roberts, S. (1999) 'Re-shaping welfare provision: risking the market', Paper presented to ESRC programme conference on *Risk and Human Behaviour*, London.

Forrest, R. and Kennett, P. (1996) 'Coping strategies, housing careers and households with negative equity', *Journal of Social Policy*, vol 25, no 3, pp 369-94.

Forrest, R. and Murie, A. (1990) *Selling the welfare state: The privatisation of public housing*, London: Routledge.

Forrest, R. and Murie, A. (1994) 'Home ownership in recession', *Housing Studies*, vol 9, no 1, pp 55-74.

Forrest, R., Kennett, P. and Leather, P. (1997) *Home owners on new estates in the 1990s*, Bristol/York: The Policy Press/Joseph Rowntree Foundation.

Forrest, R., Kennett, P. and Leather, P. (1999) *Home ownership in crisis? The experience of negative equity in Britain*, Aldershot: Avebury.

Forrest, R., Murie, A. and Williams, P. (1990) *Home ownership: Differentiation and fragmentation*, London: Unwin Hyman.

Franklin, J. (ed) (1998) *The politics of risk society*, Oxford: Polity Press.

Freund, P. (1990) 'The expressive body: a common ground for the sociology of emotions and health and illness', *Sociology of Health and Illness*, vol 12, no 4, pp 452-77.

Giddens, A. (1991) *Modernity and self-identity*, Oxford: Polity Press.

Giddens, A. (1992) *The transformation of intimacy*, Oxford: Polity Press.

Giddens, A. (1998) 'Risk society: the context of British politics', in J. Franklin (ed) *The politics of risk society*, Oxford: Polity Press.

Gilbert, G.N., Burrows, R. and Pollert, A. (eds) (1992) *Fordism and flexibility: Divisions and change*, Basingstoke: Macmillan.

Green, H. and Hansbro, J. (1995) *Housing in England 1993/94*, London: HMSO.

Green, H., Deacon, K. and Down, D. (1998) *Housing in England 1996/97*, ONS, Social Survey Division, London: The Stationery Office.

Green, H., Bumpstead, R., Thomas, M. and Grove, J. (1999) *Housing in England 1997/98*, London: The Stationery Office.

Green, H., Deacon, K., Iles, N. and Down, D. (1997) *Housing in England 1995/96*, London: The Stationery Office.

Green, H., Thomas, M., Iles, N. and Down, D. (1996) *Housing in England 1994/95*, London: HMSO.

Gregg, P. and Wadsworth, J. (1994) *Opportunity knocks? Job separations, engagements and claimant status*, London: National Institute of Economic and Social Research.

Gregg, P. and Wadsworth, J. (1995) 'A short history of labour turnover, job tenure, and job security, 1975-93', *Oxford Review of Economic Policy*, vol 11, no 1, pp 73-90.

Gurney, G. (1999) 'Pride and prejudice: discourses of normalisation in public and private accounts of home ownership', *Housing Studies*, vol 14, no 2, pp 163-83.

Hamnett, C. (1999) *Winners and losers: Home ownership in modern Britain*, London: UCL Press.

Hamnett, C. and Seavers, J. (1996) 'Home ownership, housing wealth and wealth distribution in Britain', in J.Hills (ed) *New inequalities*, Cambridge: Cambridge University Press.

Haskey, J. (1999) 'Divorce and remarriage in England and Wales', *Population Trends*, no 95, pp 34-40.

Heath, S. (1999) 'Young adults and household formation in the 1990s', *British Journal of Sociology of Education*, vol 20, no 4, pp 545-61.

Hills, J. (1995) *Income and wealth*, York: Joseph Rowntree Foundation.

Hirsch, F. (1977) *Social limits to growth*, London: RKP.

Holmans, A. (1997) 'UK housing finance: past changes, the present predicament, and future sustainability', in P. Williams (ed) *Directions in housing policy: Towards sustainable housing policies for the UK*, London: Paul Chapman.

Holmans, A. (2000) *Divorce, remarriage and housing*, London: DETR.

Holmans, A. and Whitehead, C. (1999) 'Who should buy MPPI?', *Housing Finance*, no 42, pp 22-7.

House of Commons Social Security Committee Sixth Report (2000) *Housing Benefit*, London: The Stationery Office.

Karn, V., Doling, J., and Stafford, B. (1985) 'Emerging problems in home ownership and contradictions in government policy', in P. Malpass (ed) *The housing crisis*, London: Croom Helm.

Kempson, E. (1994) *A foot on the ladder? A study of households on the margins of owning and renting*, London: HMSO.

Kempson, E. and Ford, J. (1995) *Attitudes, beliefs and confidence: Consumer views of the housing market in the 1990s*, London: Council of Mortgage Lenders.

Kempson, E., Ford, J. and Quilgars, D. (1999) *Unsafe safety nets*, York: Centre for Housing Policy, University of York.

Lazarus, R. (1993) 'From psychological stress to the emotions: a history of changing outlooks', *Annual Review of Psychology*, vol 44, pp 1-21.

Le Grand, J. (1997) 'Knights, knaves or pawns? Human behaviour and social policy', *Journal of Social Policy*, vol 26, no 2, pp 149-69.

Leather, P. and Mackintosh, S. (1997) 'Towards sustainable policies for housing renewal in the private sector', in P. Williams (ed) *Directions in housing policy: Towards sustainable housing policies for the UK*, London: Paul Chapman.

Lindley, R. and Wilson, R. (1998) *Review of economy and employment 1997/98*, Warwick: Institute of Employment Research, University of Warwick.

Lupton, D. (1999) *Risk*, London: Routledge.

McConaghy, M., Foster, K., Thomas, M., Grove, J. and Oliver, R. (2000) *Housing in England 1998/99*, London: The Stationery Office.

McLaverty, P. and Yip, N. (1994) 'Income multiples and mortgage potential', *Urban Studies*, vol 31, no 8, pp 730-47.

Maclennan, D. (1994) *A competitive UK economy: The challenges for housing policy*, York: Joseph Rowntree Foundation.

Maclennan, D. and Stephens, M. (1997) *EMU and the UK housing and mortgage markets*, London: Council of Mortgage Lenders.

Maclennan, D., Meen, G., Gibb, K. and Stephens, M. (1997) *Fixed commitments, uncertain incomes: Sustainable owner-occupation and the economy*, York: Joseph Rowntree Foundation.

Marsh, C. and Arber, S. (1992) *Families and households: Divisions and change*, Basingstoke: Macmillan.

Martin, E. (1998) 'Immunology on the street: how nonscientists see immune systems', in S. Nettleton and J. Watson (eds) *The body in everyday life*, London: Routledge.

Mills, C. Wright (1959) *The sociological imagination*, New York, NY: Oxford University Press.

Morrow, V. and Richards, M. (1996) 'The ethics of social research with children: an overview', *Children and Society*, vol 10, no 1, pp 90-105.

Muelbauer, J. (1997) 'A regional analysis of mortgage possessions: causes, trends and future prospects', *Housing Finance*, no 34, pp 10-16.

Munro, M. (2000) 'Labour market insecurity in the owner occupied housing market', *Environment and Planning A*, vol 32, no 8, pp 1375-89.

Munro, M., Madigan, R. and Memery, C. (1998) 'Choices in owner occupation', in P. Taylor-Gooby, *Choice and public policy: The limits to welfare markets*, Basingstoke: Macmillan Press.

Munro, M., Smith, S. and Ford, J. (2001: forthcoming) *Flexible mortgages*.

Murphey, L. (1996) 'Whose interest rates? Issues in the development of mortgage-backed securitisation', *Housing Studies*, vol 11, no 4, pp 581-9.

NACAB (National Association of Citizens Advice Bureaux) (1995) *Security at risk*, London: NACAB.

NACAB (1999) *The long shadow: Cab evidence on mortgage shortfall debt*, London: NACAB.

Nettleton, S. (1997) 'Governing the risky self: how to become healthy, wealthy and wise', in A. Peterson and R. Bunton (eds) *Foucault, health and medicine*, London: Routledge.

Nettleton, S. (1998) 'Losing homes through mortgage possession: a 'new' public health issue', *Critical Public Health*, vol 8, no 1, pp 47-58.

Nettleton, S. (2001) 'Losing a home through mortgage repossession: the views of children', *Children and Society*, vol 15, no 2, pp 82-94.

Nettleton, S. and Burrows, R. (1998a) 'Individualization processes and social policy: insecurity, reflexivity and risk in the restructuring of contemporary health and housing policies', in J. Carter (ed) *Postmodernity and the fragmentation of welfare*, London: Routledge.

Nettleton, S. and Burrows, R. (1998b) 'Mortgage debt, insecure home ownership and health: an exploratory analysis', in M. Bartley, D. Blane and G. Davey-Smith (eds) *The sociology of health inequality*, Oxford: Blackwells.

Nettleton, S. and Burrows, R. (2000) 'When a capital investment becomes an emotional loss: the health consequences of the experience of mortgage possession in England', *Housing Studies*, vol 15, no 3, pp 463-79.

Nettleton, S. and Burrows, R.(2001: forthcoming) 'Families coping with the experience of mortgage repossession in the "new landscape of precariousness"', *Community, Work and Family*, vol 4.

Nettleton, S., Burrows, R., England, J. and Seavers, J. (1999) *Losing the family home: Understanding the social consequences of mortgage repossession*, York: York Publishing Services.

Nixon, J., Smith, Y., Wishart, B. and Hunter, C. (1996) *Housing cases in county courts*, Bristol/York: The Policy Press/Joseph Rowntree Foundation.

O'Brien, M., Penna, S. and Hay, C. (eds) (1999) *Theorising modernity*, London: Longman.

Ogden, J. (1995) 'Psychosocial theory and the creation of the risky self', *Social Science and Medicine*, vol 40, no 3, pp 409-15.

Oldman, C. and Kemp, P.A. (1996) *Income support for mortgage interest: An assessment of current issues and future prospects*, London: Council of Mortgage Lenders.

Pattie, C., Dorling, D. and Johnston, R.(1995) 'A debt-owing democracy – the political impact of housing-market recession at the British General Election of 1992', *Urban Studies*, vol 32, no 8, pp 1293-315.

Pickvance, C. and Pickvance, K. (1994) 'Towards a strategic approach to housing behaviour: a study of young people's housing strategies in the South East of England', *Sociology*, vol 28, no 3, pp 657-77.

Popay, J., Williams, G., Thomas, C. and Gatrell, A. (1998) 'Theorising inequalities in health: the place of lay knowledge', in M. Bartley, D. Blane and G. Davey-Smith (eds) *The sociology of health inequality*, Oxford: Blackwells.

Potter, P. and Dreverman, S. (1990) 'Home ownership, foreclosure and compulsory auction in the Federal Republic of Germany', *Housing Studies*, vol 3, no 2, pp 94-104.

Pryce, G. (1998) 'Income support for mortgage interest and the crowding out of mortgage payment protection insurance', *Housing Finance*, no 39, pp 27-31.

Quercia, R. and Stegman, M. (1992) 'Residential mortgage default: a review of the literature', *Journal of Housing Research*, vol 3, no 1, pp 21-60.

Quilgars, D. and Abbott, D. (2000) 'Working in a risk society: families' perceptions of, and responses to, flexible labour markets and the restructuring of welfare', *Community, Work and Family*, vol 3, no 1, pp 15-36.

Rowlingson, K. (1994) *Money lenders*, London: Policy Studies Institute.

Saunders, P. (1990) *A nation of home owners*, London: Unwin Hyman.

Shaw, C. and Haskey, J. (1999) 'New estimates and projections of the population cohabiting in England and Wales', *Population Trends*, vol 95, pp 29-33.

Skinner, C. and Ford, J. (2000) *Planning, postponing or hesitating: Understanding financial planning*, York: Centre for Housing Policy, University of York.

Social Security Committee (1995) *Low income statistics: Low income families 1989-1992*, House of Commons Section 1994/95, London: HMSO.

Stephens, M. (1996) 'Institutional responses to the UK housing market recession', *Urban Studies*, vol 33, no 2, pp 337-52.

Taylor, D. (1998) 'Social identity and social policy: engagements with postmodern theory', *Journal of Social Policy*, vol 27, no 3, pp 329-50.

Taylor-Gooby, P. (1998) *Choice and public policy: The limits to welfare markets*, Basingstoke: Macmillan.

Taylor-Gooby, P. (1999) 'Markets and motives: trust and egoism in welfare markets', *Journal of Social Policy*, vol 28, no 1, pp 97-114.

Taylor-Gooby, P. (2000a) 'Blair's scars', *Critical Social Policy*, vol 20, no 3, pp 331-48.

Taylor-Gooby, P. (2000b) 'Risk and welfare', in P. Taylor-Gooby (ed) *Risk, trust and welfare*, Basingstoke: Macmillan.

TUC (Trades Union Council) (1996) *Britain divided – Insecurity at work*, London: TUC.

Walker, R., Shaw, A. and Hull, L. (1995) 'Responding to the risk of unemployment', in ABI (Association of British Insurers) *Risk, insurance and welfare*, London: ABI.

Weiss, L. (1998) *The myth of the powerless state: Governing the economy in a global era*, Cambridge: Polity Press.

White, M. (1996) 'Labour market risks', in P. Meadows (ed) *Work-in or work-out?*, York: Joseph Rowntree Foundation.

White, M. and Forth, J. (1998) *Pathways through unemployment: The effects of the flexible labour market*, York: York Publishing Services.

Wilcox, S. (1998) *Scottish Housing Review 1988-1998*, Edinburgh: Scottish Homes.

Wilcox, S. (1999) *The vexed question of affordability*, Edinburgh: Scottish Homes.

Wilcox, S. (2000) *Housing Finance Review 2000/2001*, London/York: Chartered Institute of Housing/Council of Mortgage Lenders/Joseph Rowntree Foundation.

Wilcox, S. and Webb, S. (1991) *Time for mortgage benefits*, York: Joseph Rowntree Foundation.

Wilkinson, R. (1996) *Unhealthy societies: The afflictions of inequality*, London: Routledge.

Wilkinson, R.G., Kawachi, I. and Kennedy, B. (1998) 'Mortality, the social environment, crime and violence', in M. Bartley, D. Blane and G. Davey-Smith (eds) *The sociology of health inequality*, Oxford: Blackwells.

Williams, F., Popay, J. and Oakley, A. (eds) (1999a) *Welfare research: A critical review*, London: UCL Press.

Williams, P. (1995) 'A shrinking safety net for a changing market', in S. Wilcox (ed) *Housing Finance Review 1995/96*, York: Joseph Rowntree Foundation.

Williams, S. (1998) '"Capitalising" on emotions? Rethinking the inequalities in health debate', *Sociology*, vol 32, no 1, pp 121-40.

Williams, T., Hill, M. and Davies, R. (1999b) *Attitudes to the welfare state and the response to reform*, DSS Research Report No 88, Leeds: Corporate Document Services.

Index

[Page references for figures and tables are in italics.]

A

administrative costs *109*, 114
adverse selection 87
affordability 47-8, 65
age
  arrears *33*, *35*, *37*, 39, 40
  mortgagors *13*, 14
  possessions *28*
  see also young people
Allen, J. 6
Anderson, I. 107
arrears *see* mortgage arrears
Association of British Insurers (ABI) 90, 97
attitudes to home ownership 2-3, *3*, 8, 36, 173
  knowledge and experience of costs 107-8
Australia 17, 18
Austria 17

B

Bartley, M. 153
baseline policies 97
Beck, Ulrich 3-4, 150, 170
benefits *see* welfare provision
Berry, M. 18
biographical disruption 149-50, 164
bivariate associations, arrears 34, 36, *37-8*, 38-43
Bjork, M. 18
borrowers *see* mortgagors
British Household Panel Survey (BHPS) vii, 57, 60, 61, 64, 166, 177
British Social Attitudes Survey (BSAS) 2
Buck, N. 57, 67
Building Societies Act 1986 10
Burbridge, A. 107
Burchardt, T. 86, 93
Burrows, R. 46, 48-9, 67, 108, 120, 151
Bury, M. 149

C

capital accumulations 107, 116-17, 123, 173
capital gains tax 80
Caplovitz, D. 108
care costs 80
categorical identity 148-9
Cebulla, A. 92, 95
central government, costs *109*, 114, *115*
children, possessions 113, 125, 137-48
churning 31, 176
Clapham, D. 14
class *see* social class
compulsory possession 126-7
confidence 112
Conservative Party 10, 116
consumer protection 108
contract work 68-71
control
  adults' feelings 113, 128, 129-30, 151, 160-1, 163
  children's feelings 145-6
coping strategies 130, 151
  to minimise consequences of losing home 134-7
  to save the home 130-4
  women 134
cost recovery 108
costs 107, *109*, 110, 123
  administrative 114
  financial 114, 116-23, *118*, *119*
  political 116
  social, social psychological and health 110, *111*, 112-14, 151-68
Council of Mortgage Lenders (CML)
  arrears 21, 30
  MPPI 90, 97
  possessions 121
credit market *see* financial markets
cross-border credit 18

D

demographic changes 46, 49-50, 51
Denmark 17
Department of Social Security (DSS) 30-1
deregulation 17-18
financial market 10, 12, 18, 21, 54
labour market 5-6, 54
disempowerment 165
divorce 49
arrears 21
possessions 49-50, 112
Doling, J. 18, 108
dramaturgical stress 164
Dreverman, S. 18
drinking 156
dual earner households 14, 59
employment continuity and change 60-4, *61*, *63*
precarious employment 59, *60*
Dudleston, D. 179

E

eating problems 156-7
economic cycles 1, 21-2, 170
economic trends 46, 53, 81, 172-3
see also fiscal support; inflation; labour market
Elstad, J.I. 153, 154
emotional capital 164-5
emotional intensity 128-9, 163-4
emotional security 7
emotions 157-8
employability 71, *72*, 73-4
employment 1, 8
continuity and change 60-4, *61*, *63*
flexible 77-8, 173
instabilities 56-7
low-paid 65-6, 81
precarious 57-9, *58*, *60*, 81
see also labour market
employment status
arrears 32, *33*, 34, *35*, *37*, *38*, 39-40, 78
mortgagors 57-9, *58*, *60*
possessions *28*, 29, *29*
see also full-time employment; part-time employment; self-employment; temporary employment; unemployment
empowerment 165
England 32, 176-7
equity withdrawal 16
Esping-Andersen, G. 7, 54
estate agents 114
ethnic minorities 14
European Monetary Union 8
Evans, D. 120
expenditure, and arrears 45-6, *45*
experts 6, 7
external risks 4-5

F

Family Expenditure Survey (FES) 48, 66
Family Resources Survey (FRS) 177
fear 159-61
financial costs *109*, 114, *115*, 116-23, *118*, *119*
financial markets
deregulation 10, 12, 18, 21, 54
uncertainty 7
Financial Services Act 1985 10
Finland 17, 18
first-time buyers *11*, 12
fiscal support 53, 79-80, 83
MITR 65, 81, 83
flexible employment 77-8, 173
flexible labour market 18, 54, 55-6
flexible mortgages 15-16, 179
Ford, J. 67, 88, 97, 99, 102, 108, 110, 119, 120, 121, 122
and Burrows 46, 108, 121
and Kempson 88, 90-1, 93, 94, 96, 108, 179
and Quilgars 88
and Seavers 107
and Wilcox 46, 102
and Wilson 108
Forrest, R. 14, 92, 130
Forth, J. 57
France 17, 18
Franklin, J. 4

Freund, P. 157, 163-4
full-time employment 53-4, *54*
future aspirations *111*, 113

G

General Health Questionnaire 12 166-7
Germany 17, 18
Giddens, Anthony 3-4, 5, 6-7, 150, 170-1
Gilbert, G.N. 55
globalisation 5-6, 7-8, 17-18, 19, 54, 169
government policies 8
  home ownership 10, 46-7, 116, 169
  housing 173-4, 179
  inflation 79
  labour market 54-5
  low-income home ownership 48-9, 80, 177-8
  see also fiscal support; Income Support for Mortgage Interest
Green, H. 26
Gregg, P. 56, 57

H

Hamnett, C. 1, 3, 14, 107
Hansbro, J. 26
health 130, 153, 163, 165
health costs *109*, *111*, 151, 168
  children 141
  statistical evidence 165-8
  stress 26, 113, 153-4, 155-7
health services *109*
Heath, S. 3
Henry, N. 6
Hills, J. 86, 93
Holmans, A. 22, 25, 49-50, 88, 91, 93, 108
home improvement grants 48
home owners *see* mortgagors
home ownership
  attitudes towards 2-3, *3*, 8, 36, 107-8, 173
  government policies 116, 174
  rise and stalling 10, *11*, 12-16, 46-9, 51
  risk society 7-10
Homebuy 174
homelessness 110, *115*, 116, 126-7
hours of work 67, 133
House of Commons Social Security Select Committee 175
house prices
  decreases 14, 15
  increases 15, 21, 50, 79
  inter-country differences 17
  regional differences 12
household changes
  arrears 45, *45*, 49
  see also divorce
household structure
  arrears *33*, *35*, *37*, 40-1, 43-4
  possessions *28*, 29
Housing Benefit 83, 177
housing careers 150-1, 176
housing market institutions, costs *109*, 114

I

identity *111*, 112, 148-51
ideology 7, 54, 85, 116, 173
illness, arrears 45, *45*
income
  pay flexibility 55-6
  polarisation 65
  see also low pay
income loss
  and arrears 45, *45*
  safety-net provision 88, 89
Income Support Mortgage Interest 21, 83, 84
  administrative costs 114
  curtailment 48, 85-7, 175
  effectiveness 101-5, 106
  late payment 30
  mortgagors' knowledge 87, 91-2, *92*, 96
  and MPPI 88-90, *89*, 105-6
  payments 114, *115*
  run-on 170
  work disincentive 67, 108
income to debt ratio 47-8, *48*
  arrears 42-3, 44

and inflation 79, 81
inflation 1, 15, 50, 53, 79, 81, 172
inheritance tax 80, 81
injury, arrears 45, *45*
insecure employment *see* precarious employment
insecurity
children 141
possessions 113, 163, 173
risk society 6, 108, 170
Institute for Fiscal Studies 65-6
insurance
attitudes towards 94-5, *95*, 96
inter-country differences 17
see also Mortgage Payment Protection Insurance
insurance tax 65, 80, 81
insurers
costs *109*
Mortgage Indemnity Guarantee 114, 121
see also Association of British Insurers
intentionally homeless 127, 133
interest rates
inter-country differences 17
and ISMI 103-4, *104*
and MPPI 100
rises 12, 14, 21, 65
supra-national regulation 8
Ireland 17, 18
ISMI *see* Income Support Mortgage Interest
Italy 17

J

job duration 56-7

K

Karn, V. 18
Kempson, E. 88, 93, 97, 99, 100, 101, 130, 168
and Ford 88, 90-1, 93, 94, 96, 108, 179
Kennett, P. 130

L

Labour Force Survey (LFS) 57
labour market 16, 19, 53-5, *54*, 81, 169, 172
case studies 68-71, *72*, 73-7
deregulation 5-6, 54
flexibility 18, 54, 55-6
see also employment
labour market institutions, costs *109*
Labour Party 116
Lash, Scott 4
Lawson boom 14, 43
Lazarus, R. 157
Le Grand, J. 86
Leather, P. 107
lenders
arrears negotiations 130-2
costs *109*, 114
outstanding debts 135-7
possessions 119, 121
safety-net provision 84, 85
and unsustainable home ownership 178-9
see also Council of Mortgage Lenders
lifestyle changes 110, 140
lifestyle choices 6, 150, 170
loan to value ratios 17, 21
arrears *34*, *36*, *38*, 42-3
loans *see* mortgages
local authorities
costs 9, *109*, 114, *115*, 116
homelessness acceptances 126-7
negotiations with 134-5
logistic regression analyses 34, 36, *37-8*, 38-43
London 15
arrears *34*, *36*, *38*, 41-2
possessions *29*
lone parents
arrears 40, 41
ISMI 84
low pay 65-7, 81
case studies 74-7
low-income home ownership
arrears 44
extent 14, 46, 47, *47*, 51, 65-6

government policies 48-9, 80, 169-70, 174, 177-8
income to debt ratio 47-8, *48*, 79
inter-country differences 17
MPPI 93
possessions 122
relationship breakdown 50
low-income tenants *47*, 83
lump sum repayments 15
Lupton, D. 3, 5

M

McConaghy, M. 26, 27, 64
Mackintosh, S. 107
Maclennan, D. 8, 67
maintenance costs 80
manufactured risks 4-5
marital status
arrears *33*, *35*, *37*, 39, 43-4
possessions 27, *28*, 29
see also divorce
Martin, E. 156
men, full-time employment 53-4
mental health *see* psychosocial effects
MIG 114, 121
MIRAS 14, 43
MITR 49, 65, 79-80, 81, 83
mobility 57
restricted 107
and stamp duty 80
moral hazard 87
mortgage arrears 169
aetiology 44-50, *45*
epidemiology 29-32, *33-4*, 34, *35-6*, 36, *37-8*, 38-44, 81
explanations 21-2
extent 14, 22, *23-4*, 25, 170
flexible employment 77-8
housing careers 176
ISMI recipients 102-3, *103*, 104-5
and low pay 67, 177
MPPI claimants 100-1, *101*
negotiations with lenders 130-2
social and socio-psychological aspects 26, 74-7
unemployment 64
Mortgage Code 84
Mortgage Indemnity Guarantee 114, 121
mortgage interest relief at source 14, 43
mortgage interest tax relief 49, 65, 79-80, 81, 83
Mortgage Payment Protection Insurance (MPPI) 16, 83, 84-5, 86-7, 131
effectiveness 88, 97-101, 106, 171
insurers' management 179
and ISMI 88-90, *89*, 105-6
take-up 88, 90-6, 102, 106, 175
mortgage possessions *see* possessions
mortgage rates *see* interest rates
mortgages 1, 15-16, 17
see also income to debt ratio; loan to value ratios
mortgagors
inter-country differences 17
socio-economic characteristics 13-14, *13*
Munro, M. 46, 78, 92, 179
Murie, A. 14
Murphey, L. 18

N

National Association of Citizens Advice Bureaux (NACAB) 97, 121, 135
National Housing Federation (NHF) 48
nature 5
negative equity 14, 79, 117, 120
negotiations
with lenders 130-2
with local authorities 134-5
Netherlands 17
Nettleton, S. 108, 110, 125, 151
Nixon, J. 108
Northern Ireland 32, 177

O

O'Brien, M. 4
odds ratios, arrears 34, 36, *37-8*, 38-43
ontological identity 148, 149
ontological security 6-7, 170
organisational costs *109*

outstanding debt 120, 121, 135-7, 158
overtime 68-71, 74
owner-occupation *see* home ownership

P

part-time employment
arrears 77, 81
flexibility 55
job duration 56
protection 55
rise 53, 54, *54*
payment difficulties *see* mortgage arrears
personal and family relationships *111*
Pickvance, C. 130
Pickvance, K. 130
political costs *109*, 116
Portugal 17, 18
possession orders 126
possessions vii, 169
consequences for children 137-48
coping strategies 130-7
costs 107-8, *109*, 110, *111*, 112-14, *115*, 116-23, *118*, *119*, 121-2, 123
epidemiology 26-7, *28-9*, 29, 49
experience 125-6, 127-30, 151
explanations 21-2
extent 2, 14, 22, *23-4*, 25, *25*, 170
housing careers 176
institutional context 158-9
and low pay 67, 177
process 126-7
psychosocial impacts 26, 74-7, 155-68
Potter, P. 18
poverty 112, 122, 123, 171
and health 153
precarious employment 57-9, *58*, *60*, 81
case studies 71, *72*, 73-4
and low pay 66-7
priority need 126-7
property prices *see* house prices
Pryce, G. 88, 91, 93-4, 96
psychosocial effects *109*, 110, *111*, 112-13, 151, 153-4
emotional capital 163-5
emotions 157-8
social status, stigma and shame 161-2
statistical evidence 165-8
stress 155-7
uncertainty, fear and lack of control 159-61
public policy *see* government policies
public sector workers 174
purchase date, arrears *34*, *36*, *38*, 43

Q

quality of life 110, *111*, 112
Quercia, R. 18
Quilgars, D. 88

R

rational choice theory 86, 91
constraints 91-4
redundancy, arrears 45, *45*
reflexivity 6, 8, 170
regional differences 176-7
arrears *34*, *36*, *38*, 41-2
housing market 12-13, 15
possessions *29*
see also South East
regulation 108
rehousing 126-7, 177
relationship breakdown *see* divorce
relative risk 38
rents 48
repossession *see* possessions
residual debt 120, 121, 135-7, 158
retired people, arrears 40
Right to Buy (RTB) 10, 12, 173, 174
arrears *34*, *36*, *38*, 42, 44
risk vii
risk aversion 94-5
risk perceptions 78, 81, 92
risk society 3-7, 19, 108, 150, 170-1
home ownership 7-10
risky employment *see* precarious employment
Ruonavaara, H. 18

S

safety-net provision 9, 53, 83
case studies 74-7
complementarity 88-90, *89*
effectiveness 88, 96-106
inter-country differences 17
limitations 14, 174-5
public and private 84-7
restructuring 8, 16, 46, 171
see also Income Support Mortgage Interest; Mortgage Payment Protection Insurance
Saunders, P. 1, 107, 116
Scotland 32, 176, 177
Seavers, J. 107
SEH *see* Survey of English Housing
self-confidence 141, 161, 162
self-employment
arrears 31, 41, 44, 45, *45*, 77, 78, 81, 171
extent 8, 53, *54*
job duration 56
low-income home ownership 66
nominal 55
volatility 57
self-esteem 112, 161, 162
shame 161-2
shared ownership 32, 174
sickness, arrears 45, *45*
Sim, D. 107
single parents *see* lone parents
Skinner, C. 94
smoking 156
social change 4
social class
arrears 32, *33*, *35*, *37*, 41, 44, 78
possessions 29, *29*
social costs 9, 107, *109*, 110, *111*, 112-13
social exclusion 110, 112, 123, 171
social housing 173
social psychological effects *see* psychosocial effects
social security provision *see* welfare provision
Social Security Select Committee 175
social status *111*, 112, 148-9, 151, 164, 173
case studies 161-2
children 146, 147
South East
arrears 14, *34*, *36*, *38*, 41-2
housing market 12, 13, 15
possessions 15, *29*
public sector workers 174
Spain 17
Stafford, B. 18
stamp duty 80, 81
status *see* social status
Stegman, M. 18
Stephens, M. 8
stigma 112, 127, 149, 161
stress 26, 113, 127-8, 153-7
subsidies *see* fiscal support; safety-net provision
Survey of English Housing vii, 26, 172, 176-7
arrears 30, 31
income to debt ratio 42-3
low-income home ownership 66
reasons for arrears 44, *45*
suspended orders 126
sustainable home ownership 2, 8, 108
Sweden 17, 18

T

tax 65, 80, 81
tax relief *see* fiscal support
Taylor, D. 148
Taylor-Gooby, P. 7, 16, 86, 94
technological change 54
temporary employment 55, 56-7
trading down 50, 79, 132, 172
trading up 79

U

UK Homes Repossessions Page 120
uncertainty
children 147
possessions 113, 128, 159-60, 163
risk society 7-8, 169-70
unemployment 1, 2, 8, 14
arrears 45, *45*, 64, 77, 81
employment mobility 57

and globalisation 5
and low pay 67
mortgagors 64
United States 17, 18
unsustainable home ownership vii, 1, 2, 19, 122-3, 169, 170-1
comparative perspective 16-19
lenders' responses 178-9
structural influences 8-9
see also mortgage arrears; possessions

V

voluntary possession 126-7

W

Wadsworth, J. 56, 57
Wales 32
wealth accumulation 107, 116-17, 123, 173
Weiss, L. 5
welfare provision
public attitudes 94
restructuring 7, 8, 85, 86-7, 151, 169, 174-5
see also safety-net provision
White, M. 18, 54-5, 57
Whitehead, C. 88, 91, 93
Wilcox, S. 46, 47, 48-9, 67, 79, 102
Wilkinson, R. 108, 153
Williams, F. 94, 125
Williams, S. 164-5
Wilson, M. 108
women
coping strategies 130, 134
low pay 65
outstanding debts 136-7
part-time employment 54, 55
work disincentive 108
Working Families Tax Credit 177
working hours 67, 133

Y

young people
arrears 39, 44
attitudes to home ownership 2-3, *3*, 39

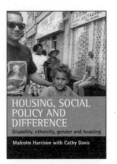